Jackie Robinson

Jackie Robinson

Race, Sports,
and the
American Dream

Edited by

Joseph Dorinson and Joram Warmund

M.E. Sharpe
Armonk, New York
London, England

Library of Congress Cataloging-in-Publication Data

Jackie Robinson : race, sports, and the American dream / Joseph Dorinson
and Joram Warmund, editors.
p. cm.
Selected papers from a conference held Apr. 3–5, 1997 on the Brooklyn Campus of
Long Island University.
Includes bibliographical references and index.
ISBN 0-7656-0317-9 (hc. : alk. paper)
1. Robinson, Jackie. 1919–1972—Congresses. 2. Baseball players—United
States—Biography—Congresses. 3. Discrimination in sports—United States—
Congresses. I. Dorinson, Joseph, 1936–. II. Warmund, Joram, 1939–.
GV865.R6A34 1998
796.357′092—dc21
98-38327
CIP

Printed in the United States of America

The paper used in this publication meets the minimum requirements of
American National Standard for Information Sciences—
Permanence of Paper for Printed Library Materials,
ANSI Z 39.48-1984.

BM (c) 10   9   8   7   6   5   4   3   2

We dedicate this book to three generations of family:

To our spouses, Eileen Dorinson and Solange Warmund,
we owe everything: love, inspiration and children.
We offer this book in gratitude.

To our parents who gave us moral values,
we offer this book as a reverse heirloom.

To our children, Hilary, Paula, Robert, Jillian and Brian, Joshua
and Amanda, who represent a better future,
we present this book as a living legacy.

Contents

Preface

Jackie Robinson: Race, Sports, and
the American Dream

On April 3–5, 1997, a conference on the Brooklyn Campus of Long Island University (LIU)—"Jackie Robinson: Race, Sports, and the American Dream"—commemorated the fiftieth anniversary of Jackie Robinson's historic debut as a member of the Brooklyn Dodgers baseball team. Although that event was celebrated throughout the year in various parts of America, it was particularly appropriate that LIU host the Jackie Robinson conference; after all, the "great experiment" had started in Brooklyn.

The conference attracted attention from scholars and students, Robinson's Brooklyn Dodger teammates and opponents, commentators and fans. They all congregated in Brooklyn, imbued with a common mission akin to a pilgrimage, to participate in the event. From the outset, the focus was deliberately extended beyond the historic event to incorporate analyses, commentaries, and reminiscences of what Gunnar Myrdal had labeled the "American dilemma" and its antidote, the promise and pursuit of the American dream. It is this broader perspective that differentiates this book from the more traditional biographies of Jackie Robinson. The selections from the conference included in this book invite the reader to reflect on issues of sports, race, and the dramatic transformation of the American social and political scene in the last fifty years. We have placed Robinson and his era in a larger historical context to provide a fuller appreciation of the man, the athlete, the milieu, the dialectic forces of change and resistance—in short, the Zeitgeist—which operated before, during, and after April 15, 1947. On that fateful date Jackie Robinson became the first African-American to play major league baseball in this century.

The authors represented in this volume reflect a wide variety of callings—scholars, sportswriters, journalists, ballplayers, and baseball fans. The presenters mirror the anticipated mix of our readers. Consequently, these chapters contain a diversity of style and a range of opinion, and do not consistently conform to a single academic standard. Instead, we offer a heady mix of journalism, scholarship, and memory. To refine and reduce everyone's contribution to a rigid formula would have diminished the authenticity of our presentations. Rather, we decided to retain the spontaneity, the flavor, and the unique perceptions of each author. Therefore, we urge academic purists to put aside their blue pencils and encourage them to concentrate on the lessons learned from a generation that is quickly passing into eternity. Also, to borrow a phrase from that North Carolina sage, Harry Golden, we invite you to "Enjoy, enjoy!"

Acknowledgments

We gratefully acknowledge the support from colleagues, students, and friends too numerous to mention. A few, however, deserve special citation. The LIU administration, including Provost Gale Haynes and Vice-President Jerry Kleinman, provided the financial underpinning for the April conference. We would also like to thank Delicia Garnes and the staff of the LIU Academic Computing Center for their help. Michele Forsten and Christopher Cory, also of the LIU family, gave their commitment at the very beginning, when it was not yet fashionable to support the project, while Joe Goldstein, America's foremost sports publicist, generated enormous response through creative publicity. Rudy Riska urged us to "think big," Marty Adler to "think Brooklyn," and Ralph Branca to "think Dodger Blue." Steve Hisler brought the players. Peter Coveney, our executive editor, gave us the green light to break into print and steered us through thick traffic to our destination; Steve Martin, our production editor, ensured consistency in style and form. And the elegant, lovely, and energetic Rachel Robinson served as an inspiration to all. Mrs. Robinson conferred her blessings on the conference at a critical juncture. Her terrific associates at the Jackie Robinson Foundation provided valuable support throughout. Will Mebane and Mike Jones, in particular, were enormously helpful. Jillian Warmund Chipman and Amanda Goldberg did the typing and retyping of the manuscript. More importantly, with their scrupulous attention to detail, they provided us with editorial expertise and literary sensibility in the formulation of the book. Finally, no acknowledgment would be complete without homage to Jack Roosevelt Robinson, who touched "the better angels of our nature" and made America—in the prophetic words of Langston Hughes—"America again."

Jackie, Do They Know?
An Ode to Jackie Robinson

Tom (Tommy) Hawkins

Do they know what you did Jackie Robinson when you broke that color line? Do they know the worlds that you opened when the Dodgers asked you to sign?

Do they know the humiliation that you suffered through the years or how it felt to "stomach" the threats and constant racial jeers?

Do they know the competitive passion with which you played the game or the host of insults you endured when they defiled your name?

Do they know that you rose above it with majestic winning style, escorting a perennial bridesmaid down the coveted championship aisle?

Do they know you were a "Black Moses" with a soul of raging fire, a man who firmly stood his ground with undiminished desire?

Do they know that you had all the tools, talent, "smarts," and skill, well blended with civility plus an unshakable iron-clad will?

Do they know that when you left the game no grass grew under your feet, you continued pioneering using the executive suite?

Do they know with respect and reverence, we document your deeds, careful to water and nourish your bountiful well-sown seeds?

Do they know that in the hall of fame you regally reside, having scaled the heights of the "grand old game" and humanity with pride?

Do they know that you left us early, age fifty-three when you passed? But, in that great half-century, what a legacy you amassed?

Introduction

Joseph Dorinson and Joram Warmund

The Jackie Robinson story invites retelling, Jules Tygiel advises, like the Passover story. Why is this saga different from all others? Because it is a major event in our nation's history. Because this "Ty Cobb in Technicolor" (in Bill "Bojangles" Robinson's famous phrase) did not get his due from society. Before the advent of Robinson, America lived absurdly. Jim Crow dominated overtly in the South, covertly in the North. Our country stood divided: black and white, rich and poor. A common slogan put it neatly if not discreetly. "If you're white, you're all right; if you're brown, stick around; if you're black, step back!"

Along came Mr. Robinson into an all-white neighborhood. Unlike previous black heroes in sports, he was neither a brute nor a clown. He was daunting, dignified, daring, different. He could carry a football with the speed and elusiveness of Gale Sayers, dominate a basketball contest with a scoop to the hoop like Oscar Robertson, out-jump everyone on the track field like Bob Beamon and hit, catch, and run on the baseball diamond— well, like the peerless Jackie Robinson. As a black man, however, in 1942 he had to step back.

Drafted into the U.S. Army, Jackie Robinson rose to lieutenant's rank. One foul day, a bus driver in Texas insisted that this black officer move to the back of the bus. Legally within his rights, Robinson refused. Belligerently, he argued with the military policemen summoned to arrest him and was charged with insubordination and put on trial. Robinson stood up to the Jim Crow system with the courage and consistency that would mark his entire life.[1]

With the assistance of an able lawyer, Robinson won acquittal but refused to remain in service. Granted a discharge, he entered the Negro Leagues as a shortstop for the Kansas City Monarchs in 1945. He excelled in all phases of the game. Attracting the attention of Branch Rickey, general manager of the Brooklyn Dodgers, he was carefully scouted. Although he did not get to see Robinson, who was sidelined by a sore arm, play, Clyde

Sukeforth, after a lengthy interview with Jackie, wrote a glowing report to his Dodgers boss, Branch Rickey. Soon, Rickey and Robinson were engaged in what Tygiel aptly calls "Baseball's Great Experiment." This encounter changed baseball history and indeed transformed America.

Dorinson remembers Robinson's debut. Ten years old at the time, he rooted for the Yankees. But his parents were "progressive"—a euphemism for left-wing politics. They taught him that racism was wrong. They sent him to a radical summer camp named Camp Kinderland where he encountered two giants in African-American life: Paul Robeson and W.E.B. DuBois. This interracial camp promoted multiculturalism long before the coinage of this relevant term. Rooting for the "Jim Crow" Yankees filled Dorinson with guilt, a storehouse amply stocked by radical European-born parents. How could he resolve this dilemma? Easily, he became a Jackie Robinson fan. He cheered for all the Negro players who followed.

In the low-income housing project located in the Greenpoint-Williamsburg section of Brooklyn where Dorinson lived with his parents and an extended family of friends, baseball generated endless debate and inspired passionate loyalties. Who was better: Pee Wee Reese or Phil Rizzuto, Duke Snider or Mickey Mantle, Roy Campanella or Yogi Berra? Occasionally, a lonely Giants fan would trumpet Buddy Kerr, Willie Mays, and Wes Westrum. They even slugged it out over the broadcasters: Red Barber versus Mel Allen. Of course, when the "Old Redhead" joined the Yankee broadcast team in 1953, this dispute became academic. No one argued over Robinson. Anticipating the advent of Ali, Dodger, Yankee and even Giant fans knew that Jackie Robinson was "the greatest." No player, black or white, could match him for sheer excitement. Neighborhood kids, mostly marginal and minority, sensed that Jackie's arrival was "the start of something big."

Robinson's entrance into major league baseball was the subject of the LIU conference and is the raison d'être for this book. Dorinson's principal spur was an earlier conference at Hofstra University, which focused on Babe Ruth. Arguably, George Herman Ruth ranks as the most important player in major league history. With his mighty home runs, he transformed the game of baseball. He helped to legitimize the sport after the ugly scandal of 1919 that threatened destruction of our national pastime. Fans came to see the "Bambino" hit one out. They preferred his style of play to Ty Cobb's. Power eclipsed speed; the home run and the runs batted in (RBIs) triumphed over the bunt and the steal.

At the April 1995 Hofstra University conference, participants offered content with a right-wing political bent. Actor Eddie Bracken denigrated President Franklin D. Roosevelt as soft on communism, and David Eisenhower discoursed on an all-star team selected by his late and dishonored father-in-law, Richard M. Nixon. Dorinson, along with his parents, victims of the "red scare" in the 1950s, squirmed at the juxtaposition. Vilified as a "little red," Dorinson was stripped of an American Legion medal he had won on merit. Marginalized by Cold War animosities, Dorinson identified with outsiders and rooted for the underdogs. No people in the United States were more maligned and mistreated—it appeared to Dorinson—than American Negros. He therefore regarded Jackie Robinson as a perfect hero for an imperfect age.

The rationale was simple. A tribute to this baseball pioneer belonged in Brooklyn, where the "great experiment" began. And a major conference was a categorical imperative. If Ruth transformed the game, Robinson changed America! Robinson not only led the Brooklyn Dodgers to six pennants and one World Series championship in ten stellar seasons, he also demonstrated the absurdity of segregation. By prying open the doors of baseball, Robinson showed the way to open other fields such as business, broadcasting, banking, insurance, and construction. Dr. Martin Luther King, Jr., acknowledged a debt to Robinson. Without the great athlete's showing the way, he confided to aide Rev. Wyatt T. Walker, there would have been a more difficult journey to justice. "Jackie made my work much less difficult."[2]

At television station WLIW, Dorinson spoke to Marty Adler, president of the Brooklyn Dodgers Hall of Fame. Both were interviewed for a TV special on Brooklyn. Both agreed on the merits of a Jackie Robinson conference. Subsequently, they met at the Downtown Athletic Club, home of the Heisman Trophy. There, Executive Director Rudy Riska encouraged these two planners to "think big." Following this advice, they elicited the support of Andrew Parton, vice-president of Chase Bank. Delighted with the proposal, Parton pledged financial support. Dorinson went on to secure commitments from the LIU administration, local political officials, and scholars from all over. Dr. Joram Warmund joined the team, providing the project with administrative expertise.

Aside from considerations of friendship and collegiality, Joram Warmund accepted co-directorship of the conference for reasons related to his personal history. Warmund belongs to a family that experienced fascism first hand and actively fought against Nazism. His father volunteered in the British Army in September 1939, fought in North Africa, was wounded and captured, and spent several years in German prisoner-of-war camps. His mother traveled throughout South America organizing Zionist rallies and activities in support of a Jewish homeland. Warmund was born in October 1939—one month after Germany invaded Poland—in the then British Mandate of Palestine. In 1943, the itinerant Warmunds—mother and son—arrived in Bolivia, where they lived with his maternal grandparents who had recently fled from Germany. Large segments of the family did not survive the Holocaust. Often, Warmund and his family suffered bigotry, persecution, and violence. The Warmunds had to endure long periods of forced separation as well.

In 1950, the reunited family came to the United States in search of the American dream. The following year, Warmund visited relatives in Norfolk, Virginia. Suddenly, it became painfully obvious to him that America, the last great hope for all the downtrodden masses "yearning to breathe free," was a land of deep contradictions if not patent hypocrisy. African-Americans could not sit on the same park benches, drink from the same water fountains, eat in the same restaurants, or even flush the same toilets as whites. America was not completely dissimilar from the Germany of 1935 in its treatment of minorities. But contrary to Germany in the mid-1930s, the generation of post–World War II Americans was on the verge of addressing—as Gunnar Myrdal had already put it in 1944—the "American dilemma." Warmund came of age during this period of great social change.

Like Dorinson a product of New York City public education, Warmund then did graduate work in German history. As a professor, he continually reflected on the fact that, contrary to Germany in the 1930s, America pursued a course that would ultimately repudiate racism. He was especially sensitive to this divergence in nationally driven historical paths. The creation of a conference he entitled "Jackie Robinson: Race, Sports, and the American Dream" therefore struck a deep personal chord within. So, this by now thoroughly assimilated American, this former Yankee fan—who idolized Mickey Mantle—now joined the boy from Brooklyn, Dorinson, to provide the conference with a perspective that far transcended the retelling of just another sports story.

Postwar America was reforming and transforming. At the vanguard of this movement was baseball, in particular the Brooklyn Dodgers management. At the cutting edge of this salutary thrust was a magnificent athlete: Jackie Roosevelt Robinson. On his massive shoulders and his bowed but mercurial legs, Brooklyn, as a microcosm of America, achieved an apotheosis. Transcending personal gain or glory, Jackie Robinson acted as a great catalyst in a noble experiment that had to succeed. His triumph translated into America's as well. Our country's response to racism contrasted sharply with the German "solution," thereby providing a positive, just, workable alternative to a world still poised on a precipice facing choices: to be or not to be inclusive or separatist. At the crossroads we must choose wisely and well. And Jackie Robinson's noble life points us in the right direction.

The conference quickly began to build momentum. In February 1997 local newspapers, radio and television started to report on the coming three-day event. Many scholars responded to calls for papers placed in academic journals and on websites. Mrs. Rachel Robinson indicated that she would attend. Major League Baseball listed the conference in its official publications, while promoting the year-long celebration of Jackie Robinson's historic mission. Radio and TV personalities called to secure interviews revealing that the LIU conference had become—in their words—the hottest ticket in town. No doubt, the large number of celebrities who promised to attend generated huge interest. The stars did not disappoint. Robinson's star waxed brighter with each announcement. In an age of hype and hypocrisy, when so many athletes function as overpaid narcissists, our hero looked better than ever.

Pledged to a continuing dissemination of Robinson's contributions, Dorinson and Warmund decided to collect a representative sample of the presentations and publish them in book form, thereby preserving and imparting Robinson's legacy. The papers that follow describe conditions prior to Robinson's arrival, offer new perspectives on the events surrounding the integration of baseball, present reminiscences of the era, explore the impact of his breakthrough, and assess how far African-Americans have traveled in Robinson's wake.

The editors believe that this book will make an important contribution to deepen our understanding of race, sports, and social mobility. If the great expectations spawned by Robinson's arrival in 1947 have not fully materialized, America is nevertheless a far, far better place because of his barrier breaking. His story renews hope and revives faith. Keeper of the flame, Rachel Robinson provides eloquent testimony to the essential truth, namely that love conquers hate.

No discussion of this historic event fifty years ago is possible without a reference to Brooklyn. A melange of ethnicities, a pastiche of cultures, the borough once known for its abundance of religious institutions proved a hospitable laboratory for the "great experiment." It can be said forcefully—indeed proclaimed proudly—that Brooklyn was central in challenging our nation's pervasive racism. One incident related to Dorinson by Joan Hodges, Gil's widow, is illustrative. Dodger wives used to meet regularly for lunch. Suddenly, this amenity ceased. "Why?" Joan Hodges inquired. "Because of Rachel" came the retort. Mrs. Hodges gave Mrs. Redneck a lesson in local civics: "This is Brooklyn, not some southern town. We don't do things like that here."[3] The luncheons resumed. Mrs. Hodges continues to live on Bedford Avenue, a few miles down the road from where the Dodgers once played and history was made by Jackie Robinson and his beloved teammates.

A number of knotty questions invite lively debate and scholarly scrutiny. Could the color line have been crossed outside Brooklyn? Why did Branch

Rickey select Jackie Robinson as the pioneer? Why did it take so long? Do we need heroes? Why did Robinson choose baseball? How did Cold War politics conspire to pit Jackie Robinson against Paul Robeson? What role did the Communist Party and its organ, the *Daily Worker,* play in breaking the color barrier? What is Jackie Robinson's legacy? Why was the Zeitgeist uniquely ready in 1947? As the youngest child asks at the Passover seder, "What does it all mean?"

In response, the articles assembled offer fresh perspectives and illuminating insights.

Notes

1. Jules Tygiel, "The Court Martial of Jackie Robinson," in Jules Tygiel, ed., *The Jackie Robinson Reader: Perspectives on An American Hero* (New York: Penguin Dutton, 1997), pp. 39–51. This penetrating study first appeared in *American Heritage* magazine (August/September 1984).

2. David Falkner, *Great Time Coming . . .* (New York: Simon and Schuster, 1995), p. 237.

3. In conversation with Joan Hodges, it was John Comer, superintendent of School District 22 and a neighbor of the Hodges family, who first called this anecdote to Dorinson's attention.

Part I

Historical Perspectives

The poet John Donne put it succinctly, "No man is an island, entire of itself." Jackie Robinson did not perform in isolation, nor did he act in a historical vacuum. Robinson's struggles and achievements need to be assessed within the historical set of circumstances in effect at his time. The essays of Joram Warmund, Peter Golenbock, Sidney Gendin, and Jack Moore combine to provide the essentials of such a backdrop.

Joram Warmund describes the historical framework of 1947, the Zeitgeist of the time, and then places Robinson within that context. He also contends that in retrospect it can be seen that 1947 was a unique, possibly even a watershed, year in world history. Jackie Robinson's breaking of baseball's color barrier must be understood within this broader perspective.

Peter Golenbock recognizes that Jackie Robinson's chances for success certainly depended on his talents and abilities, but he also required the support of a group of white men of courage and conscience. Both Warmund and Golenbock contend that the forces for change needed men of integrity who were in command positions and who were prepared to take the risk.

Sidney Gendin reminds us that Jackie Robinson was not the first black man to play in major league baseball. Moses Fleetwood Walker held that distinction. He also was the last major league black ballplayer until Jackie Robinson entered the scene. Gendin draws remarkable analogies between Walker and Robinson. Walker, Robinson's "accidental predecessor," is a tragic figure. His is the story of what might have been—indeed, one could argue, of what should have been—for Fleet Walker and also for entire generations of talented ballplayers who were banned from participating in the American pastime because of the color of their skin.

1

Jack B. Moore rounds out this section with a comparison of Jackie Robinson with two black contemporaries: Roy Campanella and Monte Irvin. Each of these men experienced similar racial slights and insults, yet each reacted and triumphed over adversity in a different way. Moore investigates three black responses to racism in America, thereby inviting reflection on a topic of continuing conflict.

Taken together, Warmund, Golenbock, Gendin, and Moore describe and analyze some of the important ingredients that were fused in the crucible of the "great experiment." The results of that process are examined in later parts of this book.

1

In the Eye of the Storm: 1947 in World Perspective

Joram Warmund

Red Barber labeled 1947 as the year "When All Hell Broke Loose in Baseball."[1] Baseball, the national pastime, a mirror that reflected the national values—and sometimes even formed them—had embarked on the "great experiment"[2] of racial diversity. The process, once begun, could not be reversed despite any encountered resistance. The game was transforming; so was society, at home and in the world.

In retrospect, Red Barber's description needs to be modified, both for baseball and for the world at large, particularly when assessed from the perspective of fifty years later. The year 1947 needs to be seen not only for what happened, but also for what did not. "All Hell" did not really break loose. Jackie Robinson *did* make his major league debut on April 15, 1947, and no major upheaval was recorded.[3] Despite threats, rumored or real, to mount a resistance, there were no strikes, no sit-downs or boycotts, no mass protests.[4] The game did transcend the event. Certainly the challenges were formidable; resentment and resistance did exist. But in the final analysis— in the year following the Nuremberg Tribunal—Jackie Robinson and the causes he represented succeeded because of intrinsic merit and good timing.

The man to lead the charge was right, and so was the time. The later transformation toward integration would not occur as smoothly nor as rapidly in society as it did in baseball. The commitment made in baseball in 1947 was accomplished because sufficient support had already been galvanized, particularly amongst the key power brokers in the game and within

3

select members of the fourth estate, to discourage potential opposition from organizing a coherent resistance. Parallel conclusions were being reached in domestic and foreign politics. It was in 1947 that America began to accept responsibility for leadership, and of moving—perhaps too slowly—in the direction of closing the gap between its professed ideals and the inequities that still existed. A similar shift was occurring on the world scene.

Modifying Red Barber's description does not diminish the significance of what happened; rather it brings into sharper focus the events of that year, which committed America and the world to a specific and irreversible direction. A storm was gathering, changes were to occur rapidly and dramatically, and had already gained momentum, but in contrast to the immediate past, and future, the year 1947 appeared relatively calm. All hell did and would indeed break loose throughout the world, but not in 1947.

In retrospect, we can now better appreciate the real significance of what happened in 1947. It was then that the critical options were made which defined the future course of the postwar world. As with Caesar, at another time—and to mix my metaphors and tenses—the "die was cast."

In 1945–1946 modern history ended. The era which historians have traditionally labeled as "modern," in contrast to "medieval" or "classical," had collapsed. The most obvious attribute of modern history was the expansion of European power and values throughout the world. By the beginning of the twentieth century, Western civilization—its power, technology, and value system—had gained global preponderance. But by the end of the Second World War this primarily European hegemony had been shattered. Could the European Humpty-Dumpty be repaired, or would a new, a postmodern, construct replace it?[5]

In the aftermath of the *really* Great War, European military, political, and economic recovery depended on non-European support, primarily from the United States and possibly, but not likely, from the Soviet Union. This need for recovery was not localized to Europe. Famine, disease, and anarchy ravaged large regions of the world. Millions of people were displaced. Relief could not be found in the former colonies, not even in those that had escaped the dislocation of invasions. Rather, the colonial regions were in varying stages of resistance to foreign rule.

The victors of the war, the Grand Alliance of the West and East, had been connected by a common Axis threat. Now, this relationship was proving tenuous. The collapse of the previous world order created an immense vacuum into which American and Soviet power and ideology were almost inexorably rushing. The struggle for victory was now replaced by new challenges: domestically, by those of reconversion and recovery, and internationally, by the need to establish new power relationships that would assure that winning the war would not lead—especially in the emerging atomic age—to losing of the peace.

The United States emerged as the most powerful force on earth. This formerly reluctant giant now needed to adjust to the notion of accepting responsibility for the well-being of the world; to lead in the securing of peace by providing relief and reconstruction to large regions of the world. To name some of the postwar international problems that would require America's attention: Continental Europe possessed approximately ten–twelve million displaced persons in search of a future with some stability. The defeat of Germany now required addressing the problem of "denazification" of an entire Central European, primarily, but not exclusively, German people. As in Europe, but even more so, victory in the East now imposed on America the responsibility for occupying and reforming Japan. Leadership in the war now placed the United States at the forefront of the movement for an international peace organization, the United Nations. The development and use of the atom bomb now obligated America to search for ways to control future uses of atomic energy. Asian crop failures in 1946 threatened 400 million people with starvation, and similar threats of famine faced millions more residing within the recently occupied European regions. The former Grand Alliance was becoming more strained as Soviet-American perceptions increasingly diverged on the appropriate formula for creating the Brave New World.[6]

Domestically, America also faced new challenges. The most immediate task was to reconvert from a wartime society, to reabsorb into civilian life approximately twelve million servicemen and women. Industry needed to switch from a wartime production to civilian markets. The pressure was great to demobilize, despite America's expanded responsibilities abroad.

Now that the war was over, could America accomplish reconversion without dislocation? Could and would America's economic system avoid runaway inflation or a return to the prewar depression? These questions needed to be answered quickly and positively. The country was changing. Rosie the Riveter would need to step aside.

Victory over "evil" abroad had created a sense of expectations that the American dream would be expanded and become more inclusive. The prewar migrations of populations from the farms to the cities, and from the cities to the developing suburbs, now accelerated. Ethnic shifts, particularly of Mexicans into the West and of African-Americans from the South to the great northern cities, would reconfigure the population mix and eventually impact on political priorities. As the white population moved out of New York City, Puerto Ricans and southern blacks filled the void. The rhetoric of the war and the promise of the great cities were combining to provide new hope for improved living conditions and a better quality of life. These aspirations were democratic in nature, appealing to all segments of the population. Would America be able to satisfy these often conflicting aspirations?[7]

And what about the rest of the world, particularly those regions that had been in the war zones? Should European recovery be accomplished at the expense of German recovery? Could it be effected without a German resurgence?[8] Would Britain and France be able to reassert their prewar colonial empires? Or would the colonies gain independence, and if so, what form of government and social structures would they establish?[9] Recovery and reconstruction were almost universal aims in the war-torn regions. National determination and social and economic development were the aspirations of what would be later known as the Third World. By the end of 1946, the prescriptions for attaining these goals—and in some cases the goals themselves—were varied and contradictory. In some cases they actually threatened each other.

By 1948–1949, many of the above questions had been answered. The wartime alliances were replaced by two power blocs confronting each other in a Cold War that would experience repeated hot points. Britain and France would not be able to resist the movement for colonial emancipation, although Britain would find a more graceful way to disengage than France.

By 1948, America was responding to the challenges and responsibilities required of a world leader. The Marshall Plan, the Truman Doctrine, the creation of the Japanese Constitution, the formulation of the Containment Policy—all these were announced in 1947 and implemented in the years to come.[10]

Domestically, the year 1947 would also serve to define America's future. The rapid and massive conversion to a civilian, consumer-oriented economy, and the increased shifts in the population did not result in a runaway inflation, or in a depression, or in a social upheaval, as some had feared and others had predicted. The number of men and women in military uniform was reduced to three million. These new civilians were successfully incorporated into society. The wartime prosperity did not end, but rather was continued and accelerated. The turning point for these dramatic changes occurred almost routinely and imperceptibly in 1947.[11]

The year 1947 would continue the technological revolution started during the Second World War. The development of atomic energy, the use of the computer, improvements in aviation and in rocketry, all had preceded 1947 and would continue afterward. But in retrospect we can now recognize that the year would also witness the "invention that changed the world," the transistor, which has become the electronic brains of virtually all the machinery used in daily life today.[12] This invention, perhaps almost typically for the year, was created in 1947 and publicly announced in early 1948. It received "scant attention" at the time.[13] Television, still in its infancy, was used for the first time to broadcast the 1947 World Series, a portent of the future when it would gain rapid preeminence as a reflector and formulator of American culture. But, again, as with so many of the other essential and substantive events of 1947, the new technology made its entry in almost muted form, to be fully appreciated only in retrospect.

More obvious and more overt changes were happening in the colonial world. In 1947, India and Pakistan gained independence, to be followed by a virtual Third World upheaval in the following years. But, in contrast to the decolonization process of later years, the one that established India and Pakistan, although filled with ample numbers of violent incidents, still can be described as relatively peaceful. It is also clear that a course of action toward worldwide national independence had been started before, but now after 1947, with England's disengagement from its largest possession, this movement could no longer be reversed.[14]

The Second World—that is, the world of the Soviet Union—also emerged by 1948 with a clear sense of direction. The challenge of reconstruction of 1945–1946 had been met in a specific way. In 1947, Russian manipulations in East Europe were especially intrusive in Hungary. A pattern of exerting control was becoming apparent. By 1948 and 1949, the "Iron Curtain" described by Churchill in 1946 had become a reality. The Soviet Bloc and the ideology it professed—which by 1950 included a newly formed Communist China—presented itself to the emerging Third World nations as a better alternative to the capitalism of the West.

Domestically, Russia was now recovering from the destruction of a war that had claimed over twenty million casualties. No other nation had absorbed greater losses. But the transition to a peace economy would not prove to be as smooth, nor would recovery be as extensive as it was in an America that had been spared that kind of devastation. Yet, Russian paranoia was perceived as a threat. So, while the post-1947 years in America would see an anti-red panic known as McCarthyism, Russian ideology and vital interests would fixate on its strategic vulnerability, insisting on an aggressive policy that included control of East European regions as an enlarged buffer zone. The resultant shift in postwar foreign policies from a tenuous cooperation between the wartime allies to a set of competing power blocs occurred, and became hardened, in 1947.[15]

Clearly, the year 1947 was the pivotal year in international and domestic affairs. It needs to be evaluated by itself and not just absorbed within the years immediately preceding or following. Options existed before 1947 that were not taken. Postwar America had choices. It could have opted to return to a form of isolationism reminiscent of its policy in the period after the First World War. Or, it could have chosen to be more accommodating to its Soviet wartime partner, recognizing Russia's immense sacrifices and allowing it greater latitude in its policy to dismember Germany. For a while, American policy concerning the future treatment of Germany was not that dissimilar to that of the Soviets.[16]

America could have opted for a system of collective security through the mechanism of the United Nations. Instead, in 1947, the United States initiated a major reorientation of its foreign policy, which committed it to accept responsibility for leadership of the West in what would emerge as a prolonged struggle against the Communist Bloc. The Truman Doctrine of March 12, 1947, committed the United States to providing support to the "free peoples of the world in maintaining their freedom."[17] In June, the Marshall Plan offered a generous, comprehensive economic assistance program for all European nations wishing to participate in a general European recovery (European Recovery Program). By September 1947, the Soviets had not only rejected the Marshall Plan, but were creating a united front of the communist parties, known as Cominform, designed to combat "Anglo-American imperialism."[18] The Cold War was under way. So, commitments were made in 1947 that would propel human events for at least the next generation. Not all these decisions may have been the best available. We may certainly assess them differently from the perspective of fifty years.

If, retroactively perhaps, 1947 can be recognized as the watershed year between the previous wartime alliances and the subsequent bifurcated Cold War world, it needs also to be recognized as a hiatus during which vital change was accomplished in a relatively calm, almost muted, form. Jackie Robinson entered the major leagues in April. Eleven weeks later Larry Doby followed suit, and the process continued that season, with three additional black players.[19] By 1959 every major league team had at least one black player. Significant as this event was, it occurred without major upheaval. The facts remain that in 1947 a black person was indeed accepted on the ball field, that within twelve years every team had at least one black player, but that in 1949 another black person was stoned and run out of town in Peekskill, New York. By 1949, the Cold War and the climate of McCarthyism made Paul Robeson not only a black performer, but also one identified with the wrong political philosophy.[20] The times were changing rapidly.

Baseball supposedly was one of the great definers and influencers of American values. Yet, it did not have the spillover effect one might have expected; certainly not in the immediate future. After 1947, a black person could be accepted on the ball field, but the country would still witness bloodshed over the issue of integrated bathrooms, restaurants or schools.

So, even if baseball was "progressive," its influence was either not that great or it was of a more subtle and long-range nature. Whatever the case, the decision to initiate integration in major league baseball was more doable in 1947 than in the period immediately preceding or following. The general receptivity for such change—almost like a window of opportunity—existed for a short period of time, that is, in 1947.

Commitments were made in that year that were to affect world politics and that were to establish courses of actions not fully completed until the 1990s. The timing of baseball's integration reflected this wider world condition. Clearly, this was more a case of baseball being influenced than of its being the influencer. The mood would shift after that year, and those changes, which had not been already effected, would become more difficult to accomplish in the next decades.

It is important to remember that in 1947 baseball and the movies were two great reflectors and shapers of American values: the concepts of fair play, hard work, rewards based on merit, and the rejection of inequities were all represented and expressed by, and through, baseball and films. The movie of the year in 1947 was *Gentleman's Agreement*, an exposé of anti-Semitism existing even among the so-called polite society of postwar America. Issues of bigotry were being reexamined, and this review was occurring in the broad historical context of a postwar world in the process of reorienting itself. As with Truman in politics, so also with Zanuck in the cinema and Rickey and Chandler in baseball, this was a change led by a cluster of men of courage and strong character who were intent on reaffirming the standards of decency. They represented a leadership with a moral conscience who took advantage of their opportunities to do the right thing. These opportunities presented themselves in the year 1947.

Minorities did gain their opportunities in the culture vehicles of baseball and the cinema; they also gained it in the military, when in the following year President Harry Truman ordered the armed forces to become integrated. The proponents of the old order, that is, the supporters of a Jim Crow America or those who adhered to more subtle forms of bigotry, were unprepared for the coming change. After 1947, resistance would stiffen against the further expansion of integration into other areas of society. In September 1945, a large anti-integration protest had already taken place in Gary, Indiana, resulting in a thousand white students walking out of classes.[21] In August and September 1946 serious racial disturbances occurred in Athens, Alabama, and in Philadelphia, Pennsylvania.[22] In the first incident, approximately a hundred African-Americans, many of them elderly or physically handicapped, were reported to have been knocked down and trampled.[23]

In December 1946 President Truman had appointed the National Committee on Civil Rights to investigate issues of racial and civil rights in America and to make appropriate recommendations.[24] The committee concluded its deliberations by the end of October 1947, and among its numerous criticisms it also strongly condemned racism in America, offering thirty-five specific recommendations for moving the country closer to the realization of its professed ideals. The document, deliberately entitled "To Secure These Rights," quantified the history of lynchings in the South—from a high of sixty-four in 1921 to an annual figure of six in the 1940s—and further identified numerous other clear subversions of civil rights.[25] The report offered specific recommendations designed to enhance "the dignity of the individual" and "for sorting out the subversive from the loyal"; it also clearly positioned itself in opposition to segregation "of any kind which is based on race, color, creed and nationality."[26]

President Truman strongly supported the findings of the committee. His personal convictions on the matter would be further tested in July 1948, when he adhered to the National Democratic Convention's strong civil rights plank, with the resulting creation of a splinter "Dixiecrat" party that seriously threatened the president's chances to gain reelection.[27] Truman was committed to taking the risk.

As things turned out, sufficient voters were willing to make the stand with him. Equally clear, resistance to integration had now also become better organized. Consequently, real integration and social justice at large would not occur without bloodshed and only after a prolonged struggle not yet fully completed. In 1947 momentous commitments were made in politics, society, and baseball, and they occurred in an almost uneventful form, because resistance was still disorganized and, more importantly, because there was a real confluence of a leadership predisposed to accept responsibility and willing to initiate and support a new course of action with a critical mass of the media and the public which was sufficiently receptive to accept such change.

The decision to play Jackie Robinson in 1947 fits in with the larger shifts that were concurrently under way. In chronological context, using the world political scene as one example, Jackie Robinson's entry into the major leagues in April was preceded in March by the Truman Doctrine and followed in June by the Marshall Plan. On the domestic scene—in a test so discreet it was almost on a subliminal level—six days before Robinson's opening at Ebbets Field, the Congress of Racial Equality (CORE) sent "freedom riders" to the South to test the previous year's decision of the Supreme Court against segregation in interstate bus travel.[28]

It was within this larger historical context that Robinson's debut occurred. The event needs to be placed within this broader setting. The decision required proper timing. In 1947, the Zeitgeist was ready for the change. The year 1947 was the right time. Branch Rickey and Happy Chandler were in place and committed to the "great experiment." Jackie Robinson was the right man, and Brooklyn was the right setting. Sufficient support now existed to meet potential resistance. America internally was becoming bifurcated, just as the world at large would be in the arena of ideological and political contradictions and confrontations. The storm was already gathering in 1945 and 1946, its direction was set in 1947, and the resultant impact would be felt by generations yet to come.

Notes

1. Red Barber, *1947: When All Hell Broke Loose in Baseball* (New York: Doubleday, 1982).

2. Jules Tygiel, *Baseball's Great Experiment: Jackie Robinson and His Legacy* (New York: Oxford University Press, 1983).

3. Arthur Daley, "Opening Day at Ebbets Field," *New York Times,* 16 April 1947, p. 32. See also Arthur Daley, "Play Ball," *New York Times,* 15 April 1947, p. 31.

4. Tygiel, *Great Experiment,* Chapter 10, particularly pp. 186–195.

5. Hajo Holborn, *The Political Collapse of Europe* (New York: Knopf, 1951).

6. For good summaries of conditions after 1945, see Ronald Steel, *The End of Alliance: America and the Future of Europe* (New York: Viking Press, 1962); Richard Mayne, *The Community of Europe* (New York: W.W. Norton, 1963), particularly Chapter 4, pp. 68–84; T.E. Vadney, *The World Since 1945,* 2d ed. (New York: Penguin, 1992), particularly the opening sections of Chapter 1–7; Glenn Blackburn, *The West and the World Since 1945,* 4th ed. (New York: St. Martin's Press, 1996); L.S. Stavrianos, *Global Rift: The Third World Comes of Age* (New York: Morrow, 1981).

7. For a close study of ethnic shifts, particularly in New York City, see Ira Rosenwaike, *Population History of New York City* (Syracuse: Syracuse University Press, 1972), especially pp. 133 passim.

8. In addition to references identified in note 6 above, see Gregory F. Treverton, *America, Germany and the Future of Europe* (Princeton: Princeton University Press, 1992).

9. See sources identified in note 6, particularly Vadney, *The World Since 1945,* and Stavrianos, *Global Rift.*

10. The literature on the origins of the Cold War is substantial. See George F. Kennan, *American Diplomacy 1900–1950,* 7th printing (Denver: Mentor Books, 1959), particularly on the development of the Containment Policy, Chapter 6, and the text of the 1947 *Foreign Affairs* article on containment, pp. 89–106; Herbert Feis, *From Trust to Terror, the Onset of the Cold War, 1945–1950* (New York: W.W. Norton, 1970); Walter LaFeber, *America, Russia and the Cold War, 1945–1966* (New York: Wiley and Sons, 1967); Walter LaFeber, ed., *America in the Cold War, Twenty Years of Revolutions and Response, 1947–1967* (New York: Wiley and Sons, 1969), a useful summary of documents concerning the coming and development of the Cold War; Charles L. Robertson, *International Politics Since World War II, a Short History* (Armonk, NY: M.E. Sharpe, 1997), particularly Chapters 1 and 2; Joyce and Gabriel Kolko, *The Limits of Power: The World and the United States Foreign Policy, 1945–1954* (New York:

Harper and Row, 1972), for a more revisionist outlook; Thomas G. Paterson, *On Every Front, the Making and Unmaking of the Cold War,* rev. ed. (New York: W.W. Norton, 1992).

11. For a general text describing the postwar era, see Samuel Eliot Morison and Henry Steele Commager, *The Growth of the American Republic,* 5th ed., vol. 2 (New York: Oxford University Press, 1962), particularly Chapters 31–32.

12. William J. Broad, "Incredible Shrinking Transistor Nears Its Ultimate Limit: The Laws of Physics," *New York Times,* 4 February 1997, pp. C1 and C5.

13. Ibid.

14. In addition to sources cited in notes 6 and 10 above, particularly Vadney and Stavrianos, also see Hans W. Gatzke, *The Present in Perspective: A Look at the World Since 1945,* 2d ed. (New York: Rand McNally, 1961), particularly Chapter 5.

15. See sources cited in note 10.

16. Treverton, *America,* particularly Introduction and Chapter 1.

17. Gatzke, *The Present in Perspective,* p. 27.

18. Ibid., p. 28.

19. Ira Berkow, "He Crossed Color Barriers, but in Another's Shadow," *New York Times,* 23 February 1997, pp. 1, 30.

20. Lynn Ames, "Beyond the Talent, Remembering Paul Robeson in an Era of Unrest," *New York Times,* 26 January 1997, Westchester edition, p. 2.

21. Alton Hornsby, Jr., *Chronology of African-American History: Significant Events and People from 1619 to the Present* (Detroit: Gale Research, 1991), p. 92. Also, see the seminal work of C. Vann Woodward, *The Strange Career of Jim Crow,* 2d rev. ed. (New York: Oxford University Press, 1966), especially pp. 129–139 covering the period of the 1940s.

22. Hornsby, Jr., *Chronology,* p. 92.

23. "Negroes Mobbed in Alabama Town," *New York Times,* 11 August 1946, p. 12.

24. Hornsby Jr., *Chronology,* p. 94.

25. Anthony Leviero, "Guardians For Civil Rights Proposed by Truman Board; Report Asks End of Biases," *New York Times,* 30 October 1947, p. 15; for text of portions of the report, see p. 14.

26. Ibid.

27. Hornsby, Jr., *Chronology,* p. 96.

28. Ibid., p. 94.

2

Men of Conscience

Peter Golenbock

At the time that Branch Rickey plotted to integrate baseball (and America), an entire society was against him. Jim Crowism was ironclad in the South, where Christian fundamentalism and the bitterness from losing the War Between the States and a slave workforce crystallized a caste system that called for Afro-Americans to be as invisible as possible to white society. In the North, even in New York City, that bastion of cosmopolitan liberalism, racism was more subtle but just as palpable. Jesse Owens, America's heralded hero against the Nazis in 1936, could not stay at the Plaza Hotel on his return. If you were black, you stayed in Harlem with your own kind.

What was incredible was not so much that Jackie Robinson ended up succeeding with the Brooklyn Dodgers, but rather that he ever got that chance to enter baseball—which was as societally mainstream as any aspect of American life. The second amazing occurrence was that Jackie Robinson, despite the opposition of much of white society, survived all manner of threats and intimidation and went on to be Rookie of the Year, then Most Valuable Player (MVP).

How then, did it happen, and who made it happen? Of course, it took all the courage and skill that Jackie Robinson could muster. But just as Dr. Martin Luther King, Jr. needed white lawmakers to pass the Civil Rights Act to accelerate the cause, so Robinson needed the support of a corps of courageous white figures in this drama: Happy Chandler, Branch Rickey, Pee Wee Reese, and Leo Durocher.

- Chandler, little recognized but without whom Robinson would not have played for the Dodgers, opened the door to the integration of

baseball (and the nation) not long after he succeeded as baseball commissioner the avowedly racist Kennesaw Mountain Landis, who died
on November 25, 1944.

• Rickey, who had foresight, courage, and the sense to pick the right
  man, walked through that door.
• Even though he was a southerner with southern prejudices, Reese had
  the decency to accept Jackie for his ability, not the color of his skin.
• And Durocher quelled a rebellion by southerners on the Dodgers that
  allowed Robinson to come to the team without incident.

The least likely hero in this drama was Chandler, who was named commissioner in April 1945. Chandler had been governor of Kentucky, long a
state with a segregationist history. But Chandler had known Satchel Paige,
Josh Gibson, and Buck Leonard, and he had a strong sense of justice.
Chandler saw that America's black soldiers had given their lives fighting
against the Axis in World War II. If they could die for freedom, he reasoned, why couldn't they have an equal opportunity to play major league
baseball. Though Chandler hadn't the power to change society as governor,
as it turned out, he had that power as baseball commissioner.

It wasn't long after Chandler was elected commissioner that Wendell
Smith and Rick Roberts, journalists from the *Pittsburgh Courier,* a black
newspaper, came to see him. Shortly before Landis' death, the two men had
asked Landis about the possibility of blacks playing in the majors. Landis
had dismissed them without discussion. But when these crusaders asked the
question of Chandler, the new commissioner told them, "I am for the Four
Freedoms, and if a black boy can make it at Okinawa and go to Guadalca-
nal, he can make it in baseball."[1]

The pool of black players that Chandler was making available to major
league baseball was breathtaking: Josh Gibson was at the end of his career
and he drank too much to be a pioneer, but there was a raft of superstars
available, including Buck Leonard, Willie Wells, Judy Johnson, Satchel
Paige, Monte Irvin, Larry Doby, and Roy Campanella. In 1944 Bill Veeck
had tried to buy the cellar-dwelling Philadelphia Phillies and to stock the
team with these men, but was stopped by National League President Ford
Frick and Landis. The team was sold to William Cox instead, as Frick
bragged all over the baseball world that he had stopped Veeck from "con-
taminating the league."[2]

After Chandler's Four Freedoms speech in 1945, only one GM saw the
exciting possibilities of the change in the air, and that man was, of course,
Branch Rickey, who made the decisions for the Brooklyn Dodgers. Rickey
had opposed racial discrimination since the turn of the century, when he

was the twenty-one-year-old baseball coach of Ohio Wesleyan University. His star catcher, Charles "Tommy" Thomas, had been stopped from registering at a South Bend, Indiana, hotel with the rest of the team the night before a game with Notre Dame.

It was the first time Rickey, and Thomas too, had experienced such blatant discrimination, and both were stunned. Rickey explained that Thomas was on the team, and the team members were guests of Notre Dame. The room clerk held firm: "We do not register Negroes."

Rickey, always clever, asked if Thomas could sleep in his room without the clerk having to register him. The clerk allowed it.

Rickey in his autobiography described what happened next. Said Rickey,

> When I finished registering the rest of the team, I went up to the room, pushed open the door, and went inside. And there was this fine young man, sitting on the edge of his chair, crying. He was crying as though his heart would break. His whole body racked with sobs. He was pulling frantically at his hands, pulling at his hands. He looked at me and he said, "It's my skin. If I could just tear it off, I'd be like everyone else. It's my skin. It's my skin, Mr. Rickey,"[3]

From this day forward, Rickey hated segregation. That baseball allowed it embarrassed him. He knew that one day he would sign black players, that it was just a question of when. He was well aware of the groundswell of opposition to it. No one in his family was for it. His wife pleaded with him, "Why should you be the one to do it? Haven't you done enough for baseball? Can't someone else do something for a change?" His son told him that if the Dodgers signed a black player, the team could forget signing any farm players from the South.

"For a while," said Rickey. "Not forever."[4]

Nothing and no one would sway him. In August 1945 he sent scout Clyde Sukeforth to scout Jackie Robinson, who had played baseball at the University of California–Los Angeles (UCLA), was a member of the Kansas City Monarchs, and had been active in the National Association for the Advancement of Colored People (NAACP). Sukeforth never got to scout Robinson, who had injured his arm, but accompanied him to Brooklyn to meet with Rickey.

Once Rickey determined that Robinson could and would play the game without resorting to retaliation for the slights and abuse that were sure to come, he signed him and sent him to play for Montreal in the International League for the 1946 season, a year in which Robinson suffered greatly from large and small indignities and loneliness.

The indignities came from the conditioning brought by a Jim Crow

America. In an initial conversation with Montreal manager Clay Hopper, who came from Mississippi, Rickey told Hopper he thought Robinson was "superhuman." Hopper replied, "Do you really think a nigger's a human being?"[5]

In Deland, Florida, in the middle of an exhibition game, a policeman stopped the game and ordered Robinson off the field, saying, "We don't want no nigras mixing with no whites here." Robinson left the game. Not a single teammate stood up for him.

Once the season started, Robinson found himself free of America's racism while playing at home in Montreal, a city that had little prejudice because it was located in Canada, a land that had never known slavery, the Confederacy, or separate white and black drinking fountains. Montreal, moreover, was spiritually connected to France, the chosen home of such black expatriates as Josephine Baker. Robinson was lionized in Montreal by the fans.

But when the team hit the road to play in cities like Baltimore and Louisville, Robinson took a terrible emotional beating. Pitchers threw at him, and he could not retaliate. After one game in Baltimore in which the Baltimore and Montreal players created a melee that had nothing to do with Jackie, the Baltimore fans stood outside the Montreal clubhouse calling for Jackie so they could "work him over."

Robinson led the league in hitting and led Montreal to the league World Series against Louisville. Before the opening game, the Louisville players staged a walkout to protest Robinson's presence. When they returned, they hurled racial insults at him.

The final game was held in Montreal and in it Robinson singled with the bases loaded to win game four, then in the finale scored twice and started two double plays to help win the championship. The Montreal fans carried Jackie off the field. Sam Malton of the *Pittsburgh Courier* wrote that it was the first time a mob chased a Negro to cheer him rather than to kill him.

As a postscript, at the end of the season Clay Hopper told Rickey, "You don't have to worry none about that boy. He's the greatest competitor I ever saw, and what's more, he's a gentleman."[6]

In January 1947 the baseball owners held a meeting at the Waldorf-Astoria in New York. Rickey had made it clear he intended to bring Jackie Robinson to the Brooklyn Dodgers, and so all the owners discussed the issue. Not a single one approved.

Several great Hall of Fame personalities—Connie Mack, Clark Griffith, Phil Wrigley, Tom Yawkey, and Horace Stoneham—were aghast at the very idea. The vote was 15 to 1 against, warning Rickey and commissioner Happy Chandler how they felt.[7]

Shortly after the meeting, Rickey flew to Louisville and then drove to Versailles, Kentucky, to plead with Chandler to let Robinson play for the Dodgers. Rickey was surprised when he discovered that Chandler had not been cowed by the vote. Chandler told Rickey, "Mr. Rickey, I'm going to have to meet my maker some day. If He asked me why I didn't let this boy play, and I answered, 'Because he's a Negro,' that might not be a sufficient answer. I will approve the transfer of Robinson's contract from Montreal to Brooklyn, and we'll make a fight with you. So you bring him on in."[8]

A few years before he died, Chandler told me that his one disappointment was that Rickey had taken full credit for breaking the color barrier in baseball. Said a prideful Chandler, "I have nothing to be ashamed of. I had the respect of the respectable people in baseball, and I protected the integrity of the game, and that's the truth, podner."

As a first step to bringing Robinson to Brooklyn, Rickey held training camp in Havana in order to escape Florida's suffocating racism. He then arranged for Robinson and his Montreal team to play a seven-game exhibition against the Dodgers in the spring of 1947. Robinson batted .625 and stole seven bases.

Rickey figured this would prompt the Brooklyn players to ask for Robinson, but he sadly misjudged the irrational, damaging nature of the hatred for blacks by the southerners on the Dodgers. Dixie Walker, who came from Alabama, demanded that Rickey trade him should Robinson come to the Dodgers. While the team was playing in Panama he initiated a petition demanding that Robinson not be brought up. Among the signees were Bobby Bragan, Dixie Howell, Eddie Stanky, Hugh Casey, and Kirby Higbe. The movement failed in part because the one southerner who wouldn't sign was the team captain, Pee Wee Reese.

You can't tell the character of a man until he is faced with a situation that demands it. When Reese had learned that Robinson, a shortstop, might even be coming to Brooklyn to take his job, Reese had told himself, "If he's man enough to take my job, he deserves it."[9]

Reese told Walker, "I don't care if this man is black, blue or what the hell color he is. I have to play baseball." Reese says that his primary motivation was to keep his nose clean and avoid the trouble that was sure to follow from the petition. "I wasn't trying to be a Great White Father," he told me. But Reese's actions were what counted—he was a southerner who refused to buckle under to the pressure brought by friends, family, and teammates—and for the next ten years Reese and Robinson came to symbolize racial harmony in America.

The petition also failed because Kirby Higbe, who had signed it, felt guilty about doing so, and he revealed the plot to Dodger traveling secretary

Harold Parrott, who instructed Higbe to tell Rickey.[10] When Rickey told manager Leo Durocher what the southerners were plotting, the crusty manager called a midnight meeting in the barracks and challenged the mutineers. Durocher had wanted Rickey to bring Robinson up during the 1946 season. He told the rebels, "I don't care if the guy is yellow or black, or if he has stripes like a fuckin' zebra. I'm the manager of this team, and I say he plays. What's more, I say he can make us all rich."[11]

After a pause, Durocher added, "An' if any of you can't use the money, I'll see that you're traded." It was Durocher who in 1944 had been quoted in the *Daily Worker* as saying he'd leap at a chance to hire a black player if he could. "Hell," he had said at the time, "I've seen a million good ones." After his remarks, then-Commissioner Landis had called Durocher into his office and forced him to say he had been misquoted. Landis then put out a press release saying there was no rule against hiring black players. But Durocher had not been misquoted. Durocher had grown up poor and lived with blacks in his hometown of Springfield, Massachusetts, and one of his great strengths as a manager was that he knew a good ballplayer when he saw one. And when he got a look at Jackie Robinson, he knew he wanted this man playing on his team. The great irony, of course, was that right before the 1947 regular season began Durocher was accused of associating with mobsters and was suspended from baseball for the 1947 season, so we never got to see how a great manager like Durocher might have utilized Robinson to have an even greater impact than he did, in the way that Durocher made Willie Mays into an instant superstar with the Giants a few years later. Had Durocher remained as manager, Robinson would have had as fierce an ally as there was in all of baseball. With Durocher's banishment, the rookie was pretty much on his own.

As soon as it was announced that the Dodgers were bringing up Robinson, the abuse began, with hate mail and threats: "Get out of the game or be killed." "Get out or your wife will die." There were also smaller humiliations. One time Robinson was playing poker with pitcher Hugh Casey, and Hugh was losing. To everyone in the room, Hugh hollered, "You know what ah used to do down in Georgia when ah ran into bad luck. Ah used to go out and fine me the biggest, blackest nigger woman ah could find and rub her teats to change my luck." Robinson became dizzy, but did nothing. "Deal the cards," he said icily.

But that was nothing compared to what he faced from the opposition. Ben Chapman of the Phils yelled to Jackie's Dodger teammates that they would get diseases and sores if they touched his combs or towels. The Phils shouted racial epithets and mimicked shooting him with a machine gun. For a second Robinson considered breaking his promise to Rickey. He pondered beating up Chapman, quitting the game, and going home to California. Later Chapman accused Robinson of being a "weakling who couldn't take it."

All along Rickey had been certain that when his teammates saw the abuse that Robinson was taking, that some of them would take his side. The first to do so was Eddie Stanky. By the end of the third Philadelphia game, Stanky screamed into the Phils dugout, "Why don't you yell at someone who can answer back?" The next to show support was Reese, and he did it in a very public way.

The Dodgers were playing at Crosley Field in Cincinnati, which is across the river from Kentucky, a hotbed of southern pride. Robinson got three death threats. So did Reese, for playing on the same field with Robinson.

In the top of the first inning, Robinson popped out. The Cincinnati fans were shouting vile epithets, shouting to Reese remarks like, "How can you play with this nigger bastard?" When the Dodgers took the field, Reese left his shortstop position and walked over to Robinson at first base, and he put his arm around him, as if to say, "This is the guy. We're going to win with him." According to pitcher Rex Barney, who told me the story, you could hear the crowd gasp. Roger Kahn, whose *Boys of Summer* about his life with the Dodgers is a masterpiece, has opined that this was "baseball's finest moment."

It didn't take long for other players to show kindness. After one game Robinson waited for all the other Dodgers to shower before he took his shower. Outfielder Al Gionfriddo said to him, "You're part of this team. Why are you waiting to be the last guy in the shower? Just because in some states Negroes can't shower with whites, that doesn't mean it has to apply here in our clubhouse." The two men went in and showered.

What was incredible was that Jackie Robinson had become accepted by most of the Dodger players by early May. One month. That's how long it took for his teammates to recognize his value and valor. They forgot about his color and instead saw him as the difference between winning the pennant or not, and though many didn't warm up to him, because he was not that kind of individual, they certainly appreciated what he did for them.

On September 12, 1947, Robinson was named Rookie of the Year. Said Dixie Walker in the *Sporting News*, "No other ballplayer on this club with the possible exception of Bruce Edwards has done more to put the Dodgers up in the race as Robinson has. He is everything Branch Rickey said he was when he came up from Montreal."

September 23, 1947, was proclaimed Jackie Robinson Day at Ebbets Field. Among the speakers was Bill "Bojangles" Robinson, who said, "I'm 69 years old but never thought I'd live to see the day when I'd stand face-to-face with Ty Cobb in Technicolor."

On September 26, Brooklyn held a ticker-tape parade at which he received the Rookie of the Year award from J.G. Taylor Spink, the owner of the *Sporting News*. As he accepted it, close observers could see tears in Robinson's eyes.

In one incredible year, by himself, Jackie Robinson had proved that the quotations cited by the Christian fundamentalists to justify segregation had been subversions of the Holy Book, that those who were pushing segregation as a policy were both wrong and un-Christian.

Robinson, moreover, gave the whites who despised bigotry—like Chandler, Rickey, and Durocher—leeway to speak out. And he gave southerners who believed in a sense of fairness—like Reese—an opportunity to see that blacks were, in fact, just like them, not a class of people to be feared, but rather people with hearts and minds and feelings and souls, just like them. And Jackie Robinson did that, and at the same time Robinson demonstrated to all thinking people that we would be stronger as a nation if all citizens were allowed equal opportunity to succeed in the job market.

It would be another twenty years before civil rights laws pushed the movement forward through government sanction, and it took men like Martin Luther King, Jr., and Jesse Jackson to convince more and more whites to abandon segregation and endemic prejudice, but it is fair to say that none of this would have happened, or at least not as quickly, without the success of Jackie Robinson.

And what did Jackie mean to black America? So great was his effect that it is almost beyond measure. Ed Charles, later a star for the New York Mets, remembered the day Jackie Robinson came with the Dodgers to play in Florida, where he lived. Charles told me, "I can recall myself talking to God, asking why things were the way they were, asking, 'When will there be a better day for our people?' And then when Jackie came, it was like, 'My dreams have come true now. We'll have that opportunity to prove to the world that given a fair chance, we can produce, we can be responsible.'"

How many other Americans have had such a powerful positive effect on so many? And where would Jackie have been without these men of conscience?

Notes

1. Albert "Happy" Chandler, conversation with the author, fall 1983. See Murray Polner, *Branch Rickey: A Biography* (New York: Atheneum, 1982), p. 174.

2. Bill Veeck, *Veeck As In Wreck* (New York: G.P. Putnam Sons, 1962), p. 172.

3. Arthur Mann, *Branch Rickey: American in Action* (Boston: Houghton Mifflin, 1957), p. 216.

4. Harold Parrott, *The Lords of Baseball* (New York: Praeger, 1976), p. 187.

5. Arthur Mann, *The Jackie Robinson Story* (New York: Grosset and Dunlap, 1950), p. 142.

6. Branch Rickey, *Little Blue Book* (New York: Macmillan, 1995), p. 85.

7. Chandler, 1983. See Polner, *Branch Rickey,* p. 188; Parrott, *Lords of Baseball,* p. 192.

8. Chandler, 1983.

9. Pee Wee Reese, conversation with author, summer 1983.

10. Kirbe Higbe, conversation with author, 1983. See Polner, *Branch Rickey,* p. 194.

11. Leo Durocher and Ed Linn, *Nice Guys Finish Last* (New York: Simon and Schuster, 1975), p. 205.

3

Moses Fleetwood Walker: Jackie Robinson's Accidental Predecessor

Sidney Gendin

The discipline of history consists mainly of political and intellectual history, but social history deserves not to be neglected, and baseball is certainly part of that social history. Recent celebrations of Jackie Robinson's fiftieth year as a major league baseball player will go far, I hope, to remedy that neglect. Robinson was named by *Life* magazine in 1990 as one of the one hundred most important Americans of the twentieth century and I doubt anything has happened in this last decade that would make *Life* feel its judgment was premature.[1]

Still, it will not in the slightest diminish the significance of Jackie Robinson's achievements as a trailblazer who did more for integration than even the celebrated *Brown v. Board of Education of Topeka, Kansas* decision for people to learn that he was not the first black man to play major league baseball. That he was not first, however, is a very little known fact, and it may be worth our while to put that fact in historical perspective.

It is Moses Fleetwood Walker, born in 1857, who enjoys the distinction of being first. There are interesting parallels in the careers of these two men as well as several profound dissimilarities. I will allude to just a few of these parallels and dissimilarities, but my focus will be on the undeserved anonymity of Walker.

Baseball is a game of mythic proportions, and although it seems nowadays to have been eclipsed in popularity by basketball and football, it continues to be the titular head of sports, wearing the grand title of "national pastime." Whatever its right to that distinction, baseball's early years were hardly glamorous. Its beginnings are shrouded in unrecoverable history although it probably has its origins in the old English game of rounders. It took the form it largely has today through the inventiveness of Alexander Cartwright, despite the fact that the legend of Abner Doubleday has somehow prevailed, and the city Doubleday claimed to be the origination point, Cooperstown, is the site of baseball's Hall of Fame.[2]

Most likely baseball's authorities had invested so much time and energy into promoting the Doubleday legend and so much money in preparing the Hall of Fame that when the facts emerged clearly, as they did in the late 1930s, it was deemed that there was no particular reason truth should prevail over fable. Interestingly, however, Cooperstown, while not the first place where baseball was played, is the place where Bud Fowler spent his childhood years. Fowler, born in 1854, never played in the major leagues, but he became the first professional black baseball player when he played for an otherwise all-white barnstorming team headquartered in New Castle, Pennsylvania.[3]

He then had a long and successful career in several minor leagues and was just the first of at least sixty blacks who played on teams in organized white baseball leagues before the turn of the century. Baseball may have been a good way to pass time in its early years, but it was hardly a noble sport. Cartwright introduced its rules in 1846 and referred to it, not as baseball, but as the "New York Game." It was in the city of New York that the game principally flourished, although it soon spread throughout the Northeast. In its first thirty years or so, baseball had very little organization. In the 1850s and 1860s there was something called the "National Association of Baseball Players," which never had a formal league or championship but claimed a membership of about 300 clubs. Baseball was a wild thing in which drunken fans and drunken players took turns threatening to kill umpires. Ropes or barbed wire separated fans from the players and umpires, and umpires frequently had to run for their lives before a game was over. Gambling was commonplace and players placed their bets as openly as they placed their beer bottles alongside themselves in the field. In the 1860s there were probably at least a dozen baseball teams in the New York area, and they cannot properly be characterized as either amateur or professional. Such labels would be anachronistic. Whether players were paid or not was a matter of private agreement between them and their sponsors.

Among the New York teams was the Brooklyn Uniques, an entirely black club. When the Philadelphia Excelsiors, another black team, arrived for an exhibition game against the Uniques in 1867, the *Brooklyn Daily Union* had this to say:

> These organizations are composed of very respectable colored people . . . and include many first-class players. The visitors will receive all due attention from their colored brethren of Brooklyn; and we trust, for the good of the fraternity, that none of the "white trash" who disgrace white clubs, by following and brawling for them, will be allowed to mar the pleasure of these social gatherings.[4]

After the Civil War, whites of all classes still took separation of the races as the preferable norm, but those in the North had no problem with blacks joining in their games. Thus the Brooklyn Uniques and other black teams regularly met white teams in exhibition games.

Baseball, intending to improve its image and end rowdiness, and still largely confined to the Northeast, became organized in 1876 with the advent of the National League. Henceforth contracts became the standard basis for salaries of players. Real stadiums were built, championships were held, and leagues were classified as major or minor although "farm" teams in their present form did not exist. By 1884 the two strongest leagues were the National League and the American Association. The National League, in the hope of creating a genteel image for baseball, banned Sunday games and the sale of alcoholic beverages. Baseball is an early example of the cry that sports and politics don't mix, and it tried, more or less, not to incorporate the Jim Crow laws that were springing up in the South. Major league baseball has never had a formal ban against black players, but of course it could not control the racist attitudes that prevailed among fans, players, and owners alike. It is against this background that we must understand the career of "Fleet" Walker, as Moses Fleetwood Walker came to be known.

Walker was born in 1857, the son of a barrel maker, near Steubenville, Ohio. This was a rather fortunate area in which to grow up, for Ohio was among the more racially liberal states of the time. Walker's father was an ambitious man who, in middle life, made the strange career transition from barrels to physician. Thus he was able to send his two sons, Fleet and Weldy, to prominent Oberlin College. Fleet studied physics, Latin, and Greek. Since the Oberlin community had been in the forefront of abolitionism, it is not surprising that Walker was able to join the Oberlin baseball team with little fanfare about his color. By his junior year he was so addicted to the game that he no longer had time for attending classes. His grades deteriorated, and he resolved on baseball as his life's work and turned professional in about 1881. Though not a college graduate (and, by the way, Robinson never graduated from UCLA, either), Walker enrolled in law school at the University of Michigan. Baseball, however, did not permit him to devote his full attention to legal studies and he dropped out from there as well. In 1883 Walker joined the Toledo baseball club of the American Association as a catcher—a position I wouldn't wish upon my worst enemies because catchers rarely used a glove or a chest protector in those days. The National League accepted the American Association as a co–major league in 1884, and in this way, rather than through promotion, Walker became the first black major leaguer. He was eventually joined on the Toledo club by his brother, Weldy. Although Walker's joining a white team caused no great uproar, playing for one brought him as much forthright, unashamed animosity as Robinson was ever to experience. Newspapers openly referred to him as "the coon catcher," and enemy fans unabashedly screamed, "Kill the nigger," when he took his place on the field. Walker's presence on a semipro team a few years earlier had already given him his first taste of segregation as a baseball player. On a trip to Louisville he was denied the right to have breakfast with his teammates at the St. Cloud Hotel.[5]

Cap Anson, probably the greatest player of the nineteenth century, threatened not to let his team take the field against Toledo in an 1883 exhibition game if Walker played, but Anson reneged on the threat when Toledo inserted Walker into the game.[6] Perhaps the threat of losing his share of the gate receipts made Anson back down.

It remains unclear to this day why the Walker brothers were the only black players who made it to the majors. Neither of them was among the very best. The best were certainly Frank Grant and Bud Fowler, who played in the International League and in several lesser leagues that were defunct before the century was out. We can only speculate. Consider this excerpt from the *Indianapolis Freeman* in 1888:

> The Cuban Giants, the famous baseball club, have defeated the New Yorks 4 games out of 5, and are now virtually champions of the world. The St. Louis Browns, Detroits, and Chicagos, afflicted with Negrophobia and unable to bear the odium of being beaten by colored men, refused to accept their challenge.[7]

The Cuban Giants were, in reality, a baseball club whose home city was Babylon, New York, on the south shore of Long Island. The team took its strange name in the hope that it could thwart some discrimination by posing as Hispanics. Black baseball was no small thing during the 1880s. There was a short-lived black league, the League of Colored Base Ball Clubs, and the game was being played by thousands of black men. Obviously, it should not be surprising that with numbers comes strength. It is one thing for whites to admit a token black player or two among their ranks, quite another to let their leagues be flooded with them. Why, then, the Walkers? Perhaps this. In 1945, in his first interview with Branch Rickey, Robinson asked, "Mr. Rickey, you want a ballplayer who's afraid to fight back?" Rickey replied, "I want a ball player with guts enough not to fight back."[8]

I do not want to go so far as to say the Walkers were themselves once upon a time a "great experiment," as the Robinson entry into baseball came to be called. But there is a strong analogy. The Walkers were spiritual precursors of Robinson. Brilliant men, fiercely proud of their backgrounds, burning inwardly for success in an integrated world but capable of enduring enormous abuse as a condition of being accepted, they were regarded as tolerable. Tony Mullane, the star pitcher on his own team, declared many years later, in 1919:

> I disliked a Negro. . . . I used to pitch anything I wanted without looking at his signals. One day he said, "I'll catch you without signals, but I won't catch you if you are going to cross me when I give you signals." All the rest of the season he caught me without knowing what was coming.[9]

Rickey did not select Robinson to be the first because he regarded him as the best; neither were the Walkers regarded as the best. The newspapers of his time always referred to Fleet Walker as a true gentleman, affable, and the most popular man on his team. When Toledo journeyed south for a game against Louisville, Walker was hissed and booed by fans. The *Toledo Blade* wrote, "It is not creditable to the Louisville management that it should permit such outrageous behavior to occur on the grounds."[10]

Unhappily, late in the 1884 season, Walker suffered a severe injury and was released from the team. *Sporting Life* wrote, "During his connection with the Toledo Club, by his fine gentlemanly deportment, he made hosts of friends who will regret to learn that he is no longer a member of the club."[11]

Walker and his somewhat less talented brother lingered on in minor league baseball for a few years, but attitudes were hardening against black baseball players. In 1887 Cap Anson again threatened to lead his Chicago team in a boycott against the Newark club for which Walker was playing. Newark backed down and did not play him. With boycott in the air, St. Louis was not far behind, and its players pulled out of a game against the Cuban Giants with a manifesto that read:

> We, the undersigned members of the St. Louis Base Ball Club, do not agree to play against negroes tomorrow. We will cheerfully play against white players at any time, and think, by refusing to play, we are only doing what is right.[12]

By 1888 the International League and the Ohio State League openly adopted rules limiting clubs to a maximum of one black player. Since Walker and another black player named Higgins had already been signed by Syracuse, an exception was made for that club. But the Walkers had had it. Their pride no longer permitted them to find the deteriorating terms of acceptance bearable. Weldy Walker, Fleet's younger brother, sent off the following eloquent, passionate, and bitterly ironic letter to the Ohio State League president:

> The law is a disgrace to the present age, and reflects very much upon the intelligence of your last meeting, and casts derision at the laws of Ohio—the voice of the people—that say all men are equal. I would suggest that your honorable body, in case that black law is not repealed, pass one making it criminal for a colored man or woman to be found on a ball ground. . . . There should be some broader cause—such as lack of ability, behavior and intelligence—for barring a player, rather than his color.[13]

The National League and the American Association, with less courage than the minors, took the simple expedient of adopting a secret and informal ban on blacks, a ban that would last for more than half a century. As for the Walkers, their enthusiasm for the game had waned, and with that waning their skills eroded. By 1889, the Walkers were out of baseball—Fleet thirty-one years old and Weldy only twenty-eight.

Fleet Walker's post-baseball life turned out to be more intriguing than his baseball career, but that riveting story is not relevant to baseball history. It is perhaps a nice irony that Walker was not only the first black to play major league baseball but the last to play in the International League until Jackie Robinson arrived in 1946. Only a few words need to be added as a postscript. What makes Walker a particularly appealing person to study is not just the fact of his being a first but that he is every bit as fascinating and complex a man as Robinson proved to be. Walker was an inventor and held a patent on an artillery shell. Later in life he was a theater owner and a newspaper editor. In between these two stages, in fact shortly after he left baseball, he killed a white man in a street fight in Syracuse but was acquitted of all charges. A few years later he went to prison for a year for mail fraud. Despite his problems, Walker kept his reputation as a gentleman, one who mixed well with upper-middle-class white people. There is some evidence that his acquaintanceship with important white lawyers helped him gain his acquittal of the murder charge, and when the decision was announced, the courtroom crowd erupted with loud cheers and such noise that the judge ordered the arrest of several celebrants. There were but 867 blacks in Syracuse, a city with a population of about 88,000. Surely this was testament to Walker's popularity.

Nevertheless, for other blacks, things were not going well. The Walker incident took place in 1890, a year during which Jim Crow laws began to mushroom. Worse yet, outright lynchings reached 235 by 1892.[14] In the state of Mississippi outlandish segregation laws were passed, one even calling for using separate Bibles for blacks and whites when they were sworn in during courtroom proceedings. Walker had spent his whole youth fiercely battling to cross color lines in sports, and had mixed easily with whites on a social level. This turning of the tide away from social justice and the integrated society he had hoped for proved too much for him. It is perhaps less than astonishing that Walker's final claim to what small fame he had should come via a little book he published in 1908 calling for the return of black people to Africa. The last fifteen years of his life were spent mostly in the business of operating his theater but also in the promotion of an idea that preceded the work of Marcus Garvey, whose greater eloquence gave this concept so much prominence in the 1920s.

Walker is only a footnote in baseball history but he deserves better. Like Robinson, he was extraordinary as a human being: intelligent, charismatic, trailblazing. His entrance onto the baseball scene was not the triumphal procession that Robinson's was. Indeed we may say that, since his club became a major league team only after he was on it, Walker is Robinson's accidental predecessor. But his trials and tribulations were akin to those of Robinson's even if not quite their equal. In some way Walker may even have helped to prepare the way for Robinson's triumph. To some small degree, at least, baseball's hostility to black players and the eventual informal ban that lasted for fifty-six years, was a fearful reaction to the obvious skills of Fowler, Grant, Walker, and dozens of other men who threatened the "purity" of the so-called national pastime. Had it not been for fear of them, it is possible that no color barrier would have been erected. Moreover, undoubtedly, as the unearthing of the history of black baseball from 1920 through 1945 has established, given fair opportunities, many dozens or perhaps hundreds of black men would have poured into the major leagues during those years, in which case Robinson's triumph would have been based on his being possibly the best and certainly the most exciting player of his time. For us Brooklynites, and for baseball fans in general, that would have been more than enough.

Notes

1. "Jackie Robinson: The Ball Player Who Put Blacks in the Big Leagues," *Life,* 13, 2 (Fall 1990), p. 28.

2. Harvey Frommer, *Primitive Baseball* (New York: Atheneum Press, 1988). This is only one of many books correcting the Abner Doubleday myth.

3. John Holway, *Voices from the Great Black Baseball Leagues* (New York: Da Capo Press, 1992), p. 1.

4. As cited in Robert Peterson, *Only the Ball Was White* (Englewood Cliffs, NJ: Prentice-Hall, 1970), p. 31.

5. David Zang, *Fleet Walker's Divided Heart: The Life of Baseball's First Black Major Leaguer* (Lincoln: University of Nebraska Press, 1995), p. 27. This is the definitive account of the life and times of Walker.

6. The Anson boycotts are reported in every standard history of early baseball, but the best original source is the *Toledo Blade,* 11 August 1883.

7. Peterson, *Only the Ball,* p. 34.

8. There are at least a dozen or more books giving the same verbatim account of the incident. Cf. Arthur Mann, *Branch Rickey: American in Action* (Boston: Houghton Mifflin, 1957); Harvey Frommer, *Rickey and Robinson* (New York: Macmillan, 1982); Jules Tygiel, *Baseball's Great Experiment: Jackie Robinson and His Legacy* (New York: Oxford University Press, 1983).

9. Chalk Ocanica, *Pioneers of Black Sport* (New York: Dodd, Mead, 1957), p. 8.

10. Peterson, *Only the Ball.*

11. Ibid., p. 24.

12. Ibid., p. 31.

13. Zang, *Divided Heart,* p. 27.

14. Ibid., p. 70.

4

Monte Irvin: Up from Sharecropping

Jack B. Moore

Among the black baseball players who first broke baseball's color barrier in the late 1940s and successfully integrated America's peculiar national pastime, Jackie Robinson, Roy Campanella, and Monte Irvin stand out for their Hall of Fame abilities, for the significance of their contributions to integrated baseball and to the larger civil rights battles they participated in beyond their periods of play, and for the differing patterns their lives provide as exemplary or symbolic heroes. Their lives can be interpreted variously. One way is to see Robinson as a hero who triumphed over racism by overcoming its obstacles, and who then died prematurely and tormented, a late victim and sacrifice to the pressures he had endured in his struggles. Roger Angell depicts this Jackie Robinson in *Five Seasons,* describing him crazily shouting obscenities on the field one day, "without warning" and for no immediate reason either his teammates or the opposition or the umpires could determine. "After that moment, I knew that we had asked him to do too much for us," Angell says.[1]

One of Robinson's autobiographical books was angrily and accurately titled *I Never Had It Made.* The title of Roy Campanella's autobiography, *It's Good to Be Alive,* similarly suggests Campanella's perceived role as an American hero, which is, in the classic sense, comic, for his story portrays a happy man raised high and then smashed as low into the dust as humanly possible without destroying him completely. In fact, showing a man so crushed that death would seem deliverance, Campanella then triumphs over the kinds of horrors Job endured, which reaffirms the greatness and goodness of life. Arguably the most skilled catcher of his day, he lived through the nearly total paralysis of his body at the end of his baseball career, and experienced—as did Robinson—the sad public fall from grace of at least one of his children, and yet is revered as one who did not succumb to adversity, whose cry at the end of the story of his life that "It's good to be alive" (p. 215) incredibly enough seems supported by his own triumphant, spiritual vitality.

Monte Irvin's life is less well known than Robinson's or Campanella's. So far it has been told in one book (an autobiography, written by Irvin with James A. Riley[2]) but has inspired no films or television shows. Yet it offers another interesting picture in the mosaic of images that comprise the narrative of black America's contribution to American baseball and life, a narrative that is made up of many stories that are at some points strikingly similar but are also significantly dissimilar, because the black experience is so often the same and so often different. Here I would like to focus mainly on Irvin's earliest years, occasionally comparing his experience to that of Robinson's or Campanella's when such comparison seems particularly illuminating in setting forth the nature of Irvin's response to the racism he had to deal with during his career.

Monte Irvin was born February 25, 1919, less than a month after Jackie Robinson, and only about eighty miles to the northwest, in Haleburg, Alabama, a town of less than a thousand inhabitants, on the Chatahoochie River near where Alabama, Georgia, and panhandle Florida meet. Campanella was born two years later in a section of Philadelphia called, conveniently but not totally accurately, Niceville. Robinson's father Jerry was a sharecropper, as Irvin's father was. Campanella's father was an Italian-American peddler of vegetables. All three mothers were apparently pious churchgoers. Robinson's father left Cairo, Georgia, and his wife and five children six months after Jackie's birth, and Jackie never saw him again. In *I Never Had It Made,* Jackie labeled sharecropping a "kind of slavery" and called his father a "victim of oppression," but admitted he always thought of his disappearance with "bitterness" (pp. 15–16). His attitude resembles, incidentally, Richard Wright's memory of his father, so eloquently dramatized in *Black Boy (American Hunger).* Mrs. Robinson eventually took her family to Pasadena, California, where Jackie grew up and knew poverty as a young boy, but where his mother, trained him to respect himself and his African-American culture.

Campanella describes both of his parents in *It's Good to Be Alive* as warm, loving people, and his mother as a benevolent disciplinarian. He says that as a child it never occurred to him that his father was white, only that he was a "wonderful man" (p. 35). With one brother and two sisters, Campanella lived in a family that ate well, and never experienced that grinding poverty that the Robinsons apparently sometimes did, though clearly the family had to work hard and needed constantly to economize.

Like Campanella, Monte Irvin had two strong parents living at home. The third youngest in a family of six boys and four girls, Irvin told me that his "father couldn't make a living sharecropping," that he

> always stayed in debt. It's the same old story. You couldn't progress, you couldn't feed your family, race relations were bad over and over again, and people just never learned. It's like the situation [was] in South Africa. You can't treat people like that. [My father] could see that we weren't going anywhere.[3]

In 1926, Irvin says, "My father got into an argument with this guy he was sharecropping for, and it came to a point where he had to leave right away. [The argument] came up over a matter of money. He said that [my father] owed money, and [my father] said, 'Well I don't owe you any money because I didn't make any money.' " The simplest and quickest way to indicate the danger Irvin's father and his family were in is to report that one city they escaped to in 1926 was Albany, Georgia, the focus of civil rights turmoil through the 1960s and a city of despair for Martin Luther King, Jr. The Irvins had family in Albany and they stayed there about a month. Monte Irvin's oldest sister had previously married and moved to New Jersey, where she and her husband, a construction worker, owned their own house. So one of Irvin's older brothers traveled to New Jersey, and when he had earned a little money he loaned part of it to his and Monte's father, and then the father went, and finally the rest of the family rode the Jim Crow railroad car north. They "went on over," in Monte Irvin's words, eating fried chicken and teacakes. "When my mother was cooking," he said, "they smelled really great. You can have teacakes and coffee, and that's your breakfast. She made a lot of those, and some bread, and we took off."

Irvin's sister met them at the train station in Newark, "and they had a house waiting for us. It was wonderful, I tell you, and that's where our new life began. It was like a renaissance. It was just wonderful. I started to school right away, started to play sports, I started in the first grade. I was six or seven years old." First the family lived in Bloomfield, then in Orange, New Jersey, both suburbs of Newark, with relatively few blacks. The schools were integrated, but there were segregated restaurants and there were theaters where blacks had to sit in the balcony. "There wasn't anything we could do about it, so we accepted it. [My friends were] black and white. And I was a good athlete, so I never really had that much of a problem. I found that since there were not great numbers of blacks, the

problems were less. I lived in an Italian neighborhood, and they were strug-
gling [too], you know, just had come over from Italy.

Irvin's father, a small man who "had great common sense or motherwit"
but little formal education, worked in a dairy. His mother had more school-
ing, and in the South, where "if you knew how to read" and were black, you
could teach, she taught. In New Jersey she stayed home and ran the house.
"My father," Irvin said, "earned his little salary, and he'd come home and
give her all the money, we all would give her all the money that we earned.
[I worked] in a bowling alley setting up pins, on a farm pulling weeds, that
kind of thing, you know, dollar a day. [My father] just let her run things,
since he was working. [He said] you just run things, and he was happy with
the arrangement. [If there was a problem with the children] she'd handle it,
or if it was too big she'd wait until he would come home, and the two of
them would try to talk about it and settle it."

Irvin performed well in the Orange public schools, and enjoyed them. He
was probably the greatest athlete in the high school's history, earning letters
in football, track, basketball, and baseball—where he was the star pitcher
and the leading hitter. Still, on graduation night, when he and his date, and
two other African-American couples, went to a restaurant near the school,
they were refused service because of their color. After that, they simply
returned to their homes, too depressed to enjoy what is traditionally a peak
evening for high school students.

He played during the summers for the Orange Triangles, the only black
squad in the fast semipro Suburban League. The Triangles were managed
by Jesse Miles, who had also been a star black athlete for Orange High
School. Irvin said, "Miles . . . gave us, all the guys who were interested in
sports, he gave us an outlet. . . . Instead of getting into trouble, we played
sports." The University of Michigan offered Irvin a football scholarship,
which he reluctantly had to decline because he lacked the money necessary
to travel to Ann Arbor. He was disappointed, because he had wanted to play
with Tommy Harmon and Forest Evershevski, Michigan's great stars in
those years. He attended Lincoln University in Pennsylvania instead, a
black college, incidentally at the same time as Ghana's future president,
Kwame Nkrumah, (who, he said, made no great impression on him). Irvin
left after a year and a half for a variety of reasons, including disagreements
with his football coach and frustration at being unable to maintain his
athletic scholarship and enter the predentistry track that had been his original vocational goal. A number of the Negro professional teams sought him,
and ultimately he signed with Abe and Effa Manley's Newark Eagles. The
Manleys were too cheap, he said, to offer him a bonus for signing as several
other teams had promised, but they pointed out how much money he would

save because he could live at home in nearby Orange most of the season while playing for the Eagles.

Abe Manley was in the numbers racket in Newark, a common occupation for black major league team owners, who, according to Irvin, often "tried to cheat the poor players out of the little money they did make." Still, Irvin was aware that the numbers racket was practically "the only way a black man could accumulate any money. . . . It was acceptable [in the black community]. This man had made some money and he was doing something with it. . . . You know, at least he started something, creating jobs for other people." Since Irvin's earliest playing days had been in Orange, only about ten miles from Newark, the Manleys were familiar with his talents. He had worked out in 1937 with them, and in 1938 he "started to play with them on the road under an assumed name because I didn't want to lose my amateur standing." He chose the name of Jimmy Nelson, a white fellow from nearby East Orange, whom he admired for his strong appearance and good ball playing.

Irvin became a dominating player with the Eagles, particularly after he learned to pull the ball better, an achievement he mastered mainly through his own superb and seemingly inherent skills, and partly from closely observing Joe DiMaggio's more open stance and the way he flicked his wrists to power the ball to left field. He played Negro ball during one of the game's finest periods immediately before, during, and just after World War II, and he was one of the Negro major league's outstanding stars.

In the black leagues he continued to learn about race in America. He learned "a big lesson from Willy Wells," one of his managers at Newark. "Wells . . . had not that much book learning, but he [could] handle a situation." Playing against a white team he wanted "a fair shake," so [after] he went up to home plate to receive game instructions from the white umpire, he'd say, "Look, let me ask you something. Are you prejudiced?" The umpire said no. Wells said, "Well, let's have a good game today . . . I don't want you to give us anything, but neither do we want you to take anything away from us. . . . When [the game] gets tough and Leon Day throws a fast ball right there [indicating the heart of the plate], don't say ball four." And that was the situation that came up: Last of the ninth, the Eagles leading by one run, bases loaded, the count three and two, two outs, and Day threw the ball, "right there, and [the umpire] called it a strike, strike three, where before he probably might have called it ball four. . . . That's really using strategy. . . . We knew you had to have a sense of humor. In 1946 we bought a new bus. Now we're traveling to Meridian, Mississippi. We're riding this air-conditioned bus, the seats [tilt] back, and here comes a bunch of . . . [pause] farmers, all of them in an old truck, seven or eight of them sitting in the back, and they looked in and saw us, you know, in this relaxed atmosphere, and they said, 'oooohhh look at the jigaboos.' [laughs] And this son of a bitch [was] out there, it's hot, and we're in comfort. And we laugh. . . . Like I said, there's no point in getting mad, because what was getting mad going to prove? . . . You stay mad for two or three days. And if you laugh at it you'll make *them* mad. . . . So we laughed like hell, and we told the bus driver, 'Take off for Christ's sake,' because you don't know what these bastards are going to do. That's the way it was. We learned that. It's the first lesson you learn. Early."

More chilling was the night in 1941 when Irvin and the black pitcher Max Manning were driving through Daytona Beach, Florida, from a movie to their training camp home. A young white policeman stopped them and asked were they were going. Irvin replied, "home" and the policeman said, "Goin' home? Don't you know how to say sir?" Irvin said, "Yes, sir," but Manning could not. He was too nervous, too angry. "What's the matter with your buddy?" the policeman asked. "Can't he say it?" Irvin explained they were just staying in the area to learn to play baseball, that they wanted no trouble, and that his friend would say "sir," which Manning finally did after the policeman began to unbuckle either his gun or his billy club. Irvin remarked to me that to him the potentially incendiary situation presented "no problem. You understand it? Because I know the son of a bitch is ignorant, you know what I mean, and no skin off my teeth to say sir. It's not going to make me a lesser man."

Irvin's language in describing the scene to me, four decades after it was originally enacted, was strong but controlled, reflecting his emotions at the time when he diffused or deflected the white policeman's racist verbal attack, during which Irvin's teammate "quivered"—Irvin's term—from a combination of rage and possibly fear. Irvin was aware that placation was not always an acceptable strategy. "If you get to that point, now, if you say to yourself, well, I'm going to stand up and be willing to lose my life, or walk away from this ignorant confrontation—you see what I mean?" you had to decide carefully what to do, because the point would be reached many times. In this instance, for Irvin the alternatives for the two black ballplayers were to defy the policeman, strike at him, perhaps kill him, and risk their own lives, or to "look . . . right at him" and tell him they wanted no trouble, and go on. "We could have hit this man and knocked him out, you know, we could have killed him, we could have killed a man, but we knew that wasn't a route to take. . . . I mean, my father would tell us how he would have to talk himself out of situations, you see. Now, you're not compromising your manhood. You're just, I think you're just being intelligent. And you're being more intelligent than the guy that's trying to castrate you. That's all. Pshaw."

The mode of response, with elements in it of firmness and flexibility, humor and deadly awareness, carries its own risks: for African-Americans, whether ballplayers or not, all responses to racism carry risks. After he took his physical for armed forces duty in March 1943, Irwin did not think he would be drafted and sought at least to play ball in Mexico while his draft board decided his situation. "I said, well, if you need me, you can send for me." The board said, in effect, "Better stick around." He was drafted, quite probably as a result of the board's racial jealousy over his financial success in the integrated Mexican league (the Pascual brothers were offering him $500 a month, when he was paid about $150 in Newark). Additionally, his first child had just been born, and he had a bum football knee. Irvin experienced—with the Army Engineers at Camp Clairborne, Louisiana, and in England, Belgium, and France, during his three-year tour of essentially meaningless duty—racism of such shocking completeness and intensity that he wondered, "What the hell are you fighting for? . . . Why did they want to put you in a situation like this? Where's the incentive to fight? You're going to fight to preserve the system?" To get into town at Camp Clairborne, soldiers waited under a sign that read "Seven to One," meaning seven white soldiers had to be transported on the buses before one black soldier could ride. And if there were many more whites who wanted to make the trip, the black soldiers were excluded completely. Irvin arrived at this camp just around the time that a frustrated black tank company (possibly the 761st Tank Battalion) drove their vehicles over the camp's whites-only PX, demolishing it. Nearby Alexandria had itself been the location of a white race riot against blacks in 1942.

Irvin's regiment of African-American soldiers—the 1,313th General Service Engineers, in which he was a demolition expert—was stationed for a time in Redruth, southwest England. The soldiers' duties were to train for action that they would never in fact see in Europe, but more often they were used to "mop up" a camp where some white unit had been previously stationed. One day, Irvin remembers vividly, their company commander, a white lieutenant named Black, called the men together and delivered a speech in which he said, "We're in southern England, where no blacks have ever been. So you are to accept no invitations. You are not to go to any dinners, any movies, any social functions." The men were enraged, but then their chaplain—a black captain—stepped before them and told the men to disregard everything the officer had just said. "I will assure you 100 percent, that Lieutenant Black will be gone shortly." The men thought their chaplain was crazy—but he spoke the truth to them. Within a few days, the bigoted company commander had vanished, whisked away by his superiors. Still, the way he had attempted to treat his men had not been completely inconsistent with the U.S. Army's behavior toward segregated black soldiers. Often, he said, "it was like you were nothing."

The "war nerves" Irvin said he contracted in the Army made him feel he was not ready for the white major leagues when the Dodgers contacted him after the war. Clyde Sukeforth interviewed him, he said, prior to Robinson's signing. Living again in Orange, Irvin went in 1945 with an older brother to Montague Street in Brooklyn, to sign a statement indicating he would let the Dodgers know when he was ready to play for them. Irvin felt something had happened to him in the Army that affected him more "psychologically, not physically. I didn't have that intensity. I didn't have that star quality." What finally rehabilitated him, Irvin said, and made his late entry into major league ball possible after many of his peak years were over (he entered in 1949, when he was thirty) were his family upbringing, his good marriage, his wonderful children, and the "experience that it doesn't prove anything to be bitter. It only makes any kind of situation worse. Now, you can be strong, and you can speak out, . . . but don't cut off your nose to spite your face." When Irvin played in the black leagues and his team had to travel to the South, his strategy was, "You had to take low, or there was no point in your going. . . . They're going to deny you anything to eat. . . . They'll say all kind of things to you. Now if you can't take that, don't go down South. Don't go. So we conditioned ourselves. Well, now, we said, we're going down South. We'll have to put on our down-South personality, and they demand a lot of places that you say 'sir' to them." That was how they determined how they would act on the outside, but in his own mind, by his own will, and in his own estimation, Irvin was never down South, that curious place where he said whites attending black baseball games would have a special section behind home plate or around first base reserved for them.

Irvin respects both Jackie Robinson and Roy Campanella. To him, Jackie was a brave man who became a great ballplayer after he joined the Dodger system, and "an angry man. See, Jackie would provoke situations. Now for instance, after he'd finish play, he'd come down South, and he'd stir the people up, and then he'd leave. The people, the local people, had to stay there. Had to be there. Now he's going back to his home in Connecticut. Now the next day these people'd have to deal with the establishment. Campy told him one day, you know, dammit, you ought to be ashamed of some of these things you're doing. 'Well, [Robinson said], you're an Uncle Tom.' [Campanella said], 'What do you mean I'm an Uncle Tom? . . . I have no hang-ups about race.' [He said], 'my father was Italian. And furthermore, my name is damn near as big as yours. You don't tell me what to do, you go ahead and do, Jackie, what you want to do, and Campanella will do what he wants to do.' [Jackie's way] killed him, it killed him."

Once, in a game, when Leo Durocher and Robinson were violently razzing each other,[4] their tirade escalated to the stage where each man bitterly hurt the other. Robinson attacked Durocher's masculinity, and Durocher was shocked and humiliated to discover he was taunting Robinson racially. Durocher was embarrassed particularly when he saw his own black teammates, Henry Thompson and Irvin, listening, yet he claimed they supported him finally for what was unfortunately a part of the game. Irvin told me that in this series Robinson was a marked man because he had banged viciously into Giant second baseman, Davey Williams. Durocher exhorted his team to retaliate against Robinson. Then Durocher looked at Irvin and Thompson, wondering how they felt—and Irvin said he told Durocher, "We have New York written on our jerseys, Leo." They were loyal to their team. But Irvin also said that when sportswriter Joe Reichler told and retold the story years later, always concluding it with Robinson being knocked into the bleachers by Alvin Dark's barreling body, Irvin had to ask him, Joe, were you there? Dark had launched his body and spikes at Robinson, Irvin reminded him, but he also insisted Jackie had dodged nimbly out of harm's way, nowhere near the bleachers. And Dark, Irvin said, was left sprawling on the ground. Loyalty is clearly a complicated matter for Irvin, as doubtless it was for Robinson and Campanella, another area of delicate balance for friends, players, and human beings with sometimes opposing allegiances.

At the turn of the century, the activist W.E.B. DuBois and the more moderate Booker T. Washington were often pitted against each other as differing models for Negro (that day's term) behavior and leadership. They came to see each other as antagonists, and were often presented in that light by white commentators. More recent scholarship, while not denying their differences, has also emphasized the congruencies of their thought, particularly on the need for black self-help and the efficacy of at least temporary or limited concepts of segregated black institutional self-rule in a segregated society. In *Shadow and Act*, Ralph Ellison stressed that black Americans needed elements of Washington's pragmatism, and elements of DuBois' radicalism. Blacks would profit from the best ideas each man had to offer and could not afford their split into opposed forces, just as, in the sixties and later, black—and white—America needed to accept some of the strategies of both Martin Luther King, Jr., and Malcolm X, in the continuing struggle for civil rights and racial justice. Similarly, the sometimes divergent routes Irvin, Robinson, and Campanella took in the directions of their lives are well worth study in determining historically how black Americans responded to racism in the past, and how they might best respond in the present and the future.

Monte Irvin's life, which I have described only fleetingly here, is exemplary in several important ways. First, its course embodies and humanizes historic movements in a particularly interesting fashion, since it dramatizes so many elements of the second black diaspora that saw over 800,000 African-Americans emigrate from the South, most of them locating in urban centers in the North in the racially bloody decade following World War I. Later, Irvin would be one of the 2.5 million African-Americans to register for the draft, and one of the 909,000 to see duty in the Army. Of these, approximately 78 percent were placed in service branches such as the quartermaster, engineer, and transportation corps. Second, he represents a black American success story in terms of his rise from sharecropper's son to become one of the greatest black ballplayers and a member of the Hall of Fame. For many years (1968–1984) he was the lone black administrator in the baseball commissioner's office. As such, he can be perceived, paradoxically enough, as signifying the larger surrounding American culture's possibilities for satisfying black aspirations and also the limits it has placed and is still placing on them.

Together with Jackie Robinson and Roy Campanella, Irvin represents three of many black responses to racism in America, models for some to emulate and others to avoid, paradigms doubtlessly needing adjustments to fit into current conditions, strands woven with others into a picture of black life that has a coherence and integrity of its own, while it also forms an important part of the national American picture. Robinson soared to high triumph but finally died in part from the racial poison which America had force-fed him and which in his anger he could neither assimilate nor dispel. Campanella, whom Irvin called "happy-go-lucky," became permanently immobilized but still praised God for the glory of life. Irvin traveled a behavioral route, I think, somewhere between the two. Through a very conscious act of will, he did not permit the bitterness that threatened and could have dominated his life to overwhelm and destroy him, while he has worked to wear down the causes for that bitterness. This response seems, for him anyway, the most successful of his many accomplishments.

Notes

1. Roger Angell, *Five Seasons* (New York: Simon and Schuster, 1997), p. 54. Future quotations from all books are given in Angell's text. This includes quotations from Roy Campanella, *It's Good to Be Alive* (Boston: Little, Brown, 1959); Leo Durocher with Ed Linn, *Nice Guys Finish Last* (New York: Simon and Schuster, 1975); and Jackie Robinson, *I Never Had It Made* (New York: Putnam, 1972). I was also greatly aided by Jules Tygiel's *Baseball's Great Experiment* (New York: Vintage Books, 1984), and, of

course, by Monte Irvin (with James A. Riley), *Nice Guys Finish First: The Autobiography of Monte Irvin* (New York: Carroll and Graf, 1966).

2. Irvin, *Nice Guys Finish First.*

3. Nearly all my information concerning Monte Irvin, other than what can be found in standard sources such as baseball encyclopedias, comes from personal interviews I conducted with Irvin at various times in 1986–1987 and in 1997. Quotations from Irvin are slightly edited from tapes made of those interviews.

4. See Durocher, *Nice Guys,* with some additional details added by Irvin in my interviews with him.

Part II

Fans' Remembrances

Memory is distinct from history. Yet, like its mythological offspring, memory serves the dual functions of binding us with the past and defining our present. The five essays in this section are all examples of memory. The individual remembrances presented have clearly helped define each author's concept of himself. In the aggregate, these recollections create a composite description of a recent, but already vanished, era.

There probably is no World War II movie which did not feature "the universal platoon" including the ethnic-accented boy from Brooklyn. Invariably, this son of first-generation immigrants, usually of working-class background, would exhibit and express the basic and simple values of solid character and hard work. Brooklyn was different, unique; it was also America, the home of the American melting pot. Here, cultures clashed and merged, eventually forming a new Brooklyn ethos. These authors come from that world. Their collective memory evokes the Brooklyn of the 1940s and 1950s.

Robert Gruber remembers Brooklyn fondly, though, in his words, "A happy melting pot it was not"—but it was the place where the various, separate, ethnic enclaves did agree and identify with their neighborhood team, the Brooklyn Dodgers. Brooklyn, the home of the unsophisticated working masses of different ethnic groups, was connected by the existence of the team. Players and fans traveled together via public transportation to the ballpark. The Brooklyn Sym-Phony, and the crowd, were part of the game, part of the entire experience of being at Ebbets Field. It was the team, especially the multiracial team of the Robinson era, that changed diverse ethnic identities into Brooklynites. It was Ebbets Field that functioned as the melting pot for the transformation.

Peter Williams reinforces this assessment with a personal recollection of the well-known 1951 season, which ended with Bobby Thomson's climactic, sudden-death home run, marking defeat for the Dodgers and victory for the Giants. The loss was imprinted in the collective and individual psyches of Brooklynites. But out of the ashes of defeat, Jackie Robinson—representing the spirit of Brooklyn—emerges defiantly, forever "refusing to give up."

Peter Levine relives his "field of dreams"—his memories of Brooklyn; of his father, his family, and his friends; and of his early struggles. Levine evokes those teenage formative years in Brooklyn, the home of the social underdogs, yet also the residence of the championship team.

Ivan Hametz, the son of Greek-Jewish immigrants, remembers the Dodgers as the "passport to Americanization." It was his generation that witnessed—and identified with—the passage of the Dodgers from bums to champions. The lessons learned of the hope represented by America and its contrast with the realities of racism are consciously interwoven into the father-son (immigrant–first-generation American) relationship. To Hametz, Brooklyn was a place of diversity, where everyone lived together, not always in harmony. Jackie Robinson became the "surrogate champion" of this ten-year-old and of a generation of new Americans. The two generations bonded through the "shared medium of baseball."

Henry Foner concludes Part II with a spiritual linkage to Robinson. The banners of racism in baseball were coming down at the time of Passover. The liberation from slavery of the Jewish people and the "tumbling down of Jim Crow in America's national pastime" become indelibly linked.

Even if memory is not history, it serves as a matrix for history. In this case, these essays provide insights into the elusive mind-set of a generation of people who resided in a peculiar and unique place called Brooklyn, who recognized in Jackie Robinson and the Dodgers a kindred sense of commitment to social justice and the quest for the American dream.

5

It Happened in Brooklyn: Reminiscences of a Fan

Robert Gruber

Bill Veeck, Jr., said it best: "If Jackie Robinson was the ideal man to break the color line, Brooklyn was the ideal place." Why was Jackie Robinson so fervently embraced in Brooklyn? The Brooklyn in which I grew up in the 1940s had a special feel and texture.

Each year, from New York to Florida to California, there are growing numbers of reunions of middle-aged adults who attended Brooklyn high schools forty or fifty years ago. These former students—no matter their station in life or their distance from Brooklyn—will exclaim almost in unison, "Was I *lucky* to be brought up in Brooklyn!" To this day, when people ask me if I'm a native New Yorker, I reply, "Not really, I was born and raised in Brooklyn."

Historically, the heralded completion of the Brooklyn Bridge in 1883 opened Brooklyn for further expansion but, conversely, signaled the end of its independence. In 1898, Brooklyn, then the nation's fourth largest city, joined Greater New York. To many of Brooklyn's citizens, this was known as the "great mistake."

Brooklyn became known for its diverse and unsophisticated immigrant working classes. Most of its neighborhoods were ethnic enclaves, a kind of ad hoc segregation. A happy melting pot it was not.

In contrast to the worldwide popularity of Manhattan, Brooklyn was unfashionable and known for its zaniness. Brooklynites had a chip on their shoulder; they were different, as was their "Brooklynese" language. Two of early television's most popular characters naturally came from Brooklyn, Ralph Kramden and Ed Norton. But being the butt of a national joke didn't bother Brooklynites. Perhaps it was reverse snobbery. When we saw an offbeat character from Brooklyn on the movie screen, we'd feel a sense of pride. Our attitude was: "Hey, he's one of our guys. You wanna make something out of it?!" And Jackie Robinson was to become one of our greatest guys.

The disappointing Dodgers added to our borough's greenhorn reputation. Under Uncle Wilbert Robinson, they were known as the "Daffiness Boys." Later they became "Dem Bums." But what was of greater significance was that the Dodgers anchored Brooklyn, and the camaraderie of its wildly loyal fans united its insulated communities. The reader can probably understand why many Brooklynites rooted against our former tormentors, the Yankees, in the World Series in the fall of 1996 and in the playoff series in October 1997, even though their manager was a Brooklyn guy.

Our family lived on Winthrop Street, off Bedford Avenue, about ten short blocks from Ebbets Field. Lying in bed at night listening to a Dodger game, I'd hear the roar of the crowd on the radio seconds before the cheering wafted through the bedroom window. My first Dodger hero wasn't Jackie Robinson. It was Dolph Camilli, the National League's Most Valuable Player in 1941.

We were to become Jackie Robinson fans even though the only blacks most of us knew were caricatures who visited our homes each week via the airwaves as "Amos 'n' Andy"—and the actors on radio were white. The supreme black athlete of our youth was the reserved Joe Louis, always introduced as the "Brown Bomber" and as "a credit to his race." How quickly did the assertive Jackie Robinson destroy many of our racial stereotypes!

The only real southerner most of us knew was another radio personality, Walter Lanier Barber, the "Old Redhead." He was born in Mississippi, raised in Florida, and beloved in Brooklyn.

Demographically, in the late 1940s, Brooklyn's population was about 2.7 million. In this so-called borough of churches, the largest single ethnic group was Jewish, numbering almost a million people. The black population was about 200,000.

In my Brooklyn, doctors made house calls; teachers were held in esteem, and Chinese restaurants served only Cantonese food. Few of our parents had cars, and most of our relatives lived within walking distance. On Sunday afternoons, all three generations would eat at grandma's house. Marriage between young people of different religions was strenuously discouraged, and I didn't know of any interracial couples. Drugs were not a problem and I can testify personally that there was no teenage sex.

Some memories of our youth are forever etched in our minds. When Hugh Casey's pitch eluded Mickey Owen in the fourth game of the 1941 World Series, we were sitting on a bench across the street from my grandparents' apartment on Ocean Avenue on a Sunday afternoon listening to my uncle's large portable radio. At that time, October 1941, Jackie Robinson was playing semipro football for the barnstorming Los Angeles Bulldogs.

Two months later, on another Sunday afternoon, the family was gathered in my grandparents' living room. I was listening to the Dodger-Giant football game. The broadcast was interrupted with news of Japan's sneak attack on Pearl Harbor. It was the first time that I heard some of my relatives curse. At that moment, Jackie Robinson was on a steamship two days out of Hawaii, sailing for home after having completed the football season with the renamed Honolulu Bears.

On October 21, 1944, President Franklin Roosevelt, running for an unprecedented fourth term, was campaigning through Flatbush. It was a cold, rainy day, but Roosevelt, wrapped in his big navy cape, insisted on campaigning to dispel rumors about his health. His final campaign stop was Ebbets Field, and the baseball season had recently ended. He began his speech, "I have never been to Ebbets Field before, but I have rooted for the Dodgers. I hope to come back here some day and see them play." At that time, Army Lieutenant Jack Robinson was coaching black athletic teams in Camp Breckinridge, Kentucky, awaiting his honorable discharge the following month.

Roosevelt, of course, never returned to Ebbets Field; he died on April 12, 1945. We were playing stickball in the P.S. 92 schoolyard when we received the news. We went home immediately. FDR was the only president we had ever known. On that same day, Jackie Robinson, a rookie shortstop with the Kansas City Monarchs Negro League baseball team, was awaiting a tryout in Boston with the American League Red Sox. Ostensibly because of Roosevelt's death, the tryout held by the Red Sox was delayed for a few days. Finally, on April 16, it took place. Robinson and two other Negro League players performed well, but they never again heard from the Red Sox. In retrospect, it was a sham tryout held by the Red Sox under pressure from a local politician. The Red Sox were the last major league team to integrate, fourteen years later, in 1959. Ironically their last World Series title came in 1918.

The sense of excitement at a Dodger game was often described by Red Barber: "Anything can, and probably will, happen in Ebbets Field." Under the stands there was an open runway for the players between the clubhouses and the dugouts. Many times I would thrust a pencil and paper through the bars and my uncle Larry would shout, "Leo, sign it for the kid." The field was incredibly green, and we were so close we could hear every word of the infield chatter (a wonderful tradition which has vanished).

The Dodgers were truly a neighborhood team. There was hardly any parking at Ebbets Field, and it is estimated that a third of the fans arrived on foot from the teeming vicinity. I understand that today no one walks to Dodger Stadium.

I remember, during a World War II scrap metal drive, a bunch of us twelve-year-old kids carrying a heavy old boiler ten blocks to get into the game free. Others may recall similar free admission for bundles of newspapers or cans full of cooking fat.

One sweltering day in the bleachers, Hilda Chester, with her ever-present cowbell, wouldn't let us kids take our shirts off because of the threat of sunburn. Hilda Chester, my first dermatologist. And there was Gladys Goodding at the organ, and the Brooklyn Sym-Phony was appropriately seated in Section 8. Long after the wrecker's ball demolished it, we realized that Ebbets Field was a shrine.

Optimism reigned after the war. Two unspeakable dictatorships had been destroyed, the economy was expanding, and returning black veterans wanted greater equality. It was in this environment that, weeks after the war ended, Branch Rickey first met with Jackie Robinson. The "great experiment" was fraught with risk. At the time, there were no black players in organized baseball or professional basketball or football.

With Robinson playing second base, the Dodgers' top farm team, the Montreal Royals, opened their 1946 season at Jersey City. Robinson, under great pressure, had a sensational game, a portent of a season in which he won the International League's Most Valuable Player award.

The following spring, on April 9, 1947, Manager Leo Durocher was suspended for a year for "conduct detrimental to baseball." The next day, during the sixth inning of a Dodger-Montreal exhibition game at Ebbets Field, it was announced that Jackie Robinson had been promoted to the Dodgers.

A day later, on Friday, April 11, I was walking south on Bedford Avenue on my way to Erasmus Hall High School, where I was a freshman. As I passed Martense Street, a young black man in a late model car stopped and, in a distinctive voice, asked me, "Excuse me, fella, which way to Ebbets Field?"

I replied, "Keep going about a dozen blocks up Bedford. You can't miss it." As he thanked me, I realized that it was Jackie Robinson. He was to play as a Dodger for the first time that afternoon in an exhibition game against the Yankees.

As Jackie pulled away, I was too excited to shout encouragement. When

I told the story in the school lunchroom that day, the few black kids came over and shook my hand.

That week the local news coverage of Robinson's promotion was overshadowed by Durocher's suspension. The season opener was against the Boston Braves at Ebbets Field the following Tuesday. Robinson was the Dodger first baseman, and this game has been called baseball's finest moment. On hand were 26,623 fans, reportedly many of them black. The "great experiment" had its first success; Ebbets Field became a happy melting pot.

Robinson kept his distance in the clubhouse. Many of the Dodger players had never shaken hands with or taken a shower with a black man. A committed segregationist, Dixie Walker, known as the "People's Choice," was one of the most popular Dodgers. On the field, the naturally hot-tempered Robinson turned the other cheek to avoid controversy, keeping his agreement with Mr. Rickey (as he was always called). Columnist Jimmy Cannon wrote, "Robinson is the loneliest man I have ever seen in sports."

Robinson thrived under the immense pressure of the "great experiment;" his play was extraordinary. He exemplified the subtleties of black baseball. The opportunistic bunt and the audacious steal caused many a pitcher to lose concentration.

As the 1947 season progressed, there were numerous teenage players on all-white sandlot teams in Brooklyn who adopted Jackie's bat-held-high stance as well as some who wore uniform number 42.

The unlikely Dodgers won the pennant over the favored Cardinals in 1947—and Robinson was the first Rookie of the Year. His ability and courage were recognized. One postseason poll named him the second most popular American after Bing Crosby. He was also the embodiment of "Black Pride," long before it became a popular movement.

So why was Brooklyn the ideal place to break baseball's color line? Significantly, its citizens were not content with the status quo. They were strivers: hard-working, first- and second-generation immigrants. They were ridiculed outsiders. They were underdogs who could sympathize with an underdog. More than a third of the Brooklynites were Jewish, with their tradition of social justice. Finally, frustrated Dodger fans wanted a winner and Robinson helped to bring them six pennants—and one world championship—in ten years. Winning can be a powerful force for tolerance.

But Brooklyn's glory didn't last. The *Brooklyn Eagle* stopped printing in 1955, after 114 years. The last trolley—the source of the Dodger name—stopped running in 1956. And when the team went west after the 1957 season, Brooklyn's unique identity seemed to disappear. Are there any jokes about Brooklyn anymore?

The question that lingers is whether the "great experiment" could have been successful if the pioneer black player were not Jackie Robinson or if the city were not Brooklyn. It would have taken longer and would have been more difficult. But without both Robinson and Brooklyn, I believe that the "great experiment" would have failed. It has been said that Babe Ruth changed baseball, but that Jack Roosevelt Robinson changed America. He also added to our pride in being from Brooklyn.

6

The Interborough Iliad

Peter Williams

The Middle of Things

On August 11, 1951, a pleasantly seasonal Saturday, both the Giants and the Dodgers were playing at home. Up at the Polo Grounds, Robin Roberts shut out Leo Durocher's team in less than two and a half hours, moving his Phils to within a game and a half of second-place New York. Across the river in Ebbets Field, it took even less time for Ralph Branca to outlast a number of Braves pitchers, including one named Spahn—who took the loss—in an 8–1 rout. Joe Sheehan of the *New York Times* said that the Giants, having already been "knocked completely out of sight as a pennant contender by the Dodgers earlier in the week . . . found themselves in danger of being evicted from their long-term tenancy of second place."[1] The Dodgers' win, which put them a startling thirteen and a half games in front, was the first baseball game ever televised in color; if you didn't have a color wheel to stick in front of your set, you could have caught it either at Columbia Broadcasting Systems (CBS) headquarters at 485 Madison Avenue or on the main floor at Gimbel's on Herald Square. An estimated ten thousand fans *did* catch that first colorcast, either at one of those two locations in the city or by using their converters at home. The fact that the Dodgers lost the second game of their doubleheader that day, reducing their lead to a mere thirteen, seemed absurdly irrelevant; Charley Dressen's unbeatable team was already in the World Series, and it had arrived there in living color, like Dorothy landing in Oz.

The Great Offensive

Back in April 1951, the Dodgers had by no means been regarded as a shoo-in, and the National League race had seemed up for grabs, with last year's Whiz Kid Phils just as likely as not to repeat and with the Giants, similarly strong in pitching, also given a good shot. In fact, on opening day Robin Roberts beat Brooklyn easily, 5–2, and since the Pirates won their second (they had opened and won the day before in Cincinnati), the Dodgers began their summer one and a half games back and tied for either fifth or seventh, depending on which way you look at the glass of water. The only bright spot was the performance of Jackie Robinson, who went two for four and accounted for half the Dodger runs with a homer.

The great Dodger-Giant interborough rivalry began, as it was always scheduled to, early in the season, on April 20 at the Polo Grounds. Dressen, reminded that Durocher had beaten him in all three games they'd played in Florida, bristled. "Those three don't count," he said. "It's tomorrow's game that we're after."

That game, played on a sunny but breezy spring day, started an hour late to accommodate those who might have wanted to watch the morning's ticker-tape parade for the recently fired General Douglas MacArthur. The old soldier seems to have had little impact on these fans, though, since over thirty thousand of them showed up at the ballpark. The traditional colorful bunting was hung from the boxes in the upper and lower tiers, and it flapped in a brisk wind; a marine color guard led the parade of officials to the flagpole for the flag-raising ceremony, and Francis J. Sullivan's Seventh Regiment Band, as they did every year, played the anthem. A marine who had been wounded three times in Korea (the war was still going on) threw out the first ball. It was a typical early-season game, in that both pitchers were off and nobody hit a home run, but Bobby Thomson had an RBI for the Giants, and Robby had another good day for the Bums, going two for four again and batting in two. Brooklyn won it, 7–3.

They won again the next day, again by 7–3, and the subheading in the *Times* read, "ROBINSON IS BATTING STAR." It *was* a fine game for Jackie, who came up in the fourth with Duke Snider on and his team behind by one, and hit a 400-foot drive into the upper-left-field stands. The game was tied again after seven, but the Dodgers scored 3 in the eighth, and 2 of them were directly attributable to Robinson, who doubled Snider home and then took off for third, drawing a wild throw from catcher Wes Westrum that allowed him to keep coming and score.

The third game was a lot closer. The Giants took a 3–1 lead on Bobby Thomson's first home run of the season, a long fly over the roof in short left. That lead lasted until Sal Maglie started tiring and gave up a run apiece in the eighth and ninth and then, in the tenth, fed Carl Furillo a gopher. Newcombe shut New York out in the bottom of the inning, and the Dodgers had swept the Giants in their first series.

It was the sort of beginning that Frank Sullivan's cliché expert would have called auspicious, but the Dodgers had still not reached the top of the league, and when the next Giant series started in Ebbets Field on April 28 they were no higher than third, a half-game behind both St. Louis and Boston. During this period the Giants had been awful—they had lost nine straight, and were dead last—and they didn't get much better as their Brooklyn vacation began. They dropped the first game, 8–4 (Robinson homered, but Thomson went zero for four), and the second (despite a two-run homer by Thomson), 6–3. They finally beat the Bums the following day (despite another homer by Jackie), but a victory that can only be celebrated either as the end to an eleven-game slide or as the avoidance of a three-game sweep is a pretty hollow victory, a couple or three notches *below* Pyrrhic.

Remarkably, as strong as the Dodgers were, they were still not in first place. On the third of May they got their first shutout of the season, beating the Reds, 8–0 (Robby batted in two), but they were still trailing both the Braves and the Cards. By May 10, they were *still* in third, and now they were *two* games back. The game that finally invigorated the club wasn't played until May 13, a month into the season. In Boston and down by six runs, they rallied to within one in the fourth. Then, in the sixth, Robinson singled home the tying run, and the team went to town. They eventually won it 12–6, with Jackie going two for four with a double and two RBIs.

They would never be out of first place at the end of any working day again. By June 4, they were four games ahead of St. Louis, four and a half ahead of New York; by July 3, they were five and a half up on the Giants, with the Cards seven and a half back in third. Then at Ebbets Field on July 4 they began another three-game series with the Giants, starting with a doubleheader.

The first game went into extra innings. Finally, in the eleventh, Bobby Thomson homered to put his team ahead, 5–4, and things looked bad for the locals—until, in the bottom half, Jackie Robinson did these things: he singled Snider home with the tying run; he took second after a bad throw by Irvin (could it have had anything to do with Irvin's decision to throw?); he took third when a rattled Giant catcher (not the veteran Westrum) threw a pickoff attempt into center field; and then he scored on a squeeze. Brooklyn, 6–5.

After this, the Giants seemed to throw up their hands. The Dodgers won the second game that day, 4–2, and the one the next day, 8–4, to sweep, and this sweep put them seven and a half games ahead of New York.

Nor were the Bums neglecting last year's champs, the Phils. Between July 6 and July 8 they swept a series with them, too, and in Philadelphia. In the last game of that series—the last game before the All-Star break—they had to wait until the tenth to win it, which they did courtesy of Robinson's two-run homer. Brooklyn, which placed more men (seven) than any other team on either All-Star squad, was now in front by eight and a half.

Nobody was willing to ice the champagne just yet, however. In the *World-Telegram,* Joe Williams warned that a big lead midway through the season wasn't that important. He noted that the 1945 Dodgers were in first in July but a full eleven games back in October, adding that, "Inasmuch as I do not wish to have my press-box card picked up I cannot permit this discussion to end without reference to the Braves of 1914." He was refer-ring of course to the miracle team that moved from last place on July 4 to first on the last day of the season. The Dodgers, confident that miracles belonged to an earlier age, paid no attention. By July 13 they were nine and a half games up, and the Giants had slipped back to third, behind the Cards; by August 9, although they were back in second, the Giants had fallen eleven and a half games behind. This was the biggest lead any Brooklyn team had ever had. Two days later, on August 11, during the first color telecast of a baseball game, that gap grew to thirteen and a half games.

The Dogged Pursuit

On August 12, both Roscoe McGowen and Joe Sheehan of the *Times* added a couple of notes to their accounts of the game the Dodgers and Giants had played the day before. McGowen said that Jackie Robinson was "recover-ing rapidly from minor surgery," and "wouldn't want to miss" the upcom-ing series with the Giants; Sheehan noted how "Bobby Thomson's hitting has picked up sharply since he took over third base on July 20"—Thomson, who already had twenty-two homers, had batted .350 since then—and Sheehan added that Bobby was "also brilliant afield."

Both players were instrumental in the fact that both of their teams kept winning. Although Robby was still out of the lineup, Newcombe beat Johnny Sain and the Braves on the 12th; however, Thomson made sure his team lost no ground, winning one for Maglie with a two-run homer. Both teams won again on the 13th, and then, on the 14th, they opened another three-game series with each other, this one at the Polo Grounds.

This time the Giants won the first game, although Joe Sheehan said, "with the Dodgers so far ahead, the triumph was not of unusual significance." Even after they won the second, Sheehan said, it was just "a case of locking the flag hamper after the pennant had been stolen." But after they swept the series on August 17 to cut the lead back down to single digits, Sheehan had to admit that "maybe the National League is going to have a pennant race after all."

The Dodgers were far from collapse, of course, and not even very close to concern. On the 18th they rallied to beat Boston, first taking the lead in the eighth—on a healthy Robinson's fourteenth home run—and then putting it away in the ninth. The next day, though, they lost, and Thomson's two-run homer gave the Giants a 5–4 win. By now the Dodgers were, ever so slightly, getting nervous. On the 20th Sid Friedlander of the *Post* ran a story about Dressen under the headline, "SLUMP DOESN'T WORRY CHOLLY."

On the 22d of the month the Giants, who had lost eleven in a row in June, won their eleventh straight, but the Dodgers, who took two that day— Robinson won the second game with an RBI single in the home half of the tenth—were still eight games in front. Still, the Giants were not just a *little* hot, and before their streak ended at sixteen straight on the 28th, they had moved to within five games of first.

Nonetheless, the Dodgers seemed relatively unfazed. The last game they played in August was the 13–1 savaging of the Reds in which Gil Hodges tied and then broke Babe Herman's record for most home runs by a Dodger. They got a game back that day, and finished August six up on the Giants. As Joe Williams pointed out in the *Telegram,* a plural number of contestants can feel pressure, and he implied that it had hurt the Giants, who had been "upended" by it, more than the Dodgers, who had only been "slowed." Further, he said, measuring the Giant's eleven-game losing streak against their sixteen-game winning one, the Giants were far less consistent than the Dodgers. But he admitted that the Giants "can still do it," and he admitted it three separate times in his last three paragraphs.

As the teams and the season moved into September, more writers started saying that New York could "still do it," particularly after they took two more from the Dodgers on the 1st and 2d. Game one was played at Ebbets Field, and after Maglie beat Branca, 8–1, Gene Ward of the *New York Daily News* compared the Giants to a guy who had been hanging by his fingers to Coogan's Bluff, but who now had an arm up, and who could have an "unshakable grip" if they won the next day. When they did, beating Newcombe, 11–2, at the Polo Grounds, a headline in the *Daily Mirror* read: "PANIC MAY BE ON! GUARD THE GOWANUS!" At last there seemed reason to panic—two of the Bums' starters had lost games by a combined score of 19–3, and the team that had beaten them seemed to have no particular preference as to which field was to be used as a shambles.

But the Dodgers were still five up, and it was September, and the next day they recovered a game by taking a doubleheader while the Giants split. Thomson stayed hot, however. On the 7th he went five for five with a double and a triple, and the next day he got his eighth consecutive hit before he was shut down. The problem was that he was shut down by Newcombe, who threw a two-hitter to beat the Giants at the Polo Grounds, 9–0. The lead had grown even more respectable, six and a half now, and it was getting late. Now the *Mirror*'s headline read, "A PENNANT TREE BLOOMS IN BROOKLYN."

On September 9 the Giants went over to Ebbets Field to play the next game, which may have been the most important game of the season for both clubs. Branca was pitching well, but for one mistake: he'd thrown Monte Irvin a bad pitch in the fourth with one man on and Irvin had hit it out. Maglie was doing even better. In the bottom of the eighth, with one out, Snider got only the second hit Sal had allowed, a double. The next man in the lineup was Robinson, whose esteem for Maglie was similar to what he had for Durocher, and who could channel his adrenaline constructively.

Robinson tripled Snider home, and now the Dodgers were behind by only one. Since there was only one out and Andy Pafko was up, however, Robby was less of a threat to steal, and Dressen was unlikely to ask a pretty good hitter to try to squeeze him home. It was a good bet that Pafko would swing away.

Durocher went to the mound to talk to his pitcher, and the fans started waving handkerchiefs in the stands. When the club announcer said, "Please do not wave handkerchiefs from the stands," over the loudspeaker, more handkerchiefs came out. Durocher, who wanted to be absolutely sure Robinson wouldn't run, motioned his infield in. Then he went back to the dugout.

Pafko saw a pitch he liked, swung, and hit a hard ground ball to third. It looked like a sure hit, and Robinson started for home, but somehow the third baseman, a tall man, got to it. He tagged Robby coming back for the second out and had plenty of time left to get Pafko at first. The man who had been playing third for the Giants since July 20 and who tagged Jackie was, of course, Bobby Thomson, and he saved that game for the Giants.

The writers all recognized what a terrific play Thomson had made, and they said so. Some also realized that if later hindsight should ever indicate that this season had had a turning point, this game might well be it. Recognizing the game's potential importance, the *Mirror*'s headline that day was "GASPING FOR FLAG BREATH," and the reference was to Brooklyn. But a column in the *News* was even more prophetic.

Bobby Thomson himself is an unusually modest man, so it's significant, not only that he, too, thinks he made a great play, but that he particularly remembers what the *News*' Dick Young said about it; in fact, Bob is the bibliographer who suggested that I look up Young's story in the first place. Considering that fact—as well as what Young says—I'll quote the column at some length.

> If by some mammoth miracle, the Giants should go on to win the National League flag, the exultant Giant fans among the 34,004 who sat chewing their nails at Ebbets Field yesterday will look back at this stomach-bubbling, 2–1 triumph over the Brooks and remember one thing. Not Sal Maglie's gritty pitching which made him the first 20-game winner in the loop; not the circuit-smash by Monte Irvin which produced both Jint runs—but a spectacular play by Bobby Thomson, which sent the Giants West with a long-shot chance at 5 1/2 games back, when a defeat would have put them an impossible 7 1/2 in the rear. That play by the outfielder turned infielder is the one that has the Jints still breathing—faintly, it's true, but breathing.

If the Giants went on to win the pennant, in other words, they would owe it all to Bobby Thomson's glove.

But Thomson had an occasional good day at the plate, too. On September 16 the Giants took a doubleheader from the Pirates, and he homered once in each game. Meanwhile, Maglie continued to win (he got his twenty-second game on the 23d) and the Dodger pitchers continued to suffer. In a doubleheader on the 25th, for example, Ralph Branca lost his fourth straight game and then Carl Erskine dropped his eleventh game of the year.

During this time, though, Jackie Robinson, not the youngest of men, was playing with passion, often playing hurt. In the doubleheader on the 25th, he went two for four in the game Branca lost. Then, in the first inning of the second game, he was hit under the heart with a fastball, and the *Times* reported that he "writhed on the ground for several minutes." After he finally got up and went to first, he stole second—on the first pitch.

A couple of days later, on the 27th, after a very questionable call by home plate ump Frank Dascoli and his subsequent ejection of a livid Campanella had cost the Dodgers a game, Robby was accused of kicking in the door to the umps' dressing room. He was innocent, and although it may not have been unreasonable for the United Press International (UPI) reporter to guess that a man of Robby's fire was responsible (in fact, Harvey Rosenfeld says Jack was the angriest of the Dodgers), that reporter forgot he was covering a player as well known for heroic self-control as for the will to win. When Jackie located the writer, he straightened him out with some energy, at the same time refusing to blow the whistle on the real culprit.[2]

Brooklyn should have been a game ahead of the Giants, who didn't play that day, but because of Dascoli's call and possibly because of his thumbing of Campy (who would have come up with two men on in the following inning) they lost, 4–3, and their lead was only half a game. On the 28th the Dodgers opened their last series of the season, a three-game affair with the Phils in Philadelphia. They lost by a run again. Again, the Giants didn't play. When the sun came up on September 29, the Giants and Dodgers were tied for first place in the National League.

The Showdown

On September 29, Maglie beat the Braves in Boston, 3–0, and Newcombe beat the Phils, 5–0. The next day, September 30, was the last of the season. The Giants won again, beating Boston 3–2 at Braves Field. The Dodgers played the Phillies later that afternoon at Shibe Park in what more than one observer has called the greatest game of big-league baseball ever played, on a day Harvey Rosenfeld accurately calls the greatest Jackie Robinson ever had in baseball.

At first, it looked like an ordinary game, or from the Brooklyn perspective, a humiliating one—it seemed that the Phils were going to sweep this final series, that they were going to be personally responsible for costing the Dodgers a pennant for the second year in a row. In the Philadelphia second, with two runs already over, the scoreboard showed a change in the Giants game in Boston. It was now even at one; Thomson had just hit a home run. Whether the Phils were responding to that information or not, they did get 2 more to go ahead of the Dodgers, 4–0. By the fifth inning, both Preacher Roe and Branca had been knocked out of the box—it looked as though Roe had left crying—and Philadelphia was still ahead by four, 6–2 now. In the fifth, though, the Dodgers got three runs back, with Jackie Robinson batting in one and scoring another—but then the Phils scored 2 more in the bottom of the inning. That made it 8–5, Phillies.

Erskine was pitching in the top of the sixth when, at exactly 3:35 P.M., the crowd roared. The Phillie fans naturally wanted their team to be spoilers again, and the final score of the Giants game had just been posted. Now that the Dodgers knew that the Giants had won, they knew both that they could no longer win the pennant outright and that they had to win just to get into a playoff. Roscoe McGowen heard the roar, then saw Robinson look over his shoulder at the scoreboard.

In the eighth, hits by Hodges, Cox, Rube Walker and Furillo got the Dodgers the three they needed to tie the score, and in the bottom of the inning, Dressen brought in Don Newcombe to pitch. The game stayed even for eleven innings. In the bottom of the twelfth, Newcombe started tiring. Although he got two men out, he loaded the bases for Eddie Waitkus. Waitkus, a tough customer who had once been shot by a jealous woman (and who therefore may be one of Malamud's sources for Roy Hobbs), hit a hard drive toward the gap between first and second that looked as sure a hit as Pafko's hard grounder to Thomson had on September 9.

I was an auditory witness to that game, a kid listening on the radio in an era when we were at the mercy of something called a coaxial cable and away games were never televised. For me, this game is as much a benchmark as the Kennedy assassination would be a dozen years in the future: I can tell you precisely where I was and what I was doing. I was lying flat on one of two twin beds in my parents' house in New Jersey. The one I was on was nearest the door, which was on my right as I lay there. Also on my right, on a little bedside table, was a small, cream-colored plastic radio. Although it wasn't a hot day, and although I was very quiet and very still, I remember sweating.

There were three Brooklyn announcers then, Red Barber, of course, and, after him, Connie Desmond and Vin Scully. I'm pretty sure Connie Desmond was calling the twelfth inning. "IT'S A BASE HIT TO RIGHT," he yelled— and then, "NOO! ROBINSON'S GOT IT!!!"

Jackie had lunged to his left on those reliable halfback's legs, speared the ball on the fly, and flipped it by the feet of umpire Lon Warneke to Reese before collapsing in pain because he had fallen hard on his shoulder, jamming his elbow into his side. He'd had the wind completely knocked out of him. It took him a couple of minutes to get up, and when he walked back to the dugout, he looked unsteady, even a little groggy.

Roscoe McGowen called Jackie's play "the most vital put-out of his career." Harold Rosenthal in the *Herald Tribune* called it a "sensational" catch, and, in an implicit acknowledgment of Robby's will power, added that he "simply had to make that catch, and he made it." In the *Post*, Arch Murray just said (most unnecessarily) that Jack's catch had "saved the game," although of course he knew it had also saved both the Dodgers' season and their image as a great team.

"Saved" doesn't mean "won," though, and this game wasn't over yet. As noted, Robinson had been badly shaken up, and it took him some time to snap out of it. For a while it looked as though he might not be able to take the field in the bottom of the inning. Milt Gross of the *Post*, who later rode the train back to New York with Jackie and his wife Rachel, wrote that, while another player might have agreed to leave the game, might even have wanted to, "this [was] Robinson":

He was slumped in the Dodger dugout, and the others were looking at him, wondering whether or not he could go on after knocking himself out on that superlative play in the twelfth inning. Doc Wendler, the Dodger trainer, held a piece of cotton soaked in ammonia under Jackie's nose. The horrible, penetrating smell of the medication brought Jackie around.

"Let's go," Pee Wee Reese shouted to the Dodgers. They all ran from the dugout to their positions in the field except Reese and Robinson. Pee Wee paused at the top of the dugout steps and said, "Push him out here, Doc. He'll be all right once he gets on the field."

Doc looked questioningly at Jackie and heaved him to his feet. And Jackie went out on the field in uncertain steps.

Reese knew Robinson. He knew what this game meant to Jackie—if for no other reason than that Leo Durocher's Giants would get the chance at the Yankees if the Dodgers failed. Then Jackie did it.

On the train coming back Robinson said, "It's more than a baseball game to me. It's something personal."

No more had to be said. I had heard Jackie and I had heard Leo. I knew this was meant to be. Destiny had a hand in this vendetta, and it must be contested to an end—hand to hand, if need be.

So Jackie played second in the bottom of the twelfth, and in the thirteenth, too. Then, in the top of the fourteenth, it was his turn to bat. There were two men out and nobody was on when he hit a ball that Arch Murray said "rode high and far into the upper deck." It won the game, of course—how could any deity or fate have denied Robinson and the Dodgers this day?—although they all had to wait until Eddie Waitkus flied out in the bottom of the inning, and with a man on second at that.

Some game! Murray's headline read, "HOLLYWOOD COULDN'T HAVE DONE IT BETTER FOR JACKIE." Red Smith in the *Tribune,* echoing the Dodgers' famous 1934 taunting of Bill Terry, pointed out that Brooklyn was, in fact, still in the league. The very perceptive ex-Philadelphian Walter Smith also noticed something that nobody else in Shibe Park seems to have seen—that none of the patrons seated there made any attempt to get up and leave until some time after all the players and officials had left the field. "Brooklyn's still in the league," he said, with apparent satisfaction, "and the crowd is still in the ballpark. . . . The season's over, but they won't go home."

What a game! Milt Gross confessed, in print, that it had left him with a lump in his throat, but he realized he didn't have to apologize for that Robinson-induced lump, and so he didn't try. Me, I stayed flat on my back in New Jersey for at least as long as the Phillie fans stayed at the park, looking at the ceiling and thinking how great school was going to be in the morning.

Ritorno

The rest, as they say, is history, and very unpleasant history indeed for the congregation gathered here today. I wish I could remember the game of October 3 with the same delight it gives me to think back on the one played in Philly that put me into a teenage fever, but I can only remember sitting on a plastic sectional couch with my face practically inside a cumbersome, black-and-white Dumont TV, watching while Andy Pafko stood there, looking up, as motionless as if he'd just seen the Gorgon, while I listened to that cruel Hodges repeat the Giants' mantra, myself unable to move or say anything for what seemed a matter of several minutes. Probably one of my friends from Montclair High called me and snapped me out of it, or maybe I called one of them, but I have no memory other than of kneeling on that half-couch, one arm across the back, chin on the arm. I doubt if I knew what "rite of passage" meant in the tenth grade, but this was like realizing there were tigers in the world as well as lambs, a premonition of the dark side of the force, a promise that, although there would be Woodstock, there would also be Altamont. It was an irremediable melancholy and entry into the world of pain that continues until this moment, changed, maybe, even a little diminished, but certainly not forgotten, and the only fact that partly restores my faith in the remote possibility of justice in this world of Terrys, Durochers, and O'Malley's is the fact that Bob Thomson would never have had the opportunity to hit that home run on October 3 if Jackie Robinson hadn't given it to him on September 30.

Even so, Jackie, the great hero for the now vanquished Brooklyn Dodgers, actually made the last great play of the season. The still photo shows him standing behind second, hands on hips, watching the pandemonium with apparent calm—although it was very likely not calm at all, but rather very quick thinking under enormous pressure, more of his legendary self-control. A couple of years back Ira Berkow saw a movie of Bob Thomson's great home run, and while he watched it he saw clearly what Jackie was up to. After this "single most dramatic moment in baseball history," Berkow says, the Giants are "jubilant" while "the shocked and despairing Dodgers trudge to the clubhouse":

> Jackie Robinson, though, stands near second base, back to camera, hand on hip. Why?
> In all the confusion, Robinson *alone* [emphasis added] watches keenly to make sure Thomson touches all the bases. It was one of baseball's greatest unnoticed, unknown, unrealized plays.[3]

Wow. In this, the powerful climactic action of a great war, right after

Achilles has struck the fatal blow, we see the great hero on the losing side, Brooklyn's Hector, stoically resigned to what seems to be inevitable, but, at the same time, adamantly and absolutely refusing to give up.

Notes

1. All contemporary sports column quotations appeared in print on the day after the game to which they refer.

2. Harvey Rosenfeld, *The Great Chase* (Jefferson, NC: McFarland, 1992), p. 182.

3. Ira Berkow, "Baseball's Beauties and Beasties," *New York Times*, 28 September 1994, p. B11.

7

Father and Son at Ebbets Field

Peter Levine

By now every baseball aficionado worth his salt has seen *Field of Dreams,* a marvelously maudlin film about fathers and sons and the possibility of reconciliation provided by baseball fantasy. Although the movie remains remarkably true to W.P. Kinsella's wonderful novel, *Shoeless Joe,* it does take a few liberties. Most significant for me, as I remember it, it places the birth of Ray Kinsella, the main character, in Brooklyn. In both the book and the movie, Ray is the son of John, a father whose passion for baseball is no less intense than the battles between himself and his boy. John dies before father and son have a chance to resolve their conflicts. Ray seeks penance and ultimately finds reconciliation by building a baseball diamond in his Iowa cornfield; providing a place where the ghosts of Shoeless Joe Jackson, his father's hero, other major league greats, and eventually even his father return in their prime to play the game they love. It is here, too, that Ray and John have the catch that a young son refused to have with his father and find peace with each other.

Maybe it would have happened anyway, but this small detail about Brooklyn birth, accompanied by the movie's opening credits featuring a snapshot montage of a smiling father and son in front of the facade of Ebbets Field, evoked my own "field of dreams"—pieces of reality, remembrance, and possibly even a little bit of fantasy about Brooklyn, baseball, Jackie Robinson, and my own father that provided me the possibility of our own reconciliation long after his death deprived us of the opportunity of realizing it in the flesh.

Every spring, members of the Free Sons of Israel, a fraternal lodge of second-generation New York Jewish men that provided monthly opportunities for pinochle, corned-beef sandwiches, and shmoozing, as well as cemetery plots for the entire family, took their sons to Ebbets Field to see the Brooklyn Dodgers play baseball. I eagerly awaited this annual event, even though I grew up a Yankee fan in Brooklyn, worshiping at the altar of Mickey Mantle, Yogi Berra, and Whitey Ford, despite real risk to life and limb. My *Zaide* (grandfather) was responsible for this heresy. On countless Sunday afternoons, when the entire family *shlepped* from Ocean Avenue to Sackman Street to visit my father's Russian parents, he and I sat in front of his small Dumont television set and together cheered his favorite baseball player, Mickey "Mendl."

The chance for this rare opportunity to be with my father in a world of Jewish men that smelled of Schaefer beer ("the one beer to have when you're having more than one"), Harry M. Stevens hot dogs, the sweat of a humid spring night, and the familiar, acridly, sweet odor of Bering Plazas and El Productos (the cigars of choice in my father's world) was too special to pass up.

As always, we walked the mile from our apartment house on Ocean Avenue and Avenue S to the BMT subway at East 16th Street and Kings Highway. The stop was an elevated, outdoor station flanked by Dubrow's Cafeteria (the same restaurant I rushed to a few years later to catch a glimpse of John F. Kennedy during his campaign for the White House) and by candy stores at each corner that stocked the cigars my father was never without and the spaldeens, egg creams, pretzels three-for-a-nickel, and charlotte russes that were my preferences ("A little piece of Paris in Flatbush," Mr. Ring always told me).

We boarded the Brighton line for the twenty-minute ride to Seventh Avenue and the walk to the ballpark up Empire Boulevard, a trip I made many times in my childhood with my friends, when Borden "Elsie the Cow" ice cream wrappers and our public school identification cards got us into the bleachers for next to nothing. Side by side, we sat quietly on the shellacked yellow wicker benches of the dirty, begrimed, but grafitti-free green subway car along with other Dodger faithful. Suddenly, the stillness was shattered by the taunting shrieks of a bunch of Italian "hoodlums" who came bounding through the car, knocking fedoras off left and right as they made their way through the train.

Now I mean no disrespect to Italians. Even then, some of my best friends like Richie Taverna and Carl Zarillo, were Sicilian. But in my neck of the concrete, Italians were the enemy of Jewish boys like me—these swarthy, thin kids with greased-back duck's ass haircuts and names like Paddy Joe Finelli; cheeks seemingly sunk permanently from the perpetual cigarettes they dragged on; dressed in black leather jackets, white tee shirts, pegged black pants, thin black belts, and, of course, pointed black Italian shoes with white socks; and who had more sex in school stairwells than we ever dreamed possible. These were kids who never made "Special Progress" or S.P. (the chance to skip from seventh grade to ninth, an intellectual leap that retarded many of those who made it both physically and emotionally); who hung out in the school bathrooms; who were destined to major in "shop" and receive general rather than academic diplomas; and who, by some perversion of the Board of Education, won the right to employ their muscle and intimidation in the service of schoolyard and hallway discipline as school marshals—vocational training as prelude to their lives of crime. These same kids who terrorized us to the point that we never risked going to the bathroom in school now threatened not only me but my father as well.

It was 1956, a year before my bar mitzvah. I was not quite a man. Yet it was I who felt protective of my father, while he did not say or do anything, either in this brief instant of terror or in its aftermath, which suggested that he felt the same toward me. No arm around my shoulder, no reassuring words, no brave stand against (you should pardon the expression) the goyim—only the bowed head and silence that made me both ashamed and angry at him and unsure about my own feelings. After all, I wasn't the father; he was.

The renegades passed on to the next car. The train continued on to Parkside Avenue, Prospect Park, and finally Seventh Avenue, with not a word spoken about what had taken place. We made it to the game on time, took our reserved, upper-deck seats down the right-field line, and watched the "Bums" bash the Milwaukee Braves by the score of 11–8.

Even now, certain details of that evening at Ebbets remain vivid. Fondly, I remember looking down on a Brooklyn infield that included Roy Campanella, Charlie Neal, Junior Gilliam, and an aging Jackie Robinson, with my father telling me how proud he was to live in a place that fielded baseball's first integrated professional baseball team and, in the 1950s, one of baseball's best teams.

That night, another black ballplayer, with his own memories of Jackie Robinson, stood out more clearly than the "Boys of Summer." Eight years earlier, as he tells it, he had cut high school classes in Mobile, Alabama, to hear Robinson speak in a corner drugstore. The Dodgers were in town for a spring training game, and Jackie never missed a chance to offer himself to local blacks, particularly youngsters. As Hank Aaron recalled,

> I can't remember exactly what he said, but I do know my mouth was wide open. I was in the back, but I felt like I was hugging him, you know? Holding

his hand. I saw a concerned citizen. He was saying something like, "Hey, just give yourself a chance. If I can make it, all of you can make it. It may not be in sports, but it can be in something."

In his autobiography, *I Had a Hammer,* Aaron wrote,

That same day, I told my father I would be in the big leagues before Jackie retired. Jackie had that effect on all of us—he gave us our dreams. Before then, whenever I said I wanted to be a ball player, Daddy would set me straight. I remember sitting out on the back porch once when an airplane flew over, and I told Daddy I'd like to be a pilot when I grew up. He said, "Ain't no colored pilots." I said okay, then, I'll be a ball player. He said, "Ain't no colored ball players." But he never said that anymore when we sat in the colored section of Hartwell Field and watched Jackie Robinson.

Aaron did make it to the majors before Jackie retired, and that night, with the Free Sons of Israel and their sons in attendance, the young slugger, then in his second year with the Braves, came up three times—each time smacking the ball over the chain-linked fence above the right-field scoreboard onto Bedford Avenue. The fourth time up, with a major league consecutive home run record in his grasp, he smashed a shot that hit the Bulova clock atop the scoreboard. He pulled into second as Duke Snider fielded the ball that bounced over Carl Furillo's head and threw it to Pee Wee Reese who was covering second base.

My father and his friends—men he had known since grade school at P.S. 184 and the playgrounds of Brownsville and the Lower East Side—animated now by the game, the beer, and the freedom of the moment; ties loosened; their white, starched, long-sleeve shirts open at the neck and rolled up to their elbows, cheered the Dodgers' good fortune and reveled in their missed opportunity to witness baseball history. What I recall most is the simple thrill of being part of my father's world—for me an exhilarating counterpoint to the evening's earlier disappointment.

My father and I never talked about this evening that occurred almost forty years ago. He has been dead for twenty-four years. It's even possible that time has blurred my memory of those yearly baseball outings that marked my passage through adolescence. Maybe it wasn't three home runs; perhaps the Braves won. You could look it up. It doesn't really matter. For me, *Field of Dreams* reminded me of my own Brooklyn moments and helped me understand what my father and I missed as well as what I obtained from him: botched opportunities for expressing mutual respect and love; encouragement to live and enjoy every moment of life to the fullest; and a respect for humane values and racial equality, nurtured by baseball pioneers like Jackie Robinson and Hank Aaron, that I have come to appreciate long after that Brooklyn night faded into memory.

We all know that the struggle for civil rights in this country was far bigger and more complex than the efforts of the man who broke baseball's color line. But like Brooklyn and Ebbets Field, Jackie Robinson's heroic efforts on and off the field have made him an enduring symbol of that struggle. Consider in closing one final bit of Hollywood film magic that confirms his status as cultural icon and reaffirms the reason we honor him today. In *Shoeless Joe,* when Ray Kinsella "convinces" J.D. Salinger to come to Fenway Park with him, he reminds the famous author that he once gave an interview in which he said, "When I was a kid, I wanted more than anything else in the world to play baseball in the Polo Grounds." By the time *Shoeless Joe* became *Field of Dreams,* Salinger had become Terrance Mann, played by James Earl Jones, a black activist and novelist from the 1960s whose memories had also been altered by screenwriters and film directors. "When I was a kid," he admits to Ray, "I wanted more than anything else to play baseball at Ebbets Field with Jackie Robinson."

8

A Ten-Year-Old Dodger Fan Welcomes Jackie Robinson to Brooklyn

Ivan W. Hametz

One Sunday morning late in March 1947, I walked into the living room of our apartment at 187 Ten Eyck Walk, Williamsburg, Brooklyn. As usual, my Greek-Jewish immigrant father was reading the *New York Times*. I wanted to ask permission—a rarity today—to do something with my friends that afternoon. Before I could pose the question, he said, "The Dodgers are going to have a Negro first baseman this year." Smugly, I looked at him with that "Yes, so what?" attitude I had developed in my tenth year of life in Brooklyn. My father, in a thick Levantine accent, raised his voice in the stentorian manner of Pericles in Athens, "He is going to be the first non-white to play in the major leagues!" Knowing that the Howie Schultz—Eddie Stevens combo had performed admirably in 1946 made me stubbornly indifferent to his oracular tone. In an effort to communicate in my lingo, I retorted, "Can he hit?" Though trigger-tempered at times, my father was infinitely patient with me. "Think," he countered. "Please stop and think. This is a giant step [one of our favorite games] toward ending inequality in the United States. It is what we were fighting for in World War II. Justice!"

No stranger to injustice and to inequality, my father had come to America to build a new life. He loved America but was keenly aware of our country's limitations. He also loved baseball, his passport to Americanization. An avid Dodger fan, he followed the fortunes of Dodgerdom from bum to heroic status in a single generation. Like an ancient soothsayer, he predicted that Rickey's choice of Robinson would bring glory to Brooklyn. As the years passed, my father's judgment proved prophetic.

Within two weeks, as I recall, Jackie began to vindicate the judgment of Branch Rickey and my father. Though playing out of position, at first base, Robinson fielded brilliantly. But it was at bat and on the base paths that the Negro rookie emitted a special glow. He hit .297 and stole twenty-nine bases, leading the league in the latter category. Darting off a base, he drove pitchers crazy. As the National League's best rookie, he led the Dodgers to the World Series. Though our team lost to the Yankees in the seventh game after taking a 2–0 lead, it was a glorious season.

Following the poet Wordsworth, I recollect that emotional season in tranquillity. Rachel and Jackie Robinson received a lot of media attention, more than most veteran players. I did not realize at that time that Mr. and Mrs. Robinson were not permitted to stay in the same hotels as other Dodger couples. When my father informed me of this blatant discrimination, I felt a keen sense of outrage. My father explained that the "great experiment" had to succeed because America had strayed from its high principle of equality and justice for all. That I understood. But why, I wondered, did skin color have so much weight in the way people were judged?

In retrospect, 1947 represented a turning point in my life. A safer city then allowed a ten-year-old to attend Ebbets Field with older friends to watch the Dodgers play. I admired Pee Wee Reese, Ralph Branca, Cookie Lavagetto, and Dixie Walker (before I learned that he was a fierce racist). I adored Jackie Robinson. Why? He won my admiration with a combination of speed, courage, and competence. He was a blur on the base paths. He seemed to get hit by more pitches than any other player. Did he bail out against some inside "heat"? Perhaps. But who could blame him? It bothered me that certain Dodger pitchers did not defend Robinson with retaliation pitches. Often, he seemed isolated from his own teammates. Opponents came at him with spikes flying. If Robinson did not fight back at first, he stood his ground and earned the respect of both foe and fan.

Williamsburg, my neighborhood, was a microcosm of Brooklyn. In a place of diversity, we lived together—not always in harmony. On certain occasions, Halloween for example, the ugly face of anti-Semitism surfaced. A bunch of thugs would chase Jewish kids with socks filled with chalk and beat us. Passive and nonviolent, the Jews did not retaliate. It was a humiliating experience. As a *shtarker*, bigger than most of my friends, I fought back and taught my tormentors a lesson in retributive justice. Now, as an adult, I do my fighting in a court of law. At the tender age of ten, however, I needed a surrogate champion. As a Jew, vulnerable to mob mentality and group oppression, I discovered Jackie Robinson. In his quest for recognition and respect, he fought for us. A beacon, he shone the light of liberation on us all: Jew and Christian, black and white, Yankee and Dodger fans alike.

Besides battling bigotry in our neighborhood, we also contested for supremacy in baseball—not as players, but as fans. Among my friends I could count only one Giant fan. All the rest were either Dodger or Yankee supporters, with a surprising majority of the latter. I remember, as the summer of 1947 progressed, endless arguments over which was the best team. Though the Giants hit a record 221 home runs, their mediocre pitching placed them in fourth place in the National League and last place in our neighborhood. Regardless of which team we favored, all of the Williamsburg boys of spring rooted for Jackie Robinson. Fifty years later, I *kvel* with pride that we shared this reverence for a baseball pioneer.

Although the season ended on a sour note for Dodger fans, we rejoiced in Robinson's successful breakthrough. Ever resilient, we chanted, "Wait till Next Year!" To be sure, "next year" did not arrive until 1955. By that time, age and injuries had taken their toll on Mr. Robinson. He was thirty-six years old and on the downside of a meteoric career. But he left a legacy of lasting accomplishment and unconquerable spirit. He was—and is—a hero for all seasons.

The "Silent Generation" of the 1950s followed the crowd. In the spirit of Thoreau, Robinson had no crowds to follow. He marched to a different beat. Regardless of the consequences, he did what was right as he saw it. Clearly, he did not "go gently into that good night." With Dylan Thomas, he "rage[d] against the dying of the light." Criticized constantly and often vilified, Jackie remained a rebel to the end. Much like Paul Robeson, who chose to attack a vicious system from without, Jackie Robinson challenged it from within. Rejected by militants in the 1960s, just as he had been abused by bigots in the 1940s, he never lost either his moral or political compass. Though blinded by diabetes and felled by a broken heart, his soul force carried on.

For a young lad growing up in Brooklyn, vintage 1947, Robinson was the quintessential hero. My father, the Delphic Oracle, taught me, long before Martin Luther King, Jr., entered center stage, that we must judge people on the "content of their character," not the color of their skin or the house in which they worshipped. Jackie's character and skill impressed this rabid Dodger fan in the making. As I grew to manhood and bonded with a father from another culture through the shared medium of baseball, through the common reverence of Robinson, this writer developed a heightened appreciation of number 42. I read about his years at UCLA and his struggles in the Army. I learned about his post-baseball career as a pioneer in business and civil rights. Always on the cutting edge, Robinson starred on and off the field. A role model with crossover appeal, Jackie was ranked as the second most popular person in 1947. Bing Crosby was first. Popularity should have thrust Robinson into the history books as the first black manager in major league baseball. I agree with the poet who wrote, "The saddest words: it might have been."

The death of his eldest child and namesake, followed by his own demise at an early age—only fifty-three—conveys a tragic coda to an heroic life. In his departure and in the passing of Gil Hodges, Roy Campanella, Billy Cox, Junior Gilliam, and Carl Furillo, we witness the twilight of the gods.

Recently, I survived serious—indeed, life-threatening—surgery. This experience compelled me to contemplate on life's mysteries and wonders. In search of a happy, perhaps Faustian moment, I conjure up a vivid memory. I see Jackie Robinson, a young lion, dancing off third base. Everyone in the park, everyone listening to Red Barber's dulcet description on radio or Vin Scully's resonant baritone on television knows what's coming. Jackie stops. Jackie roars home. Safe! Opposing pitcher, catcher, and manager shake their heads in disbelief. Yogi Berra continues to argue that he was out. Thousands cheer. I raise my hand in triumph. I am young again. My father is at my side explaining the game's finer points. Brooklyn is green and fragrant and jubilant. I seize the day and freeze the play with an ode to joy.

Although crowds no longer cheer in Brooklyn for the Dodgers and Jackie Robinson, he needed no crowds. Jackie was a crowd, all by himself.

9

Mah Nishtanah

Henry Foner

The year 1947 has already gone down in baseball history as the year in which Jim Crow was sent packing by professional baseball. It will be so designated here in Brooklyn this coming April when the borough marks the fiftieth anniversary of Jackie Robinson's ascension into the major leagues.

For me, it will help keep alive the memory of a day forever etched in my mind. I was a substitute teacher in stenography and typewriting at Prospect Heights High School, six blocks from Ebbets Field. I had a spiritual if not racial kinship with Robinson. Just as he was battling seemingly insurmountable odds to become a big-league baseball player, I was engaged in an uphill struggle to become a "regular" teacher, despite a Rapp-Coudert witchhunt that had already (temporarily) laid waste the careers of my brothers, Philip, Jack, and Moe, formerly, respectively, two history professors and one clerk in the registrar's office at City College.

Rapp-Coudert, for those of you who came after, was an earlier incarnation—the New York State version—of the McCarthy Committee. The former flourished briefly in the early 1940s and took with it some forty to fifty of City College's finest teachers. You don't have to take my word for it—even the trial committees that dispatched their careers were compelled to acknowledge their academic virtuosity. One of their proudest accomplishments was winning a place on the City College faculty for its first African-American instructor, Max Yergan, brought aboard to teach a course that was then called "Negro History."

Against this background, it is not surprising that the news of Robinson's exploits struck a particularly responsive chord in me. I couldn't help feeling that fate had placed me within walking distance of a historical event, and, as I drilled my students that day in the fine points of the "l" and "r" hooks in Pitman stenography, I looked forward to my visit to Ebbets Field that afternoon.

Finally I was seated in the left-field stands. Robinson came out on the field, resplendent in his Montreal uniform. The Royals, then a Dodger farm team, were on hand for an exhibition game and were expected to give up their prize shortstop to their seigniorial lieges at the end of the day. All went according to plan. From my seat in the stands, I watched the brief ceremony on the field marking the tumbling down of the walls of Jim Crow in America's national pastime—and then went home to prepare for my family's Passover seder that evening.

The Foner family seders, being inhabited by scholars and political activists, often became battlegrounds for the expression and rebuttal of various pet theses. On that night, however, things were different. As the youngest in the family, it devolved upon me to ask the *fir kashes,* or four questions. That night, they took on a different meaning. After the first question, "Why is this night different from all other nights?" I proceeded to elucidate, describing my experiences of the day. My parents told me it was the most harmonious seder in the family's history.

And there it remained for more than four decades, until one day, I attended a session at the New York Public Library where the guest speaker was *New York Times* sports columnist Ira Berkow. Part of his talk dealt with the importance of Robinson's breakthrough, and during the question and discussion period, I told the story of that day in 1947. When it was over, I was approached by a young woman who said she was working with historian/filmmaker Ken Burns on his forthcoming video on baseball and asked if I had any objection to having my story included. Of course, I agreed, and so it was that when *Baseball* aired on Public Television in the fall of 1994, in the segment entitled *The Bottom of the Sixth Inning,* there was a scene showing curtains billowing in a room in which candles were burning, and a voice intoned something like,

> That evening, at 1574 50th Street in the Borough Park section of Brooklyn [our address], as the family sat down for its Passover seder, the youngest member asked the traditional question, "Why is this night different from all other nights?" and replied, "Today, the first black American baseball player entered the major leagues."

Part III
The Radical Press/Agenda

Traditional accounts of the integration of the major leagues give little space to the active campaigns conducted for that cause for more than a decade by the American Communist Party, particularly by the staff of the *Daily Worker* and the *Sunday Worker*. According to Kelly Rusinack, however, "the communist writers were among the first of the voices which grew louder each passing year to end Jim Crow in baseball."

Rusinack describes a ten-year process of consciousness raising, spearheaded by writers such as Lester Rodney and Bill Mardo, the other two presenters in this section. Rodney and his readers continuously wrote letters and petitions to Branch Rickey—general manager of "New York's workingman's team"—as well as to other baseball leaders in an attempt to gain a breakthrough. The effect of all this hard work was to keep the issue alive at a time when major league baseball seemed uninterested in reforming itself. Rusinack concludes that Rodney's and his colleagues' zeal and integrity were "unparalleled by their contemporaries and surpassed only by the civil rights movement of the 1960s."

Lester Rodney and Bill Mardo offer their reminiscences as activists in the struggle for reform. In contrast to the remembrances of the Dodger fans covered in Part II, Rodney's and Mardo's recollections address specific issues in which they were personally engaged. Rodney and Mardo were fighters for a cause, and that cause was to democratize baseball.

Rodney recalls how it looked, sounded, and felt to work for and witness the social transformation of baseball. He points out that the ban in baseball was rarely mentioned or challenged by the establishment press; only the Negro and communist papers kept the issue consistently alive. In Rodney's words, "The conscience of American journalism on baseball apartheid, sorry to say, was not in the hands of America's big daily newspapers." Rodney also offers a revisionist perspective of Branch Rickey—a viewpoint made even stronger by Bill Mardo—that argues that Rickey seized the moment and placed himself at the head of an inevitable cause, in contradistinction to the picture of the crusading integrationist biding his time.

Bill Mardo's revisionism is even more direct. The traditional story of Rickey's conscience-driven decision to integrate baseball is described as an example of the *bubbameise,* or old wives' tale, version of history. Mardo insists that Rickey "saw the handwriting on the wall" and acted accordingly. Rickey deserves credit for embracing the inevitable, but not for the years of preparation that preceded the event. Mardo's recollection of the Robinson-Robeson relationship also revises the standard versions of a personal animosity between these two black icons in 1949. Indeed, Mardo considers Robinson's finest moment to be the day he openly supported Robeson's rights of free speech; a statement carried only by the *Daily Worker* and omitted by the establishment press.

The historical correctives suggested in these three essays bring to light additional considerations, particularly on the issue of the degree of influence exercised by the dissident press. Were these protests and agitations effective in bringing about reform, or was the communist identity of the proponents an automatic excuse for ignoring their "radical" agenda? Finally, if the linkage with communism did make the baseball leadership either averse or deaf to their pleas, what alternative pressure existed to make some of them rise to the occasion?

Whether one accepts or rejects the Rodney, Mardo, and Rusinack versions, the fact remains that on this issue, the *Daily Worker* staff fought the principled fight when it was not yet popular to do so. They were—to borrow Golenbock's phrase—true men of conscience.

10

Baseball on the Radical Agenda: The *Daily Worker* and *Sunday Worker* Journalistic Campaign to Desegregate Major League Baseball, 1933–1947

Kelly E. Rusinack

The 1930s fear of fascism, the devastation caused by the Depression, and failing faith in the contemporary system served to facilitate receptivity to radical politics and progressive social reform; the traditional means to socio-political order were in chaos. It was out of this atmosphere of distrust in the established system, domestic social disorder, and the ideological influences brought by a great migration of foreigners that the United States Communist Party (CPUSA) sought to achieve legitimacy. The persecution of Bolshevism during the "red decade" following World War I, however, determined an uphill battle for the CPUSA to gain even a smidgen of respectability. The radical Communist philosophy of equality of all people attracted a small but significant following, especially in New York City, among American social progressives who could not find solace in mainstream social ethics, for it was the American Communists who championed the cause of class, gender, and interracial solidarity as the best means of social progress.

The vehicle through which the New York–based CPUSA disseminated its cultural and political information to the masses was the Party's newspaper, the *Daily Worker,* and its Sunday edition, the *Sunday Worker*. While the *Worker* headlined news of the escalation of Nazi hostilities in Europe through Communist eyes, it also sought to filter American news through its radical focus in order to influence its targeted audiences, the American working class and African-Americans. By devoting much of the *Worker*'s coverage to news and social issues of interest to these groups, the CPUSA turned its outspoken, radical perspective to the U.S. media, attacking the tattered social fabric of the United States from the platforms of the minorities from which the Communists sought to gain support. Certainly, the CPUSA saw the possibilities of increasing its popularity by appealing to blacks and nonracist whites in its efforts to end discrimination, but many rank-and-file members, the majority of whom were white, also sincerely believed in the cause of the equality of all races.

No American institution was too sacred to be rooted out for violations of Communist ideals, not even baseball. By the time that Hitler was rising to power in Germany, the CPUSA found it propitious to champion the cause of ending the segregation of baseball as part of an all-encompassing campaign to end discrimination against African-Americans in all phases of American life. Party members such as the *Worker* sportswriters saw in the issue of ending discrimination in baseball a way to make a truly revolutionary change in American society. Attacking it with an impassioned and often coarse approach that characterized Communist propaganda, the Communist writers were among the first of the voices that grew louder each passing year to end Jim Crow in baseball.

By 1933, the *Worker* began to comment on the injustice of racial segregation in baseball. A commentary by Ben Field in the August 23, 1933, *Worker,* entitled "The Brooklyn Dodgers Win a Game," described the scene at Ebbets Field, the Dodgers' ballpark:

> A Negro rushes about with a whisk-broom currying you down. He's got to earn his few cents. He chants: "Anything at all. Nothing is too small." You spot a few Negro fans. Negro workers make good athletes. But where are the Negroes on the field? The Black Yankees are fine semi-pro players. But the big leagues will not admit Negro players. There is something else to chalk up against capitalist controlled sports.[1]

That article set the tone for over a decade of *Worker* sports articles, which rarely mentioned major league baseball without commenting upon the exclusion of African-American players, also comparing African-American players with major league players. The issue of African-Americans participating in all facets of American society open to whites was as much a concern of the sports staff as it was of the news staff of the *Worker*.

Presenting the argument within the bounds of Communist ideology became easier for these writers, as a special mandate of the Communist International in 1935 allowed the CPUSA, through the *Worker,* to focus some attention on the subject of capitalist sports. As noted by the editorial staff, the sports coverage quickly became an overwhelmingly popular feature to *Worker* readers and by 1936 was granted one entire page, as the writers and readers of the *Worker* came to see the sports world as an integral and fundamental part of American society, and not as insignificant or divorced from more important concerns.

The Communist sportswriters superimposed the capitalist hierarchy upon the U.S. professional sports establishment, declaring that professional athletes were workers, too, who physically labored but did not receive much of a share in the fruits of their labors, the same as any factory worker. The athlete-workers did not have unions to protect their interests, and were at the mercy of the wealthy team owners or of crime-ridden managers and other sycophants who would take advantage and live off the profits of the athletes' work. By characterizing professional, and even amateur and collegiate athletes, in such a manner, the Communists could, with a clear conscience, provide sports coverage and commentary in the *Worker* without appearing to approve of capitalist values. Once this was party policy, the synthesis of sports and racial oppression was a logical next step.

The year 1936 proved to be a watershed year for racial issues in sports news, providing a starting point for the *Worker*'s aggressive campaign to spotlight the injustice of Jim Crow in baseball. Hitler's Germany hosted the 1936 Olympics, in which African-American athletes won numerous medals and set new Olympic world records. Hitler's apparent snubbing of Jesse Owens, the African-American track star who won four gold medals, gave the U.S. Communists a rallying point around which to focus their campaign against discrimination in baseball.

On Sunday, August 16, 1936, readers of the *Sunday Worker* awoke to the banner headline, "Fans Ask End of Jim Crow Baseball," flanked by pictures of Martin Dihigo of the New York Cubans and Oscar Charleston of the Pittsburgh Crawfords Negro League teams. A page 1 article entitled "Fans Oppose Jim-Crow in Big League Baseball" included comments gathered by a *Worker* reporter from fans at Yankee Stadium.[2] The article began with the pronouncement, "Jim Crow baseball must end," a dramatic beginning for the *Worker*'s new campaign.

The approach taken by the *Worker* was threefold. It argued that African-Americans had proved their worthiness to participate in all facets of professional American sports through their successes in the 1936 Berlin Olympics, and leveled political criticism at American society for being racist; to the Communists, discrimination and democracy could not coexist. Racism was a major component of Nazi propaganda, and support for Jim Crow was thus support for Hitler.

There is not much difference between the Hitler who, like the coward he is, runs away before he will shake Jesse Owens' hand and the American coward who won't give the same Negro equal rights, equal pay and equal opportunities.[3]

The article also asserted that admitting blacks would boost the level of play in the major leagues. In this respect, and as would be demonstrated in the future, the *Worker* sportswriters showed a remarkable knowledge of Negro League baseball and baseball history in general.

The CPUSA's campaign proved from the beginning to be virtuous and conscientious, characteristics Americans did not usually associate with Communism. As the world moved toward another war to end all wars, and as the United States would be called upon to defend democracy, Americans would have to face up to their own hypocrisies; the U.S. Communists intended to use those weaknesses to champion the cause of leftist ideals.

In the years following this auspicious article, the *Worker* intensified its active involvement in and commitment to the issue of the need to desegregate baseball, which soon became the most recurrent topic in the *Worker* sports page. Writers for the sports page—including Ted Benson, Charles Dexter, Bill Mardo, and most importantly, sports editor Lester Rodney, who proved to be the paper's most vociferous champion for the cause of ending Jim Crow in baseball—offered articles tracing the history of Negro League baseball and highlighted the fact that many contemporary Negro League players were thought of as major league star quality, the most beloved of whom was the pitcher Leroy "Satchel" Paige.

Lester Rodney was certainly breaking new ground. A Jewish-American who personified the U.S. Communist as social progressive, Rodney was more interested in seeing justice done for African-Americans than in just seeing better baseball. He was more than willing to go out on a limb to rant at U.S. society for its tyranny, and to place his personal reputation in the hands of an unpopular movement that reflected his native values. Rodney had an instinctive sense of social justice, an articulate, sensible, yet passionate style of writing. When he was made sports editor of the *Worker* in 1936, he acquired a forum through which to advance his ideals of racial equality and the true meaning of democracy in American sports. Rodney helped to further legitimize sports as a social concern, and purposely gave a voice to the opinions of athletes formerly considered to be stupid and shallow. Rodney's efforts, sincerity, and fair reporting earned him the respect of the athletes he interviewed, as well as of other journalists, black and white.

Once the *Worker* took on the issue of discrimination in baseball, it flourished. Reader letters often thanked the *Worker* for informing them of the inequality of Jim Crow baseball, and for alerting them to the existence of the Negro Leagues and special players—Satchel Paige, Josh Gibson, Johnny Taylor, and many more. Though the *Worker* proved just as wanting in the ability to provide Negro League scores as it was for the major leagues, at least the issue of ending separate leagues was at the forefront of most *Worker* articles written about baseball for over a decade.

The *Worker* sportswriters repeatedly blamed the owners of the teams, or "magnates," for perpetuating Jim Crow, and absolved the players of all blame in the persistence of segregation. Showing a sophistication for picking through decades-old Jim Crow rhetoric to expose the unfounded fears against drafting blacks into the system, the *Worker*'s sportswriters claimed early rhetorical victories of their own in their quest to effect changes in the hiring practices of big-league clubs.

One such victory came in an interview with Joe DiMaggio, the Italian-American son of immigrants and a young New York Yankee sensation, published September 13, 1937, in which he told Lester Rodney about his barnstorming days against Negro League players on the West Coast in the off-season, declaring, "Satchel Paige is the greatest pitcher I ever batted against."[4] It was well known by that time that Dizzy Dean lamented that he could not play against Paige in the majors, but DiMaggio's statement acknowledged the superiority of a black player over the greatest white players of his time, and offered proof that there were more white players whose baseball sense belied the standard Jim Crow rhetoric that racial separation was desired by the players. Rodney reiterated DiMaggio's claim often, for it sparked a trend of openness about black players among major leaguers for the next several years.

Rodney also exposed the more political side to Satchel Paige, who publicly challenged major league baseball to prove the inferiority of African-American baseball players in a September 16, 1937, article entitled, "Paige Asks Test for Negro Stars."[5] Though Paige was always characterized as easygoing and nonpolitical, Rodney quoted Paige as saying, "Let the winners of the World's Series play [the Negro League All-Stars] just one game at Yankee Stadium—and if we don't beat them before a packed house they don't have to pay us!" Coming from a man who played baseball almost 365 days a year, that was a serious all-or-nothing challenge. Paige's offer to major league baseball was never accepted, but Rodney often revisited the notion in response to unfounded racism.

Throughout the years of the campaign, as more and more white players and managers were quoted in the *Worker* as being in favor of ending segregated baseball, Rodney alerted his readers to the fact that these were not new opinions, just never before published opinions.

> Now I'm not naive enough or dumb enough . . . to think that the Sunday and Daily Worker sports page brought about a miraculous transformation in the mental life of America's athletes. . . . The past two years have seen their views in print. If there had never been a Daily and Sunday Worker sports page, it is more than conceivable that Joe DiMaggio might have remarked to some sports writer or other, "Satchell [sic] Paige, the Negro pitcher, is the greatest pitcher I ever faced." But you never would have seen it in print.[6]

Lester was only partly correct—the African-American press had been writing on the subject for decades by that time. However, the readership of this press was largely black, keeping the issue within the same community that was being oppressed and ignored. Though Rodney's official readership was by no means equal in size to that of the more popular black papers, some of the progressive whites who read the *Worker* were better able to effect changes in the white system than were disenfranchised blacks.

Thus, Rodney cultivated a genuine working relationship with the black sportswriters in his effort to educate the white public to the inhumanity of segregation. In addition to gathering new information with which to splinter Jim Crow, the *Worker* also followed up on stories published in the black press supporting the desegregation of baseball. Articles that appeared in the *Washington Herald* and the *Pittsburgh Courier,* by Sam Lacey and Wendell Smith, respectively, were reprinted in their entireties in the *Worker.* Rodney's support of Smith's series of interviews with major league managers and owners prompted an August 20, 1939, letter of thanks from Smith, whose editor, Robert L. Vann, was no fan of communism. Smith praised Rodney's joint efforts with the black press in presenting the issue of ending Jim Crow baseball to the public.[7]

Rodney and his readers continuously wrote letters to Branch Rickey, the general manager of the Brooklyn Dodgers—the New York working man's team—to hire African-American players such as Satchel Paige or Josh Gibson. In 1938, antidiscrimination pamphlets were handed out at baseball games in New York City major league ballparks, and beginning in 1939 and continuing through 1947, petitions were circulated for signature by New York baseball fans and sent periodically to Judge Kenesaw Mountain Landis, then commissioner of Organized Baseball, and to Ford Frick and William Harridge, presidents, respectively, of the National League and the American League. The Communists attempted to shame baseball into ending segregation. The petitions read, in part:

> Our country guarantees the rights of life, liberty, and the pursuit of happiness to all, regardless of race, creed or color.
> Yet in our national sport we find discrimination against outstanding Negro

baseball players who are equal to or surpass in skill many of the present players in the National and American League.[8]

Another influence endorsed by the *Worker* was that of Paul Robeson, the incomparable athlete, actor, and singer, who outspokenly expressed his support of Communist-supported programs. Robeson, whose career would eventually vanish based partly on testimony by Jackie Robinson before the House Un-American Activities Committee during the Cold War, even attended major league baseball's winter meetings in December 1943, to plead the case of desegregating baseball. Though eloquent, earnest, and impassioned, even Robeson's voice could not persuade baseball to break the color barrier.

In October 1939, the *Worker* began to tout young Jackie Robinson, UCLA's four-sport standout athlete, as a potential major league baseball player. That month, Dave Farrell, a Communist journalist in California who sometimes sent columns to the *Worker,* devoted an entire column to the possibility of Jackie's success in major league baseball. Farrell's son noted, "in my studying the [UCLA] box scores the name of Jackie Robinson was rather prominent in the hit and run batted in columns," remarking on a particular game that, "He got four for five, three of them being nothing but long singles, which he made go for doubles with real classy base running. . . . He's just like you said Cobb used to be."[9] Almost a year later, accompanying a picture of Jackie, the *Worker* again lauded Robinson:

> The Pacific Coast [Conference] ... is sure to boast one of the country's greatest [collegiate athletes] in Jackie Robinson of UCLA, one of the most amazing athletes in the land. Rated ready to equal or surpass the great Kenny [Washington] as a back, the 20-year-old Jackie also was the leading scorer on the Coast in basketball, is a shortstop of big league caliber and a track ace.[10]

World War II brought a new dimension to the campaign: if African-Americans were good enough to die in battle for their country, certainly they were good enough to play baseball for it. Though Lester Rodney, like many U.S. Communists, eagerly entered World War II, his successors, Nat Low and Bill Mardo, continued the campaign.

As the New York state legislature and Mayor Fiorello La Guardia's council began independently investigating baseball's hiring practices, Nat Low and Joe Bostic, Communist sports editor of the New York *People's Voice,* a black paper, as well as other members of the black press, began aggressively attempting to arrange tryouts with major league clubs for Negro League players. At least two previous attempts had been made to get Jackie Robinson some attention in Boston and New York, while yet another involved Newark's Terry McDuffie and Cuban Stars' Dave "Showboat" Thomas. None of these pushy attempts was welcomed by the gentlemen of baseball, who considered the brashness and pomposity of the Communists to be out of place in their world.

When Senator Albert "Happy" Chandler was appointed commissioner of baseball in 1945 after Landis's death, he quickly announced his desire to see baseball desegregated, which the *Worker* broadcast to its readers.

> I believe Negroes should have a chance like everybody else. . . . I believe that this is a free country and everybody should have a chance to play its favorite pastime. . . . There are reasonable men in baseball, and the ways and means of bringing this about must be worked out.[11]

Nat Low challenged Chandler to back up his words with actions, such as a mandate to the owners to desegregate immediately, an act for which the commissioner had no authority.

Two months after the bombings of Hiroshima and Nagasaki, Branch Rickey signed Jackie Robinson to a minor league contract. The *Worker* prided itself and the Communist Party upon their role in bringing about this momentous occasion, and an editorial praised one of their own as the champion.

> It was Lester Rodney, then sports editor of the Daily Worker, who started the campaign something like ten years ago. . . . [H]is life has been important in the anti-fascist struggle. We owe a big bouquet to Lester Rodney.[12]

Not just to Lester Rodney, but also to radical New York politicians, such as City Councilmen Pete Cacchione, Ben Davis, and Michael Quill, who helped to establish the mayor's commission, and State Representative Vito Marcantonio of the American Labor Party, who helped push the Ives-Quinn antidiscrimination law through the New York state legislature. This legislation and the direct threat that the New York City Council organized against major league baseball's hiring practices were perhaps the most significant and substantial contributions to ending discrimination in baseball in any way attributable to the U.S. Communists.

Nat Low warned, however, that the "victory" was not yet secure; he called upon social progressives to take measures to ensure Robinson's success, such as fan clubs, letter-writing campaigns, and petition drives in support of Robinson, and involvement in Robinson's travel arrangements.[13] Obviously, Low would be in for a shock come spring, when Robinson's Jim Crowing in Florida would be at least as vicious as it had ever been.

The *Worker* sportswriters reported the signings of other African-Americans by the Dodgers' organization. Roy Campanella and Don Newcombe were signed for the Dodgers' Nashua minor league affiliate, as announced on

April 6, 1946. John Wright's signing was reported in January 1946, while Roy Partlow was later signed for the Montreal team in May; the *Worker*'s Bill Mardo followed Robinson and Wright around as much as he could that year.

The *Worker* was just as brash as always in reporting the discrimination that these men faced as minor league baseball players in the South during spring training. Mardo's editorial about the Sanford neighborhood in which the black players were forced to stay, away from the rest of the team, was eloquent and emotive, describing the disparity and despair of the Jim Crow South.[14] Every time a game was canceled due to racism, Mardo was there, blasting away at the narrow-minded and senseless southern tradition of segregation.

Reviewing Robinson's first minor league regular season performance, Mardo started off his article by asserting, "Almost everything he did was pure gold."[15] Unlike most of the mainstream white papers, not only did the *Worker* sports page publish a full report on the game, but the Communist writers heaped enthusiastic praise on Robinson's every move. Rodney later pointed out the absurdity of, for instance, the refusal of the *Sporting News*, the "bible" of American baseball, to accept it that baseball was desegregating, and that this was an inevitable step in the right direction.[16]

Such reactions, as well as the obvious discrimination faced by the black players, highlighted to the Communist sportswriters the need to keep drumming away at their campaign, for the battle was far from over. Charles Dexter reiterated the *Worker*'s duty to its principles:

> The fight for real racial democracy in baseball, however, will not be won until other major league clubs have signed Negroes.... [I]t certainly behooves the progressive forces which consider the Jim-crow fight in baseball an important aspect of the general struggle for Negro equality, to resume their places and to carry on the organized campaign which brought such good results one year ago.[17]

Mardo reminded his readers that "Sports IS a Weapon," explaining that arguments against desegregation are shattered as Robinson et al. take the field in minor league uniforms, which, "in one fell swoop, does as much to arm and educate the American people against this monstrous lie [racism] as do all the pamphlets in the world."[18]

When Lester Rodney returned to the *Worker* sports page in the summer of 1946, he was still in his prewar journalistic form. He reprinted an article by Roger Treat of the *Washington Daily News,* of thumbnail sketches of the players to be seen at the Negro League's annual East-West All-Star Game. Among them, Larry Doby, a 22–year-old four-sport star and college product, like Robinson, then playing for the Newark Eagles. Rodney predicted that Doby's signing was not far off. Speculation was also rampant that Robinson would be with the Dodgers for the 1947 season, and that the Dodgers and Royals were to train in Havana in order to avoid a repeat of the discrimination and scrutiny Robinson faced the previous year.

The *Worker* sportswriters did not forget the Negro Leagues, though, and kept reporting Negro League scores and highlights as before. The Communist sportswriters believed that the Negro Leagues would continue, and that they could serve as a farm system of sorts for the major league system, where African-American players could keep honing their skills. While the *Worker* tossed around the idea that the Negro Leagues might fold without its stars, or without compensation for the players, their primary occupation was in seeing major league baseball desegregated. The *Worker* also did not cover the issue of including African-Americans in coaching and management positions, not for any racist beliefs, but again in general oversight in the midst of just desegregating the ranks.

Robinson remained their main highlight, delivering in grand fashion. The *Worker* documented well Robinson's MVP season for Montreal, and the misery which Robinson endured during spring training in Havana. During the sixth inning of a Montreal-Brooklyn exhibition game in 1947, when a slip of paper was passed around the Dodgers' press box announcing Robinson's promotion to Brooklyn, a couple of New York sportswriters came up to Lester Rodney and told him, off the record, that he could be proud of that moment. While Rodney was proud of Robinson, he was concerned for the other African-American ballplayers, contemporary and future, who needed the same chance. He and Bill Mardo and their staff relentlessly petitioned the fifteen other major league clubs to follow suit. Though Doby signed directly into Bill Veeck's Cleveland Indians club six weeks later, making him the first African-American in the American League, it would not be until 1959, twenty-three years after Rodney set his campaign going, that all major league baseball clubs had included at least one African-American on their roster.

The *Worker*'s campaign focused many eyes and many hearts, of blacks and whites, to the unfairness of separate baseball leagues, and kept the issue of discrimination in the forefront of its sports reporting for more than eleven years. However, its relatively small readership and the stigma attached to communism even during the Depression decade most likely undermined any direct influence the *Worker* might have had on major league baseball. While the sincerity of the Communist Party's interest in minority issues was often questioned, the integrity Lester Rodney and his colleagues brought to this campaign was evident in their zeal and tenacity, unparalleled by their contemporaries and surpassed only by the civil rights movement of the 1960s.

Notes

1. *Daily Worker,* 23 August 1933, p. 2.
2. *Sunday Worker,* 16 August 1936, pp. 1, 15.
3. Ibid., p. 15.
4. *Daily Worker,* 13 September 1937, p. 8.
5. *Daily Worker,* 16 September 1937, p. 8.
6. *Sunday Worker,* 30 January 1938, p. 14.
7. *Sunday Worker,* 19 August 1939, sec. 1, p. 8.
8. *Sunday Worker,* 11 June 1939, sec. 1, p. 8.
9. *Sunday Worker,* 15 October 1939, sec. 1, p. 8. For an article by Dave Farrell, Sr., praising Robinson for his football prowess, calling him "little short of sensational," see *Daily Worker,* 19 September 1939, p. 8.
10. *Daily Worker,* 17 September 1940, p. 8.
11. *Daily Worker,* 5 May 1945, p. 10.
12. *Daily Worker,* 26 October 1946, p. 7.
13. Ibid., p. 10.
14. *Daily Worker,* 7 March 1946, p. 10.
15. *Daily Worker,* 19 April 1946, p. 14.
16. *Daily Worker,* 21 May 1947, p. 10.
17. *Daily Worker,* 14 August 1946, p. 10.
18. *Daily Worker,* 11 September 1946, p. 10.

11

White Dodgers, Black Dodgers

Lester Rodney

As we celebrate the day fifty years ago when Jackie Robinson quite literally changed the complexion of what was called our national pastime, and examine its meaning for America, historians will provide the indispensable underpinning. As one who was there, in the Ebbets Field press box, in the dugouts, and around the batting cages before the games in those faraway sepia years of 1947, 1948, and 1949 and beyond, I may perhaps best contribute by recalling how it looked and sounded and felt.

I suppose someone in attendance here who was born in 1947, now a fifty-year-old Baby Boomer, would want to know: Was there actually a sense of history happening, an exciting feeling of change and of new community?

My best shot at an answer would be, "Yes, but not all of that in the beginning." It came gradually, perhaps growing along with the changes in the ballplayers and in the people who came to see them. Certainly there was no exultant, celebratory aura around that oddly constrained first day. Curiosity, of course. A warm yet almost tentative welcome for the dark-skinned newcomer as he took the field with an artificially low-keyed persona and a new, unfamiliar first baseman's mitt. There were no signs of casual, intimate teammate relationships between the rookie and his fellow Dodgers.

There were clearly more African-Americans in attendance than, say, at Opening Day the year before, though hardly the overwhelming increase some had expected and some had feared. There was none of the venomous race baiting that would spew from the dugout and stands in Philadelphia, and other cities, and even from the Phillies' dugout in Ebbets Field later, spurred by manager Ben Chapman. Peering down at the black fans, many of whom were surely at their first big-league game, it was evident that they had been made aware of Branch Rickey's call for restraint in conduct. I clearly remember the first loud cry of "Let's go, Jackie!"—a piping call from a white youngster, about thirteen.

Now, to mark the change, let us fast-forward to a game more than two years later. It is midsummer 1949, a Friday night game at the same Ebbets Field against the same Boston Braves, now the defending league champs. The crumbling clipping of my article, one of a few randomly snipped and carried off when I left my newspaper in 1957, reveals that there was a crowd of 33,714. That paid attendance meant a full house, with fans perched along the sloping, concrete ramps, some standing against the back wall of the third base line, where they periodically responded to shouts of "What happened?" from people standing down below on the street. Quite different from sealed-off Dodger Stadium in Los Angeles, which cannot even be approached on foot.

It's an important game in a close race, scoreless tie top of the fifth. With one out and nobody on, Brooklyn left-hander Preacher Roe gives up a walk. Clint Conatser, a right-handed hitter, then drives an outside pitch into the open spaces of right center. Jim Russell, the Brave runner on first, after hesitating to ensure that the ball can't be caught, takes off. Right-fielder Carl Furillo catches up to it at the base of the wall, 380 feet or more from home plate, wheels and cocks the game's strongest arm as the crowd rises in anticipation.

Freeze the action for a moment. The long-legged Russell is in full cry tearing through third in a wide turn. Conatser digs toward second. Robinson, now a second baseman, eases out some 50 feet into the outfield, half facing Furillo. Shortstop Pee Wee Reese moves to cover second. Catcher Roy Campanella, the team's second black player who came aboard in 1948, waits slightly up the third base line. Roe ambles from the mound to back up the plate. It is the full panorama of baseball, a team game, in a moment that no television camera can encompass.

In the spring of 1947, Furillo had not exactly been on a welcoming committee for Robinson. Branch Rickey told him, "OK, if you don't want to play, go back to pounding railroad ties in Pennsylvania." Furillo played. It may sound like a corny movie, but one afternoon about two months later, when I hopped off the Brighton line over to Ebbets a bit early, there was number 6, Furillo, casually beckoning to number 42 to join him in warming up their arms together on the sidelines before pregame fielding practice. The abstraction was fading. Roe, out of Ashflat, Arkansas, had joined the team in 1948, and could fairly be described as acting with cool correctness toward Robinson.

All right, unfreeze. Furillo cut loose. The noise began swelling as the ball bulleted into Robinson's glove, head high, slightly to his right, making it unnecessary for him to pivot his feet before throwing. Robinson's throwing arm was the least imposing of his nonpareil skills, possibly due to two years of pounding as a running, blocking, pass-catching back for UCLA's football team, but he made the throws when he had to. Campy snatched the ball waist high and dove for the tag as Russell plummeted in feet first. Up through the dust came the thumb of umpire Larry Goetz. He's out! Sportswriters noted 9–4–2 on their scorecards, the next batter popped up, and the white-uniformed Dodgers came off the field. The crowd roar started up again. As Furillo loped in with a huge grin, Robinson, Roe, and Campanella were waiting for him at the lip of the dugout. Leaning out from the press box, you could see them envelop Furillo into the foursome, whack each other exuberantly, and step down into the dugout. You switched your gaze to the people in the stands, those raucous, salty, kidding, good-natured, integrated Ebbets Field stands, unlike any before or since. You imagined the continuing crowd roar traveling far out into the Brooklyn night to merge with the cheers and animation of those listening to radio's Red Barber in Flatbush, Brownsville, Red Hook, Bay Ridge, Canarsie, Bensonhurst, Coney Island. . . .

Here, two years later, was the full-blown aura of the magical years when a bunch of grown men playing a game of ball were the pulsing heart of a big city. It was Green Bay multiplied by a hundred, plus incalculable social meaning for America.

Answer to Baby Boomer's question: Yes, it was exciting.

The crowd inching toward the exits after the game, bubbling with *the* play, had seen the Dodgers win 4–0 en route to winning the pennant, one of six pennants in the ten Jackie Robinson years. (Should have been seven out of ten. How could you, Bobby Thomson? And if Burt Shotton had sent in a pinch runner for leaden-footed Cal Abrams in 1950s final game, how about eight out of ten?)

Emotional, unconditional attachment to the home team, in and out of itself, was not new in baseball. I remember it in Brooklyn through the mostly hapless 1930s, and it is hardly unknown at Chicago's Wrigley Field and Boston's Fenway Park, even, it should be noted, in a new time when some fans, reflecting TV's instant gratification simplistics, can be heard petulantly booing their own players when things don't go their way. (Anyone here remember when Gil Hodges went hitless in four straight Series games and the Brooklyn fans cheered him every time at bat?)

What made the Brooklyn crowds distinctive? In 1949, two added components of the magic fell into place. A mostly home-grown team of attractive athletes was maturing into greatness, the stars even living in and identifying with the city. And there was the extraordinary identification of the Brooklyn Dodgers, a sports team, as leaders and teachers of long-overdue elementary democracy in the land of the free, making baseball fans out of nonfans, and Dodger fans out of folks in Missouri and all points north, east, south, and west. Even out of a few Giant fans of my acquaintance. By the way, from their very start as an integrated team, the Dodgers were cheered lustily by a good part of the larger-than-usual crowds in the other cities, and the cheers were not just for Robinson. If Gil Hodges drove Duke Snider home with the winning run, the cheers were just as loud. They were for the *Dodgers* against their "home" team. To the discomfiture of some of the home folks. What did they expect, black St. Louisianians and Chicagoans to root for a team that refused to take on black players, against a team that had broken baseball's shameful apartheid ban? Yes, there were also more than a few whites to be seen cheering for the visitors.

Back to that tumultuous 1949 Ebbets Field crowd. Who were they? How many were aware of being part of developing history, and to what degree? There was certainly a larger proportion of blacks in the stands than in the early days of 1947. My estimate would be in the 10,000 to 15,000 range. It is safe to assume that at least some of the white fans were coming as in the past, as basic baseball fans, with the ending of baseball discrimination well back in their consciousness as they plunked down their buck and a quarter for a grandstand seat. Just as surely, some of the attending whites would *not* have been there if nothing had changed. Most would probably fall between these two categories—that is, continuous Dodger fans, but caught up with the drama of *their* team's historic new dimension. How could they not be?

Factor into the chemistry the fact that this was just a few years after a cataclysmic world war in which, while blacks in the military were still segregated, it couldn't escape anyone's attention that they fought and died for their country just as did whites. War workers on the home front, including the important Brooklyn Navy Yard and Todd Shipyards, often were force-fed an education about people—fellow workers—being people. And dare we mention it, Brooklyn in the 1940s was hardly deficient in its supply of New Deal and industrial union–seasoned liberals and radicals.

It fell to Jackie Robinson to begin the process of change in baseball, first of all among the white men who made their living in the game. The process was uneven. Backsliding was sometimes in evidence. Men who had lived in a lifelong context of racist belief did, after all, go back to the old stomping grounds in the off-season. When black second baseman Jim Gilliam arrived in 1953, prompting a decision to move a now veteran Robinson to third base, the same Preacher Roe of the armlocked foursome could be heard lamenting the possible benching of his roommate Billy Cox, with a little detectable tinge of "they're starting to take over." As with other white players in real-life dynamics, democratic growth could be a two-steps-forward–one-step-back process. Although, considering the magnitude of the initial break with the past, a more accurate description would be "five steps forward and one back."

But change most did. I saw Alvin Dark arrive on the Giant scene in 1950, a Lake Charles, Louisiana, person of his time who could not possibly have been manager of that by now interracial team. He was manager twelve years later. I remember small-town southerner Max Lanier of the Cardinals going down to Mexico for better money for a few years. There he played, ate, traveled, and lived with teams on which whites were usually a minority. When he came to the Giants in 1952, he rushed one day from an uneaten meal to the hospital bedside of injured teammate Monte Irvin, the Giants' first black star. At the gala Dodgers victory party in Brooklyn's old Bossert Hotel, after they won the seventh game of the 1955 World Series at Yankee Stadium, there was Furillo ("I ain't gonna play with no niggers") rushing to greet Jackie and Rachel Robinson as they came in. Carl and Jackie, friends, hugging ecstatically with cheeks pressed together, saying, "We did it, we did it!"

Baseball, democratic baseball, can do that. Might that have been one of the reasons policy makers clamped a Jim Crow lid on the game before the turn of the century, and fought to keep it that way for another half-century?

Of course, there were white players to whom baseball integration was pretty much a shrugging "Why not?" from the start, including Dodgers' Gil Hodges, Carl Erskine, Ralph Branca, Duke Snider, and that special Kentuckian, Harold Pee Wee Reese.

From amateur sociology to the realm of historians: There remains some murkiness about when the first serious challenge to baseball discrimination began. Up until fifteen years ago, accounts of the ending of the ban, in books and in bleached movies like *The Jackie Robinson Story*, began with the 1940s and a light bulb clicking on in the noble Branch Rickey's head. The advent of a new breed of historians, which is to say "real historians," filled in the ahistorical vacuum and accorded belated recognition to the early campaigners, starting with the creative, seminal work of black newspaper sportswriters, first and foremost Wendell Smith of the *Pittsburgh Courier*, along with Sam Lacy and Joe Bostic.

In sorrowful and verifiable fact, if one did not read the Negro newspapers or the small *Daily Worker,* which joined their campaign, one might have read nothing about this amazing ban. Yes, there were a few sporadic mentions by a couple of columnists, Westbrook Pegler and Jimmy Powers of the *New York Daily News,* but random mentions in a couple of columns, with no follow-ups, put zero pressure on the baseball establishment. Search the files of our great newspapers in the mid-1930s. You will come across factual notices in the sports pages about the Negro League Kansas City Monarchs playing the Baltimore Elite Giants, Sunday, and so on, but with never a mention that these players were barred from advancing to the major leagues, or even the minor leagues, of our national pastime. You will find no incredulous editorials blasting this un-American discrimination, no investigative articles listing the qualified and overqualified black players, no queries addressed to the commissioner, the league presidents, the team owners, the managers and the white players. The conscience of American journalism on baseball apartheid, sorry to say, was not in the hands of America's big daily newspapers.

As late as 1942, the *Sporting News,* then more than now considered baseball's "bible," editorialized that "the use of mixed teams in baseball would benefit neither the Negro nor white professional game, because of the possibility of unpleasant incidents." In fairness, it should be noted that in 1947, *Sporting News* said in effect that, inasmuch as Robinson's presence was an accomplished fact, the sporting thing was to accept him and judge him solely on his merit as a ballplayer. Before you get too carried away with this change of heart, however, note that *Sporting News* then went on to repeat its old argument that both Negro and white would really be happier apart from one another.

Wendell Smith, of the *Courier,* began the breaking of the silence by querying big-league managers and players as they came into Pittsburgh. Give a little thought to the courage and initiative of a black man intruding into the comfortable old boys' white baseball establishment, with his challenge to conscience. He sought and found some decent people. Bill McKechnie, manager of the Cincinnati team, was a historic first, saying he knew of twenty black players who deserved a tryout, and "I would use Negro players if given permission." Double no-hit pitcher Johnny Vander Meer volunteered, "I don't see why they're barred." Other players agreed.

These meaningful and exciting news breaks, bearing directly on the notion that "the white players would never stand for it," were not picked up, let alone emulated, by the big dailies. The *Daily Worker,* which, in the turbulent Depression 1930s, had an impact well in excess of its circulation, featured such stories by agreement with Smith, and joined the process by interviewing other teams as they came into New York and Brooklyn. We got good responses from managers Del Baker of Detroit and Fred Haney of the St. Louis Browns, and in 1939—bingo!—from new Dodger manager, Leo Durocher. A *Daily Worker* headline in 1937 broke the story that young

Yankee Joe DiMaggio had called Satchel Paige the best pitcher he had ever faced (in postseason exhibition play on the West Coast). A few weeks later, a *Worker* interview with Paige should have ended the stereotype myth that Satch was a Step-n-Fetchit type, content to "stay with his own." Paige offered to play a winner-take-all game with the 1937 World Series winners to show the capabilities of the black players, said he would pay his own way to any big-league spring training camp, and proposed "a vote by everyone going into big-league games in 1938, yes or no, whether they wanted us in baseball or not." Paige's challenges were ignored. It is well known that Bill Veeck, principal owner of the Cleveland Indians, signed Larry Doby as the first African-American on an American League team. Eventually, he would also bring Leroy Paige into the majors. So, eleven more years would pass before big-league fans were privileged to see a man who was arguably the best pitcher in the land make his debut as a forty-two-year-old rookie. It was great, of course, and better than nothing to see him in the bigs at about 50 percent of his capability, and thank you, Bill Veeck, but deep down, the Satchel Paige story, as well as the stories of Josh Gibson, Ray Dandridge, Buck Leonard, and countless others who never got a chance, is one of tragic waste, and America has been let off the hook a little lightly for it.

Our pinko gadfly newspaper also stimulated educational picket lines at both Negro League and big-league games. At one Negro League doubleheader in New York in 1939, more than 10,000 signatures calling for an end to the ban were obtained, including those of all the Negro players. (By 1942 Commissioner Landis had more than a million petition signatures on his desk.)

So it was that in August 1939, we published a letter from Wendell Smith congratulating us for our "great efforts" and suggesting "further joint campaign projects." I mention this only because the *Courier,* hardly a radical newspaper, would surely have preferred to congratulate the *Times,* or *Post,* or its own city's *Post Gazette.* But that's the way things were.

As an interesting "what if," the first magnate to respond favorably to a *Daily Worker* query sent to all club owners was William Benswanger of the Pirates. In August of 1939 he responded as follows: "If the question of admitting colored players into organized baseball becomes an issue, I would be heartily in favor of it. I think the Negro people should have an opportunity in baseball just as they have in music or anything else." Benswanger subsequently agreed to a tryout arranged by us for Campanella, along with Sammy Hughes and Dave Barnhill (as detailed in the book *Roy Campanella, Most Valuable Player Series, 1952* by Dick Young). The Pirate owner actually contacted the three players, but the tryout never happened. Benswanger backed out, almost certainly under pressure from the baseball establishment, though we have no hard evidence of that.

Ponder how different baseball history (American history!) might have been if Benswanger had beaten the others to the punch, and the Pirates had broken the ban. Pittsburgh at the time was the very center of black baseball, boasting the fabled Homestead Grays, who by Smith's reckoning, fielded six players of probably big-league all-star caliber, and the strong Pittsburgh Crawfords. It was thus a perhaps more logical city than Brooklyn for the breakthrough. Dipping into the available pool, with Paige at his peak, awesome catcher Josh Gibson, remarkable third baseman Ray Dandridge, and others, the Pirates might have dominated the league for years, and I suppose this conference would be at the University of Pittsburgh.

But it was Rickey who pulled the trigger. As a point of personal privilege, let me confess, half a century later, that at the time I could never fully figure Rickey out (something I would never have admitted in my days of certitude as *Daily Worker* writer). Looking back with perhaps more wisdom, I have no reason to doubt the sincerity of his deep, religion-based feelings against discrimination. He could be pompous, arrogant, and egocentric, and yes, he was guilty of big-daddy patronizing behavior toward blacks as in his 1947 dictum for fan conduct—though the context of the times, and his purpose, might induce a charitable retroactive view of that. Wrapped in his mantle of emancipator, he hated with a cold fury to acknowledge that the campaign, or "agitation" as he termed it, had anything to do with the case. Far shrewder and bolder than the other magnates, he seized the day and capitalized on what had become inevitable. No saint he. Yet, Branch Rickey is the one who took the giant step the others would not take. Perhaps more importantly, once committed, he fought uncompromisingly against all those who would sabotage the historic advance. He can rest with high marks.

So it was Rickey who led baseball into "year one," 1947, the start of what historian Jules Tygiel called the "great experiment." It may sound ludicrous today to label the implementation of elementary democracy in the mid-twentieth century into America's most popular sport as an "experiment." But, in 1947, that's what it was, and Ebbets Field was the laboratory.

The story of Dixie Walker and the other Dodgers who were initially hostile, and the incipient player strike spawned by the Cardinals, is pretty well known. We take you instead into the Dodger dugout, where I was privy to an earnest conversation by a few of rookie Robinson's teammates (out of Jackie's hearing). This was just after some crude physical provocation against Robinson by players of opposing teams, who were aware of his pledge to passivity. These Dodgers were troubled. "Well," offered Peter Reiser tentatively, "democracy means that everyone is the same, so that means that we should treat everybody the same way." Which came down to, "It's not proper for us to do anything special about Robinson." This didn't quite satisfy Captain Reese. "That's true," said Pee Wee, speaking slowly as he thought, "democracy means everybody is equal, but Jackie's the only colored guy in the league, and he's catching special grief because of it. Maybe we ought to try to make things more equal for him." This, remember, was many years before the development of the concept of affirmative action to level the playing field. It wasn't long before Reese responded to vile rantings from a Cincinnati fan by walking over to Robinson on the field and casually draping his arm around Jackie.

Ripples of the wave were to move well beyond Brooklyn and the seven other National League cities. There were remarkable moments of conflicted emotions down south in preseason exhibition games, as city after city experienced its first interracial baseball. There was a night in Atlanta during spring training in 1949, an exhibition game between the Dodgers and the minor league Atlanta team. The Klan's Grand Wizard proclaimed that the game must not take place.

Blacks had been pouring into town all day from surrounding towns and rural areas. The small segregated stands for blacks filled quickly. Perhaps because of a reluctance to turn down anyone with cash in hand, or maybe with some dim sense of history, or a combination thereof, management allowed an overflow crowd onto the field behind hastily erected rope barriers in the outfield.

When Robinson emerged from the visiting dugout, with Campanella and Don Newcombe, now also black Dodgers, close behind, a deep roar erupted from the sea of black fans. This touched off a reaction of boos from the white stands. Then, a third thing happened. Other whites began to clap, then stood up while clapping to differentiate themselves from the booers. In this continuous bedlam of sounds, in an atmosphere that can only be called electric, perhaps as many as one-third of the whites were finally standing and clapping. Remember, this was the Deep South of forty-eight years ago. Who were the whites standing and clapping? All closet southern liberals? Not likely. One can only surmise that they were sport fans, weaned on sportsmanship as well as racism, caught momentarily in a head-on collision between the two as they looked down on their visiting guests, a *big league* team.

In 1953, I chatted in Yankee Stadium with a Cleveland rookie pitcher named Dave Hoskins. The year before, he had been the first black player in the Texas League. Surviving a bad beaning and assorted other viciousness, he became a star. The first time his Dallas team played in Shreveport, Louisiana, Hoskins received three written threats to shoot him dead if he stepped onto the field. He didn't show them to anyone because he wanted to pitch.

"There was a law they were trying to pass in the Louisiana state legislature to forbid any Negro from playing in a mixed game," he said. When he took the mound, he continued, "there was quite a bit of booing, just a little applause. By the third time I came to bat, the applause was louder than the booing. We won, 3–2. A week later, they dropped that law. I don't know, but I figure the way the Shreveport fans acted might have helped."

Did baseball have anything to do with the Supreme Court decision of 1954, ruling school segregation unconstitutional? When I asked Campanella that exact question, Roy offered his opinion that baseball was *the* most important factor. "All I know," he insisted in the face of my quizzical, come-on-now-Roy smile, "is that the ball clubs going down there and playing together, and traveling together, and then eating together and all, we were the first every time, we were like the teachers of it."

So Campy the ballplayer was overstating, shortchanging the full spectrum of the civil rights movement. In calculating such things, it might be pertinent to recall that when Martin Luther King, Jr., first met Don Newcombe, he said, "You'll never know what Jackie and you and Roy did to make it possible for me to do my work."

In whatever role baseball played, the harshest burden was placed on Jackie Robinson, from day one as a rookie in spring training with the Montreal Royals. For him, there never really was a great sigh of relief, the feeling "we did it, it's over." In 1949, when he was free at last of the imposed restraint that had suppressed his very being, when the real Jackie Robinson stood up—aggressive and vocal, the kind of athlete he had been at Pasadena City College and UCLA, the kind of man he had been in a Jim Crow army—he encountered an immediate double standard. White ballplayers with the same qualities—Durocher, Eddie Stanky, Billy Martin, the old Cardinal Gashouse Gang—were invariably seen as tough, scrappy competitors: winners. The first black player was termed shrill and irritating. Several umpires took their cue from the league officials, who singled Robinson out for censure.

I even heard some sportswriters who, while acknowledging that Robinson was initially put upon because he was black, argue that he brought upon himself his later troubles. Which was to say that there was no double standard at work. May I testify that that is the sheerest of sheer nonsense.

In one 1949 game in St. Louis, ump Bill Stewart called ball four on a close 3–2 pitch by Don Newcombe to Enos Slaughter, then immediately ejected Robinson for a silent, body-English sign of disagreement, a wince. The Dodgers lost the important September game, 1–0. Before the 1950 season even began, league president Ford Frick, in an unprecedented announcement, selected one player, Robinson, to receive a public warning against rough baserunning. During that season, ump Jocko Conlon called a third strike on Robinson, who walked away silently. Conlon turned and called out, "It was right over the middle." Robinson took the bait, wheeled, and disagreed. Out of the game. Out with him went two batting streaks. He had hit safely in sixteen straight games, and had reached base in fifty-five straight. Nobody in the press box could remember an umpire so blatantly provoking a player into ejection.

No double standard? Late in 1949, I saw Yankee catcher Ralph Houk whirl on ump Bill Grieve at Yankee Stadium, scream and curse, and actually lay hands on Grieve. He had to be pulled away and restrained. He was not ejected. It was an important game, you understand, and catcher Yogi Berra was on the injured list.

In 1952, ump Frank Dascoli ejected the mild-mannered Campanella for a mild disagreement on a tag play ("But I had the plate blocked."). The Dodger bench naturally got on Dascoli's case. New league president Warren Giles, who had run a Jim Crow club at Cincinnati, censured the Dodgers, mentioning one name. "Jackie Robinson was particularly offensive," he said. In fact, the only player identified and ejected from the bench during that incident was a white Dodger, Chris Van Cuyk. When Robinson confronted Giles later about that, Giles said lamely, "Well, you were hollering, weren't you?" Dodger manager Charley Dressen, the very model of a model establishment manager, was moved to angrily testify that Jackie, while certainly up there with the good bench jockeys, never used objectionable language, or racial or personal slurs.

Some key figures in history are thrust into roles they do not seek, or even comprehend. Robinson, possessor of a fierce intelligence, understood and accepted his role—which is why, somewhere along the early road of raw racial abuse and demeaning artificial passivity, this proud man never said, "To hell with this. Who needs this? I'm out of here." Black players who followed him were not mouthing an expected cliché when they said they owed it to Jackie Robinson. They knew, as no white players could, what he went through.

He would have done enough, would be an American hero, if he had just taken the guff and performed as he did in the pressure cooker. The extra dimension he brought to the unending battle for justice was exactly in the continuing, unabated militancy that made some people uncomfortable. Jackie Robinson never lost his indignation at any racial injustice. As the ESPN special in February 1997 made clear, he never subsided into relaxed "gratitude," basking in well-earned glory. As the years went by, he became a deeper critic of the inequities in American society, and spoke out in an ever more forceful voice on what remained to be done. He knew that without "agitation," the Yankees, for one, would have held out a lot longer, that the lily-white managerial, coaching, and executive scene would have stayed that way.

He is surely one of a select number of Americans of whom it can comfortably be said, he made this a somewhat better country. And his legacy is not "Hooray, we did it!" but "Buddy, there's unfinished business out there."

12

Robinson—Robeson

Bill Mardo

"Jackie . . . Jackie . . . *puh-leeze* . . . Jackie!" Excited kids leaning over the Dodger dugout roof, imploring a smiling, ebony-skinned twenty-eight-year-old athlete to scribble his name on a white baseball . . . on an outstretched piece of paper . . . on anything. The air so thick with excitement you could almost dip your fingers in it. Ebbets Field, Opening Day of a new baseball season—opening in a whole new way. Yes, yes, on this fifteenth day of April in 1947, Jackie Robinson picked up his bat and broke the chains that had imprisoned a great American game for more seasons than anyone wants to remember.

It almost sounds like a gratuitous tease for this sportswriter to say to you, fifty years later, "You had to be there." Amazing, isn't it—that as we come closer and closer to the millennium, a nation has to celebrate the fiftieth anniversary of an event that, under civilized circumstances, shouldn't ever have had to be commemorated? A black man's right to play major league baseball, if he was good enough to come up to the bigs. You'd think that should have been automatic. It comes with your birth certificate. Sure, and who hit *you* on the head, Mister?

But to talk about Jackie, for me, means to talk about Paul Robeson, and inevitably, to talk about Branch Rickey. Too many times, the comments about Robinson and Robeson seem wrongly centered on what allegedly separated Jackie and Paul—and I'm here to tell you that rarely are two historic figures so closely *connected*.

But for openers, let me comment on Mr. Rickey—and what I call the *bubbameise* school of history. *Bubbameise* is a long-loved Yiddish expression meaning "fairy tale." A *bubbameise* is a myth, something other than the truth, and which, intentionally or not, manages to mix up your head a little.

Too many times, in too many books covering the Jackie Robinson story, there is the myth, repeated over and over, that what finally broke the back of baseball's color line, was Branch Rickey's determination to avenge an insult to Charley Thomas, a young black catcher on the Ohio Wesleyan University team then managed by the very young Rickey. The year was 1903, and when Rickey brought his team to South Bend to play Notre Dame, the desk clerk at the South Bend hotel refused to register a black ballplayer. Rickey suggested putting up Thomas on a cot in his room, thus technically avoiding the Jim Crow registration rule. When Rickey later went up to his room, he found Thomas sobbing uncontrollably. According to legend, according to myth, according to *bubbameise*, according to the baloney school of history, Rickey then and there vowed to someday avenge that horrible insult to his black ballplayer.

When Rickey signed Jackie Robinson forty-two years later, he cited the Charley Thomas incident as his motivating force in breaking baseball's color line. Baloney! A *bubbameise*! It's an insult to objective history. And quite frankly, it really begs the question when just about everything one reads about Rickey is soaked in Rickeyesque platitudes that have him sounding like a combination of Frederick Douglass, John Brown, and Martin Luther King all rolled into one.

Let's be honest, Branch Rickey saw Charley Thomas sobbing in 1903. Branch Rickey signed his first contract with Robinson in October 1945. Between 1903 and late 1945, was there ever a single public statement by Rickey condemning the hideous color line in baseball? Between 1919 and late 1942—the Rickey years at St. Louis—can anyone produce a single statement by Branch even remotely bemoaning the segregated seating policy at Sportsman's Park—the home stadium for Rickey's St. Louis Cardinals?

And in a book just published, called *The Jackie Robinson Reader*—a lively compilation of articles written by a variety of people who played roles in the odyssey of Jackie Robinson's life—there is a chapter in which Rickey's coach Clyde Sukeforth talks about witnessing the initial meeting between Rickey and Robinson. Here is what Rickey is quoted as saying upon meeting Robinson (and I must add, it's been done to death): "For a great many years I have been looking for a great colored ballplayer."

W—H—A—T??? Where were you looking all those years, Mr. Rickey? Istanbul? The South Seas? There were great black ballplayers in the Negro League teams that rented your very own stadium, Sportsman's Park, to play in when the Cards were on the road. To say nothing of just about every other major league ballpark when the home teams were away. What was it, Mr. Rickey? Cataracts? Glaucoma? How did you manage *not* to see genius black ballplayers like Josh Gibson, Buck Leonard, Oscar Charleston, Ray Dandridge, Willie Wells, Leon Day, Smokey Joe Williams, Cool Papa Bell?

Baloney, Branch! A *bubbameise*! Here, I should remind the reader that Branch Rickey, who said he spent years trying vainly to find *one* great colored ballplayer to crack the color line, was an absolute genius at spotting baseball talent. After all, it was Branch Rickey who revolutionized baseball when he invented the famous "farm system" for the St. Louis Cardinals— where promising young players would be nurtured, trained, and developed. At one time, Rickey's farm system totaled over six hundred players! The best scouts, instructors, and coaches were hired to bring those young potentials along. Rickey even pioneered in the use of batting cages and pitching machines.

And for the next twenty-two years, Rickey's farm system fed the talent to the St. Louis Cardinals that brought them eight pennants and developed baseball immortals such as Duckey Medwick, Frankie Frisch, Dizzy Dean, Pepper Martin, Enos Slaughter, Rip Collins, Lon Warneke, Terry Moore, and Max Lanier. As a matter of fact, Rickey's hunt for talent was so all-pervasive that during the 1930s he even bought out *two entire minor leagues*—the Arkansas-Missouri League and the Nebraska State League!

Is it "picky" of me to ask why this genius at spotting baseball talent couldn't seem to find one, not even one promising black ballplayer? But wait. Maybe I'm missing something here. Let us once again go back to that oft-told Robinson-Rickey introduction. After telling Jackie that he has been looking for years for a great colored ballplayer, Rickey then goes on to say (this one also done to death, and please try to keep your breakfast down): "But what I'm looking for is *more* than a great player. I'm looking for a man that will take insults, take abuse—and have the guts *not* to fight back!"

In other words, what Rickey really was looking for, during all those years, was a black player with enough self-control to avoid giving the haters an incident that would scuttle the integration of baseball before it ever really got off the ground.

Self-control? I thought self-control was practically invented by black Americans! I thought that for over two hundred and fifty years black Americans by the millions had exhibited a self-control in the face of indignities and horrors that would have reduced a lesser people to basket cases! And just on the baseball scene alone, what were the great black ballplayers of the twenties, thirties, and early forties exhibiting, if it wasn't self-control—as they traveled from town to town in claptrap buses, sometimes playing two and three games a day to eke out a living, pulling into gas stations that wouldn't let them even use the bathroom, catching forty winks on the bus or in claptrap boarding rooms in the "other part of town," eating fries on the side of the road or in a beat-up burger joint in shantytown?

No, no. The reason that Jim Crow in baseball took until 1947 to crumble wasn't that Branch Rickey for years had been vainly hunting for one great black player able to take insults and have the guts not to fight back. The reason lies elsewhere.

Let's be perfectly frank. Branch Rickey signed Robinson after a long and bitter campaign of social protest: ten years of struggle by key black sportswriters and their papers, ten years of struggle by progressive trade unionists, ten years of struggle by some politicians of conscience, ten years of struggle by the Communist Party, and ten years of struggle by the *Daily Worker* Sports Page and its sportswriters.

And from 1936 to 1946, democratic-minded baseball fans rang doorbells, pounded the pavements, picketed outside ballparks, and collected signatures on petitions urging that America's national pastime become national not in name alone but in fact.

And for all of those years, while the sign on Branch Rickey's door in St. Louis said, "Do Not Disturb," there were decent democratic major leaguers who made it clear they didn't mind going on record against Jim Crow. The great DiMaggio told the *Daily Worker* that "Satchel Paige is the greatest pitcher I ever faced and should be in the big leagues." Joe was speaking from firsthand knowledge, of course. Black all-star teams won 60 percent of the postseason exhibition games against white all-star major leaguers.

Bill McKechnie, manager of the Cincinnati Reds, said, "I know of at least twenty Negro players good enough to play in the big leagues, and I would be happy to have them on the Reds if given permission." Carl Hubbell, a Texan, and a peerless pitcher for the New York Giants, called Josh Gibson "as great a catcher as I ever saw." And while the sign on Rickey's door read, "Out to lunch—Be back in 10 years," his own pitching ace of the Cards' mound staff, Dizzy Dean, said in 1937, "Satchel Paige is a better pitcher than I am, ever was, or ever will be."

Through the late thirties, the good fight went on. By the time 1940 rolled around, baseball's high commissioner, Judge Landis, received one million signatures calling for an end to Jim Crow in baseball! And along about that time, Brooklyn Dodger manager Leo Durocher said he "would hire colored ballplayers if they were not barred by the owners. I've seen a million good ones."

This, of course, brought the flame up a little higher under the boiling pot of baseball Jim Crow. Feeling for the first time the growing pressure—and looking to deflect Durocher's statement —Landis issued his historic statement:

"Negroes are not barred from organized baseball by the Commissioner and never have been. There is no rule in organized baseball prohibiting their participation and never has been to my knowledge."

In 1943, Paul Robeson, then at the height of his popularity and quite simply the most recognizable and respected black man on the planet, except perhaps for Joe Louis, went before the annual meeting of the major league club owners and made a proud and passionate plea urging that the scar on the face of American baseball be surgically removed once and forever. Broadway's reigning Othello received a standing ovation and many curtain calls from the club owners—but they weren't quite ready to buy tickets for the run of the show. No, no, it would take more pressure, more picketing, more petitions, more everything, including a demand that the club owners actually give tryouts to some qualified black ballplayers. The tryouts tactic, as you will see, would soon signal a real problem for the now squirming club owners. Especially in New York!

After nearly a decade of social struggle, but on another front, New York legislators wrote the Ives-Quinn Law into the books, making discrimination in hiring practices unlawful. That wonderful little barrel of fire and decency, Mayor Fiorello LaGuardia, set up a committee to monitor the New York club owners. And then there was that historic morning in 1945, when black sportswriter Joe Bostic of the *People's Voice* and Nat Low of the *Daily Worker*, unannounced, went up to the Brooklyn Dodgers' spring training camp in Bear Mountain, New York, and demanded tryouts for black ballplayers Showboat Thomas and Terence McDuffie.

To his credit, a previously reluctant and mute businessman, Branch Rickey by name, saw the handwriting on the wall. Continue to keep out the Josh Gibsons, the Satchel Paiges, the Leon Days, the Buck Leonards, and the Willie Wellses, and by golly, you might wind up in court in a losing battle. It wasn't too many months later when the now Dodger boss removed the "Do Not Disturb" sign from his door, and extended his hand to Jackie Robinson.

You might ask why I critique Rickey now—on this occasion—fifty years after he made history by being the first club owner to break Jim Crow in the big leagues? A fair question—and I can only answer it one way. Anytime you separate a man's actions from the social climate he is living in—the social pressures he is *finally* responding to—you stand a pretty good chance of producing a history that is just a little astigmatic. So all I am suggesting is that we look at Rickey in a three-dimensional way—and stop treating him as an untouchable icon. There was the pre-Robinson Rickey who stayed shamefully silent for much of his baseball life—and there was the Robinson Rickey whose extraordinary business and baseball sense helped him seize the moment, jump aboard the Freedom Train as it was getting ready to pull out of Times Square, catch social protest at its apex, and then do just about everything right once he signed Robinson.

Rickey himself, up in years and confronting his own mortality, gave biographers yet another postscript to the Charley Thomas legend as his motivation for signing Jackie. "I couldn't face my God much longer knowing that his black children are held separate from his white children in the game that has given me so much."

Okay. Fair enough. But if I may respectfully use Rickey's well-known religious beliefs as a metaphor, I can envisage that on the day he finally meets his creator at those black, brown, and pearly white gates, she greets him with all the renowned insight and charity that go with the job. Embracing the Dodger boss, she says softly, "Nice going, Branch. But tell me. What kept you so silent—for so long?" Branch starts to open his mouth when his maker, with a twinkle in her eye and the sweetest of smiles, interrupts, "Branch. Please. No more *bubbameise*. Not here."

And now I'd like to briefly talk about two men who, unlike the pre-Robinson Rickey, never stayed silent: Paul Robeson, who was the son of a runaway slave from North Carolina, and Jackie Robinson, who was the grandson of a slave and who himself first saw the light of day on a sharecropper farm in Georgia. It would be easy to cite many similarities between Robinson and Robeson. Both were truly great four-letter athletes—Robeson at Rutgers plowing through the Jim Crow collegiate sports scene in the 1920s, and Robinson stunning the college sports world as a track, basketball, baseball, and football powerhouse at UCLA in the late 1930s.

But the umbilical cord connecting Jackie and Paul is much tighter than the sports scene. Both men—from the git-go—couldn't tolerate second-class citizenship. Not for them—not for their people—not for a second. Paul, singing, acting, and speaking on stages, movie screens, concert halls, and podiums around the world—one theme always reverberating like a heartbeat: "Let my people go." And Jackie—who refused to go to the back of the Army bus at Fort Hood, Texas, almost a decade before Rosa Parks made history with the same statement of defiance.

Jackie and Paul—so many connections! The day after Jackie's first hit in the majors, Robeson had a scheduled concert canceled by Illinois authorities. The anticommunist crazies were beginning to take America on a long dark ride to sickness and silence. Not too much later, the Albany Board of Education canceled another previously scheduled Robeson appearance. And was anybody surprised that, a day or so after Albany's move against Paul, new Brooklyn Dodger Jackie Robinson was disclosing hate letters filling his mailbox—and threats against his life.

Two years later—as the anti-red McCarthyite madness was reaching fever pitch—Branch Rickey persuaded a dubious Jackie to appear before the House Un-American Activities Committee to contest Robeson's suggestion at a Paris Peace Conference that it would be unthinkable for America's blacks to ever go to war against a Soviet Union that supposedly had erased racial discrimination. But Jackie—ever the militant—turned his testimony into more of a vigorous assault against American racism than an all-out attack against Robeson.

But now let's cut to the chase—to one of the most sadly ignored pages in the Robinson-Robeson odyssey, and to further testimony, if indeed any was required, of the largeness of Jackie's character and his great ability to see the bigger issue despite any personal political differences.

On August 27, 1949, on the lovely Peekskill picnic grounds thirty miles north of New York City, yesterday's "Militia Mentality" maniacs acted out their own version of Hitler's storm troopers burning the books and torturing the Jews. Only this time the "Jew" was Paul Robeson and his fans who had come upstate for an annual Robeson concert—and the "burning books" were Robeson's music sheets fed into the fires that were started with the wooden chairs of the stunned concert goers. Burning crosses blazed a few feet from the stage. People were stoned mercilessly. Cars were overturned. Blood stained the green grass red.

And it was just one day after that horror, I firmly believe, that Jackie Robinson began to see Robeson for what he really represented and for what a giant target he had become for the witch-hunters and racist thugs of his time. I remember rushing to Ebbets Field the morning after the Peekskill bloodbath and actually breaking the news to Jackie as he sat in the Dodger dugout a few minutes before gametime. Remember that only five weeks earlier, in Washington, Jackie had told the House Committee that in his opinion neither man, Robeson nor Robinson, could claim to speak for fifteen million blacks.

Reading the newspaper accounts of the symbolic lynching of Robeson at Peekskill, Jackie Robinson slowly lifted his eyes from the newspapers I had handed him and, anger written all over his face, told me: "Paul Robeson should have the right to sing, speak, or do anything he wants to. Those mobs make it tough on everyone. It's Robeson's right to do or be or say as he believes. They say here in American you're allowed to be whatever you want. I think those rioters ought to be investigated, and let's find out if what they did is supposed to be the democratic way of doing things." And then Jackie, clearly opposed to communism, nailed the insanity of those days right where it lived. "Anything progressive is called communism," he sighed (*Daily Worker,* August 29, 1949).

Let me add that the very same newspapers that had salivated over Jackie's political difference with Robeson at the House hearings—the very same wire services that had relayed to newspapers all over America the minor critique of Robeson at the House hearings—somehow "missed" Jackie's passionate defense of Robeson's rights just five weeks later! How they missed this *Daily Worker* front-page exclusive is something to think about. But one thing is certain. Jackie Robinson didn't miss spotting the lynch rope at Peekskill . . . didn't miss seeing the white sheets at Peekskill.

I leave it for others here to cross the T's and dot the I's on Jackie's phenomenal baseball career, so much of which had been fashioned under the double-standard pressures and tensions that only a pioneering black ballplayer could know in the middle and late forties. But for this sportswriter, on a Sunday morning in an Ebbets Field dugout, when the haters and maniacs and the powers that be tried to turn a black freedom fighter named Robeson into a pariah and America's public enemy number one, another black freedom fighter named Robinson refused to be silent when silence and fear was stilling so much of America. For me, that was the best day Jackie Robinson ever had . . . in any ballpark . . . anytime.

I think that if Jackie Robinson was with us today—and if Paul Robeson was here to pay tribute to his black brother's heroic achievements—both warriors would be using the moment to address a question much more urgent than batting averages and bases stolen.

Half of all African-American children—six and a half million of them under the age of thirteen—live in poverty. One-third of all black men between the ages of twenty-one and twenty-nine are in the criminal justice system. Housing in the inner cities—already a horror fifty years ago when Jackie broke in—is fifty years more horrible today! In the mean streets of Harlem, Bedford-Stuyvesant, Chicago's South Side, and East Los Angeles, many of those rat-trap tenements are crumbling beneath the weight of their own decay. Up to twenty million Americans are unemployed, underemployed, or part-time employed. Scratch away the cold arithmetic and what you see behind those numbers are America's poor blacks, poor Latinos, poor whites.

Nobody is going to front-page this one, either, but the crime rates in deeply disadvantaged white neighborhoods are almost identical to those in comparable black ghettoes. Crime is not a black thing, not a Latino thing, not a white thing. It's a poverty thing. Maybe a young gang member in the Chicago slums said it all when he told a *New York Times* reporter, "Everybody is hustling just to eat. It ain't right to sell drugs. But starving ain't right either."

Having had the real privilege of knowing both Jackie Robinson and Paul

Robeson, I know in my gut this is what Jackie and Paul would be addressing today. They might be saying, "Hey, Ebonics is a fact of black life. But c'mon, let's get real! Roots . . . street language . . . the vernacular . . . don't have a damn thing to do with what is number one on the agenda. There's a four-letter word that we all spell alike and pronounce alike. It's called jobs . . . J-O-B-S! Jobs lead to another four-letter word that we all spell alike and pronounce alike. It's called hope . . . H-O-P-E! Jobs and hope lead to something called a L-I-F-E! And maybe, just maybe, from the richest nation on the face of the earth—which with just the press of a button in Houston can get a rock-sampling jeep to do a figure 8 on the planet Mars—maybe, just maybe, that same nation can figure out how to bring a little something called "quality education" into those same starving ghetto neighborhoods!

And now, if you will forgive a writer some license, I must confess that I am haunted today by a picture that plays back and forth in my head. It's this. In the wee hours of the night . . . in a paint-peeling bedroom of a roach-infested, rat-infested apartment—the same apartment in the same decaying tenements that dot and defile the sad streets of Harlem, Bedford-Stuyvesant, Chicago's South Side—a weary welfare mother sits by a secondhand crib, her eyes burning as she fights to stay awake and guard her sleeping infant from being nipped by those relentless rats. As she rubs her eyes and pinches herself, on the radio turned down low a black station is playing Robeson's recording of "My Curly-Headed Baby." Paul's voice is so tender and gentle and so full of love for all those sleeping black babies that one wonders, was there ever a lullaby like this one? And as this bone-weary, eyelids-heavy mother sits and rocks and guards over her curly-headed baby, across her lap lies her weapon of choice, at the ready to do serious damage to those nipping night crawlers: thin at the handle; with strips of tape, the better to grip it with; wood widening gracefully out to the fat part. And as she rocks, and as Paul sings to black mothers and black babies everywhere, through the early morning darkness we dimly make out what it is she holds across her lap. Of course, of course. What it is, is a baseball bat.

Part IV

On the [Level?] Playing Field

The three writers in this section deal with Jackie Robinson and some of his contemporaries primarily, but not exclusively, on the field of play.

Joseph Dorinson offers a comparison of Jackie Robinson, Hank Greenberg, and Joe DiMaggio, representatives of three groups on the social margin. All three, by their talents, strength of character, and dignity transformed the public stereotypical notions held of their heritages. Robinson, Dorinson writes, "vaulted into our national psyche"; he "redefined baseball culture" and "destroyed the way blacks were perceived." Hank Greenberg, an American Jew, was "equally heroic to his people." In the mid-1930s, at the height of Nazi racism abroad and bigotry at home, Greenberg "transmitted a positive image" of the Jew. Dorinson presents DiMaggio as "the Italian analogue to the Jewish Greenberg." DiMaggio became the "commendable counterimage to Mussolini." Dorinson asserts that these three "constitute a noble trinity. Each emerged as a representative of a particular group; yet each earned universal appeal."

Robert Moss introduces Burt Shotton, manager of the Dodgers in 1947 and again in 1949 and 1950. Thrust into the hot seat of 1947 by the sudden suspension of Leo Durocher, Shotton was entrusted with managing the first major league team with a black ballplayer. Moss argues that the opinion held by some authors that Burt Shotton was an "aged bumbler" misses the remarkable job he did. Shotton should be judged by his accomplishments, contends Moss, and those were impressive. He inherited the challenges of 1947 and succeeded. Moss provides a reinterpretation of Robinson's first Dodger manager. Of the four who managed Robinson, Shotton was the least prominent, but he may in fact have been the most effective and important.

Lyle Spatz completes this section with a statistical presentation of Jackie Robinson's ten years on the field, "through the prism of opening day." This quantitative approach has the effect of reinforcing the assessment of the qualitative attributes that made Jackie Robinson so special. Although much had been accomplished by opening day in 1956, when the Dodgers started more blacks than whites, Spatz points out that the "roster of the opposition Phillies ... contained as many blacks as did the opposition Braves on opening day in 1947—none." The field of play was still not level.

13

Hank Greenberg, Joe DiMaggio, and Jackie Robinson: Race, Identity, and Ethnic Power

Joseph Dorinson

"A life is not important except in the impact it has on other lives," wrote Jackie Roosevelt Robinson shortly before his death in 1972.[1] His was a short life by modern standards, but what a life! In this commemoration—fifty years after—we join Stephen Spender in contemplating "those who were truly great ... who fought for life, ... born of the sun ... they traveled a short while towards the sun and left the vivid air signed with their honor."[2]

In this presentation, I will discuss three men of honor, three magnificent baseball players, three icons, and three exemplary ethnic/racial heroes. To begin, some observations on the role of heroes in our culture invite mention. A democratic society seems uneasy in the presence of heroes because, aristocratically, heroes loom larger than life. Thus, throughout our nation's history, Americans seem eager to elevate the extraordinary individual followed by a propensity to topple him or her from the pedestal. In short, we are prone to smash icons. Some heroes, however, may go into temporary eclipse though their accomplishments and their traits resist our throwaway culture.[3]

Jackie Robinson, Hank Greenberg, and Joe DiMaggio defy the debunkers and compel us to contemplate their cultural roots and historical branches. In reverse chronology, Robinson's monumental breakthrough on April 15, 1947, demands primacy. With amazing grace under enormous pressure, Jackie changed the game, bringing Negro League style—speed coupled with power, daring with panache—to the center of American baseball. Not only did Jackie change the game; he also transformed the nation.

Born in Cairo, Georgia, on January 31, 1919, the youngest of five children, Jackie moved with his fatherless family to Pasadena in 1920. His mother, Mallie, worked as a domestic; the children pitched in. Leaving welfare behind, the family purchased a house in all-white Pasadena. Eventually three branches of the Robinson family bought houses on Pepper Street. No major memorial marks the spot.[4] Perhaps 1999 will witness a tribute etched in stone.

With three older brothers to compete with, young Jackie had to improvise speed and quickness against size and strength in street games. He excelled. After two stellar years at Pasadena Junior College, he moved up to UCLA, where he played football, basketball, and baseball, and ran track. In 1940, he finished second in total yards—440 running, 435 passing—in the Pacific Coast Conference (PCC). In basketball, he led the PCC in scoring. He also won championships in golf and swimming. Financial straits forced Robinson to alter course: he did not graduate. Drafted into the Army in 1942, he rebelled. His fierce sense of justice forced him into a series of racially charged confrontations. Jules Tygiel illustrates how Robinson pursued an aggressive course of action to redress wrongs. His efforts were rewarded with a court martial, which resulted in a discharge in 1944 for medical reasons.[5]

Jackie joined the Kansas City Monarchs, a powerhouse in the Negro League, for the 1945 season. Despite a weak arm, he played shortstop. At this time, Branch Rickey decided to sign a Negro ballplayer. He informed broadcaster Red Barber, the Dodger Board of Trustees, his wife, and his family. Rickey sent out a flood of scouts in search of baseball gold. Although "the Mahatma"—as Tom Meaney called the Dodger general manager—received favorable reports on several players, he chose Robinson for several salient reasons essential to his grand plan. He wanted the right man, a positive press, and support from the Negro community. He wanted acceptance from Dodger teammates. As an officer and a gentleman; as a superior athlete and a solid family man, and as an articulate individual who sprang from poverty, Jackie Robinson became the pioneer.

On August 29, 1945, Rickey interviewed Robinson for three hours, during which he hectored, lectured, and tested the young lion. He wanted Jackie to wear a "cloak of humility" as part of a long-term strategy designed to win acceptance. To a skeptical Robinson, he said, "I want a ball player with guts enough not to fight back! You've got to do this job with base hits and stolen bases and fielding ground balls, Jackie."[6] Two months after this historic encounter, Robinson signed a contract with the Montreal Royals, the Dodgers' Triple A Club in the International League. One year later, he was promoted to the parent club, the Dodgers of Brooklyn, where this baseball pioneer ventured into uncharted territory.

Robinson broke barriers on and off the field. He desegregated road trips, spring training, stadiums, and hotels. Not only was he "nimble and quick"—in the words of Negro journalist Wendell Smith—"he also made the turnstiles click." In ten years as a Dodger, he led his team to six pennants and one—Brooklyn's singular sensation—World Series triumph in 1955. His on-base percentage of .411 ranks historically among the best twenty-five.[7]

After a dispiriting seventh game loss to those "damned Yankees" in 1956, Robinson retired with a hefty lifetime batting average of .311. As Winston Churchill once warned, however, statistics convey only half-truths. Jackie's contributions transcend quantification. Unwilling to be bartered to the Giants across the river and into the asphalt in 1957, number 42 hung up his spikes. Robinson went on to break barriers in business, banking, broadcasting, construction, the baseball dugout, and the executive suite. Our nation's premier athlete—the only UCLA Bruin to letter in four sports: track, football, basketball, and baseball—he fulfilled the American dream: rising from rags to riches. Rookie of the Year in 1947, Most Valuable Player in 1949, Hall of Fame in 1962—Robinson seemed to have it all.

It was an American success story scripted from vintage Horatio Alger just in time for the confrontation with the USSR, the bad guys, the communists—almost too good to be true. And it was. The truth was more complex, more disturbing. Racism did not vanish. African-Americans did not zip up to that elusive room at the top. To be sure, Jackie opened doors; but disparities between rich and poor, white and black, urban and suburban, grew wider. The turbulent 1960s—featuring the new gods of relevance, pleasure, and celebrity—cast aside old heroes befitting a throw-away culture, among them: Jackie Robinson. They cast lonely eyes at Joe DiMaggio but that's another part of the forest, another passage in the story.

Robinson did not manage or coach. Some labeled him a troublemaker, and the rubric stuck. Youngsters cited his conservative politics and his support of Richard Milhous Nixon. Robinson did not fit the radical chic or the new sexuality. As a devoted family man, business executive, and Rockefeller Republican, he must have seemed the ultimate square.[8] Obscured by the high salaried celebrities and targeted for low blows from mindless militants, Jackie went into temporary eclipse. A major study published in 1965, *The Negro American*, edited by preeminent scholars—sociologist Talcott Parsons and psychologist Kenneth Clark—contains no mention of Jackie Robinson! Other tomes demonstrated a strange indifference to this noble giant in Dodger uniform. An inane remark by a contemporary player coupled ignorance with amnesia. And this failure of memory was shared by many.

A reappraisal started in the 1970s with the advent of Roger Kahn's brilliant *The Boys of Summer* and continued in the 1980s with Jules Tygiel's magisterial *Baseball's Great Experiment: Jackie Robinson And His Legacy*. Maury Allen, Peter Golenbock, Bob Lipsyte, and Carl Prince (all in attendance at our conference) added to this impressive genre. These books demonstrate the danger, courage, and cost of this noble experiment. Martin Luther King, Jr., confided to Dodger pitching great, Don Newcombe, that Jackie Robinson was indispensable. In effect, he confessed, no Robinson, no King—a statement substantiated by the Rev. Wyatt Tee Walker, a close associate. Quoting the civil rights leader, he said: "Jackie Robinson made it possible for me in the first place. Without him, I would never have been able to do what I did."[9]

Indeed, crossing the color line in baseball, the national pastime, in 1947 was more dangerous than Neil Armstrong's first footfalls on the silvery moon in 1969. While the astronaut had the support of all Americans, Jackie Robinson—with the exception of mentor Branch Rickey, beloved wife Rachel, and a few crusading journalists—basically ran alone. He had enemies, a fifth column, on his own team.[10] He had to overcome the stereotype of Sambo, Amos 'n' Andy, Aunt Jemima, and Uncle Ben. Media-forged manacles had captured the soul of black folks and had beamed a benighted image of the docile Negro.

Throughout the sports arenas, "BR" (before Robinson) black athletes projected personas of brute force like Jack Johnson and Joe Louis or gifted clowns like the Harlem Globetrotters. Even the enormously popular Joe Louis was painfully inarticulate. Then came Jackie: daring, daunting, dignified. With the solid stroke of his bat, a spectacular snatch of a line drive heading over second base, and a sensational steal of home, Robinson vaulted into our national psyche. Off the field, his high-pitched tenor voice spoke cadenced sentences, imparting incisive commentary. Not only did Jackie redefine baseball culture by bringing a new combination of speed, power, and style to the national game; he also destroyed the way blacks were perceived. Italian, Irish, and Jewish kids—I was only eleven when Robinson joined the Dodgers—rooted for Robinson and our erstwhile Bums. We began to see our Greenpoint neighbors and Negro classmates differently; once through a glass darkly; now, through a lens brightly. A pioneer on the frontier of race, ethnic, and ultimately gender relations, Jackie Robinson brought us closer to that holy grail of peace, justice and the American way. He was a superman in Technicolor.

Less colorful perhaps but equally heroic to his people, Henry Benjamin Greenberg was born on January 1, 1911. The son of Roumanian Jewish parents, he grew up in Greenwich Village and moved to the Bronx, where he attended James Monroe High School. Sportswise, not a Bernard Malamud "natural" but a diamond in the rough, this 6-foot 4-inch American-Hebrew national—210 pounds of raw power and awkward gait—willed and worked himself up to star stature. It never came easy.

His parents resented the time and energy that young Henry devoted to baseball. They wanted him to go to college. He complied with their wishes, attending New York University (NYU) briefly before he signed with the Detroit Tigers rather than with the local team, the New York Yankees. A *Yiddischer kop*,* Hank realized that Lou Gehrig, a fixture at first base, would be difficult—no, impossible—to dislodge from the big ball orchard in the Bronx. After a hesitant start with four minor league years in the so-called bushes, "Hammerin' Hank" hit the big time in 1933. As a rookie, he hit .301 with 12 home runs and 78 RBIs.

His career, abbreviated by four years of voluntary service in the military, spanned thirteen (bar mitzvah) years as a star: .313 lifetime BA with 331 HRs. He copped the American League home run crown five times; the RBI title, four times. In 1938, he smashed 58 HRs and knocked in 146 runs. Greenberg led the Tigers to four pennants and two World Series triumphs.[11] His return from service in 1945 is the yarn from which legends are spun. Ranked by author Bert Randolph Sugar as one of baseball's fifty greatest games, the contest between the St. Louis Browns and the Detroit Tigers determined the pennant on September 30, 1945. Losing 3–2 in the ninth inning, the Tigers rallied. With one out, men at second and third, the Browns intentionally walked Doc Cramer to get to Hank Greenberg. After taking a "scroogie" for a ball, the Bronx slugger lined a grand salami into the left-field stands.[12] "Tigers win the pennant. Tigers win the pennant!" In the World Series, he hit another two homers to lead his team to a victory in seven games.

In 1946, Greenberg smacked 44 HRs and knocked in 127 runs, beating Ted Williams in both categories during a September rush. His reward was a trade to the Pirates of Pittsburgh (not Penzance) for a career finale. Elected

---

*Literally, a "Jewish brain" figuratively, someone gifted with survival skills.

to the Hall of Fame in 1956, Hank Greenberg was the first Jewish-American to be so honored.

Greenberg saved $300,000 of the $447,000 he earned in baseball as a player. He advised protégé Ralph Kiner that singles hitters drove Chevrolets while sluggers sported Cadillacs. As baseball's premier slugger, Greenberg earned the national pastime's highest salary in 1940, 1941, and 1946. Unmarried till age thirty-six, he lived at home with his parents.[13]

Hank climbed up to the executive suite first in Cleveland and later in Chicago, subject to anti-Semitic slurs all the way. These insults intensified Greenberg's Jewish consciousness. Raised in a secular household, he did not attend synagogue regularly, but when confronted with defamation of his tribe, Greenberg rallied to its cause. As defender of the faith, he fought opponents and teammates alike. Elden Auker, Tiger pitcher, remembered one incident with the White Sox. A Chicago player called Greenberg "a yellow Jewish son of a bitch." After the game, Hank called into the enemy dugout and challenged the anonymous name caller. No one moved. "He was damn lucky, " Auker opined, "because Hank would have killed him. Hank was a tough guy."[14]

The target of beer bottles as well as verbal abuse, Greenberg was pressed to the limit. Even his teammates harbored anti-Jewish feeling. Sitting on a personal powder keg, he nearly exploded:

> There was added pressure being Jewish. How the hell could you get up to home plate every day and have some son of a bitch call you a Jew bastard and a kike and a sheenie and get on your ass without feeling the pressure. If the ballplayers weren't doing it, the fans were. I used to get frustrated as hell. Sometimes, I wanted to go into the stands and beat the shit out of them.[15]

Hank Greenberg uplifted Jewish fans, among them Marty Glickman and Ira Berkow. He also inspired a young Negro athlete named Joe Black.[16] Perhaps marginality is contagious. Greenberg emerged at a time when bigotry was making a comeback in America and girdling the globe. Radio priest Charles Coughlin fulminated against the "international banker conspirator Jew." Fortified with Henry Ford–sponsored protocols, the mellifluous Coughlin polluted the air waves. Subject to stereotype, Jews were identified with greed on one hand and cowardice on the other, with moneyed power at one level and godless communism below. Along came Hank Greenberg. With his mighty bat and his enormous strength, he transmitted a positive image which popular poet Edgar Guest captured in these lines:[17]

The Irish did not like it when they heard of Greenberg's
  fame
For they thought that a good first baseman should possess
  an Irish name;
And the Murphys and the Mulrooneys said that they never
  dreamed they'd see
A Jewish boy from Bronxville out where Casey used to
  be. . . . In July the Irish wondered where he'd ever
  learned to play.
And with fifty seven doubles and a score of homers made
The respect they had for Greenberg was being openly
  displayed.
But upon the Jewish New Year when Hank Greenberg came
  to bat
And made two home runs off Pitcher Rhodes—They cheered
  like mad for that.
Come Yom Kippur—holy fast day world wide over to the
  Jew. And Hank Greenberg
to his teaching and the old tradition true,
Spent the day among his people, and he didn't come to play.
Said Murphy to Mulrooney, "we shall lose the game today!
We shall miss him in the infield and we shall miss him at
  the bat.
But he's true to his religion—and I honor him for that."*

Not only did Greenberg change gentile attitudes; he also bolstered Jewish pride. Ira Berkow's uncles likened him to a beacon when he drove in
183 home runs, 1 shy of the American League record of 184 and 7 less than
the National League mark of 190 set by Lou Gehrig and Hack Wilson,
respectively. As world Jewry grew less powerful by the Hitlerian minute,
Greenberg powered the Tigers to two pennants and provided American
Jewry with a heroic model:

> After all [Greenberg recalled], I was representing a couple of million Jews
> among a hundred million gentiles and I was always in the spotlight. . . . I felt a
> responsibility. I was there every day and if I had a bad day every son of a bitch
> was calling me names so that I had to make good. . . . As time went by I came
> to feel that if I, as a Jew, hit a home run I was hitting one against Hitler.[18]

---

*Reprinted from COLLECTED VERSES ©1984 by Edgar Guest. ©1985 by
Bragger. Used with permission by NTC/Contemporary Publishing Group.

When war clouds wafted over our country, Hank Greenberg was drafted in the summer of 1941. Discharged a few days before Pearl Harbor, Hank Greenberg was the first major league baseball player to enlist after we declared war.[19] A captain and bomber pilot of a B-29, he fought gallantly until July 1945. He became a genuine hero on and off the field. "We are in trouble," he proclaimed, "and there is only one thing for me to do—return to service." Although he realized that it might end his career, he put things in proper perspective: "All of us are confronted with a terrible task—the defense of our country and the fight for our lives."[20]

Greenberg's own experience at war and peace sparked support for and approval of Jackie Robinson. After an "errant" Pirate pitch hit Jackie, the Negro rookie trotted in pain to first base amid catcalls of "Coal Mine, Coal Mine." Greenberg encouraged Robinson, "Don't let them get you down. You're doing fine. Keep it up." Greenberg remembered Jackie as a "prince" with chin held high: "I had a feeling for him because of the way I had been treated." Peter Levine concludes this portion of his excellent book by identifying Henry Benjamin Greenberg as "the greatest American Jewish sports hero of all time."[21] Strangely, Greenberg has elicited only one recent biography, on which he collaborated, as he lay dying of liver cancer, with journalist Ira Berkow.

Greenberg admired his teammate Charlie Gehringer and his fellow slugger Joe DiMaggio because of their effortless skill and natural hitting prowess. Author G. Edward White cites DiMaggio as the Italian analogue to the Jewish Greenberg. The San Franciscan rocketed to stardom during the 1930s. His career was also interrupted by war service. Early in his career, "Jolting Joe" was saddled by negative stereotypes. As he became more famous, the ethnicity receded from view. Unlike the ever-curious and voracious reader Greenberg, DiMaggio preferred comic books and remained tight-lipped.[22] He never pursued a perch in the executive suite. His iconic status blossomed with a romantic but short-lived marriage to actress Marilyn Monroe. Shunning the limelight, "The Yankee Clipper" maintained his image, burnished by infrequent appearances at public events.[23] Jewish songwriters were stirred to sentiment in pursuit of the evanescent Joe DiMaggio.

Joe's parents discouraged their son's baseball activity. His father, Giuseppe, came from the Isola delle Femmine, an island situated northwest of Palermo, where he and his family worked as fishermen for many generations. Moving to America in search of a better life, he found a haven in the Bay Area of California. Joe was born in Martinez on November 25, 1914, the eighth of nine children. Maury Allen reports that Joe's parents spoke only Italian.[24] Uneasy with his old-world parents, Joe hated fishing and would sneak out to play baseball at every chance. He also disliked school intensely, as evidenced by his attendance record. He repeatedly played hookey. His father called him *lagnusu* (lazy) and a *meschinu* (good-for-nothing).[25] Following Ping Bodie and Tony Lazzeri, Joe DiMaggio became the first Italian baseball "superstar." With a career that spanned thirteen seasons, Joe hit .325, socked 361 HRs, won the MVP title three times, and set another record, this one the least likely of all records to be eclipsed: hitting in 56 consecutive games. Another amazing statistic is his strikeout to home run ratio of 369 to 361. During his career, he led the New York Yankees to ten pennants and nine World Series wins.[26]

When DiMaggio launched his meteoric career, Italians had arrived in political power at both ends of America, with Mayor Angelo Rossi in San Francisco and Mayor Fiorello LaGuardia in New York City. The 1930s witnessed an economic depression at home and the rise of fascism abroad. Americans sought and found heroes in sports—preferring the strong, silent types, winners without bluster, achievers minus arrogance. Joe DiMaggio and the other Joe—Louis—fit these traits, nicely.[27] In addition, they had to efface older stereotypes, DiMaggio more so than Louis.

To offset the strutting Caesar from Roma, DiMaggio was both strong and shy, charismatic yet self-effacing. He played baseball, which enjoyed a vast audience. This sport possessed a cleaner image than boxing, evoking the innocence of our rural past. In stark contrast to the buffoonish boxer, Primo Carnera, Joe DiMaggio exhibited an elegance in the field and high competence at the bat out of a spread stance. Early in his Yankee career, Joe was heavily identified with Italian traits—some less than flattering. As late as 1939, Noel F. Busch (as in bush league) wrote the following bilge in *Life*:

> Italians, bad at war are well suited for milder competition. . . . Although he learned Italian first, Joe speaks English without an accent, and is otherwise well adopted [sic] to most US mores. Instead of olive oil or smelly bear grease, he keeps his hair slick with water. He never reeks with garlic and prefers chicken chow-mein to spaghetti.[28]

Dan Daniel, writing in the *New York World Telegram*, equated DiMaggio with the "spaghetti society of romantic San Francisco." And the Yankee great considered Daniel a close friend.[29] Other writers constantly referred to him as Italian. Maury Allen cites Lefty Gomez, a close friend of the "Clipper" on the use of epithets. The Yankees called Tony Lazzeri "Big Dago," Frank Crosetti "Little Dago," and Joe DiMaggio just "Dago."[30]

When he held out for a substantial raise in 1938, the fans booed him. Yet, he proved a commendable counterimage to Mussolini, whose popularity alarmed loyal Americans. Enlisted in the Air Force in February 1943, the "Yankee Clipper" erased any doubts about dual loyalty. Military service also removed vestigial ethnicity. If Babe Ruth, roistering and rumbling, represented both spirit and symbol of the "Roaring Twenties," Joe DiMaggio, poised and proper, exemplified the more sobering and solemn 1930s.[31] In his postwar career, Jolting Joe jumped into the melting pot and came up solid gold. He never again achieved his prewar statistics except for a 155 RBI season in 1948. I remember that one year later, while I was studying for a rite of passage, my bar mitzvah, Joe D (my nickname too) came off the disabled list for a crucial three-game series in Boston.[32] Following Joseph Campbell's script of *separation-initiation-return*, Joseph Paul DiMaggio, still pained by bone spurs from his right (Achilles?) heel, smote 4 home runs, knocked in 9 runs, and scored 5 runs as he led the Yanks over the Red Sox, still smarting from "the curse of the Bambino." To quote Nat "King" Cole: "Unforgettable!"

As a safe symbol, DiMaggio blunted anti-Italian feeling. He moved away from the tribal ties to a broader framework of associates such as Toots Shor, Walter Winchell, and Marilyn Monroe. The Monroe connection came after his illustrious baseball career. It enhanced his iconic status. A noble and star-crossed lover, he torched after his ex-wife. He seemed to exude class. Maybe his shilling for Mr. Coffee and the Bowery Bank somewhat tarnished that image. But could one begrudge the Clipper a chance to make an extra buck? After all, Joe D had played in an era when salaries did not rise dramatically. In his autobiography, *Lucky to Be a Yankee,* this prince in pinstripes focused on God's gift, his natural talent, and on the significance of luck.[33] Hard work and self-discipline belonged to another place, another time.

Robinson, Greenberg, and DiMaggio constitute a noble trinity. Each emerged as a representative of a particular group; yet each earned universal appeal. Robinson, of course, remained a "race man"—most resistant to assimilation. DiMaggio, the only survivor of this great triad, avoided controversy and shunned conflict. Greenberg could never shed his Jewish skin despite a highly secular life. My generation remembers all three men with fondness bordering on adulation. The fiftieth anniversary of Jackie Robinson's breakthrough focuses a nation's "lonely eyes" on number 42, to be sure; but heightened ethnic awareness propels us in quest of other comparable heroes. Where indeed have you gone, Joe D, Hank G, and Jackie R?

Our landscape is graffitied with celebrities instead of heroes. Daniel Boorstin has inferred that a democratic society bears an intrinsic bias against individual heroes. Earlier, our nation's heroes arose from common origins, as Greenberg, DiMaggio, and Robinson did powered by merit.

Today, however, the celebrity devoid of talent often occupies center stage in both sports and entertainment. Character and achievement often play second string. These celebrities—Dennis Rodman springs unhappily to mind—blur the boundaries between heroes and antiheroes.[34]

Thus, we return to the poetry of Stephen Spender, who guides us through the urban wilderness:[35]

> Never to allow gradually the traffic to smother
> With noise and fog the flowering of the spirit. . . .
> See how those names are feted by the waving grass, . . .
> The names of those who in their lives fought for life,
> Who wore at their hearts the fire's center.
> Born of the sun they traveled a short while towards the sun,
> And left the vivid air signed with their honour.*

Robinson, Greenberg, and DiMaggio signed the vivid air with their honor. Forever fixed in the mystic chords of memory, they summon what Abraham Lincoln also called the "better angels of our nature." With love and reverence, we come together to sing their praise.

Notes

1. As quoted in Jules Tygiel, editor, *The Jackie Robinson Reader: Perspectives on an American Hero* (New York: Penguin Group Dutton, 1997), p. 14.

2. Stephen Spender, "I Think Continually of Those Who Were Truly Great," in *Immortal Poems of the English Language,* ed. Oscar Williams (New York: Washington Square Press, 1969), pp. 589–590.

3. According to one survey of sports scholars conducted in the mid-1970s, only Jackie Robinson of our triad made the top twenty. Number 42 ranked third behind two Babes—Ruth and Didrickson. See David L. Porter, "America's Greatest Sports Figures," in *The Hero in Transition,* ed. Ray B. Browne and Marshall W. Fishwick (Bowling Green: Bowling Green University Popular Press, 1983), pp. 248–259.

4. Maury Allen, *Jackie Robinson: A Life Remembered* (New York: Franklin Watts, 1987), pp. 17–20.

5. Tygiel, *The Jackie Robinson Reader,* pp.39–51.

6. Leonard Broom and Philip Selznick, *Sociology* (New York: Harper and Row, 1963), pp. 529–532.

7. Browne and Fishwick, *Hero,* p. 11.

8. These observations are contextualized in an op-ed essay that I wrote. See Joe Dorinson, "Jackie's a Hero Now—But He Wasn't Always," *New York Daily News,* 28 March 1997, p. 41.

9. David Falkner, *Great Time Coming: The Life of Jackie Robinson, From Baseball to Birmingham* (New York: Simon and Schuster, 1995), p. 237.

---

120   Joseph Dorinson

10. Jules Tygiel, *Baseball's Great Experiment: Jackie Robinson and His Legacy* (New York: Random House Vintage, 1984), pp. 168–173.

11. Joseph J. Vecchione, ed., *The* New York Times *Book of Sports Legends* (New York: Random House Quadrangle Books, 1991), pp. 96–98; see Ira Berkow, "A Kind of Beacon," pp. 98–100.

12. Bert Randolph Sugar, *Baseball's 50 Greatest Games* (New York: Exeter Books, 1986), pp. 170–172.

13. Harold U. Ribalow, *The Jew in American Sports* (New York: Bloch, 1949), pp. 25–32.

14. Peter Levine, *Ellis Island to Ebbetts Field: Sport and the American Jewish Experience* (New York: Oxford University Press, 1992), pp. 139–140.

15. Ibid., p. 139.

16. Maury Allen, *Jackie Robinson: A Life Remembered* (New York: Franklin Watts, 1987), p. 188. Also see Marty Glickman with Stan Isaacs, *The Fastest Kid on the Block: The Marty Glickman Story* (Syracuse: Syracuse University Press, 1996), p. 87.

17. Levine, *Ellis Island*, p. 136.

18. As quoted in Geoffrey C. Ward and Ken Burns, *Baseball: An Illustrated History* (New York: Alfred A. Knopf, 1994), pp. 250–251.

19. G. Edward White, *Creating the National Pastime: Baseball Transforms Itself* (Princeton: Princeton University Press, 1996), p. 264.

20. Ibid., pp. 276–278.

21. Levine, *Ellis Island*, pp. 131–132.

22. Stephen Fox, *Big Leagues: Professional Baseball, Football, and Basketball in National Memory* (New York: William Morrow, 1994), pp. 374–375.

23. White, *National Pastime*, pp. 260, 266–274.

24. Maury Allen, *Where Have You Gone, Joe DiMaggio* (New York: Dutton, 1975).

25. Carmelo Bazzano, "The Italian American Sporting Experience," in *Ethnicity and Sport in North American History and Culture,* ed. George Eisen and David K. Wiggins (Westport: Praeger, 1995), p. 111. Another important source for the study of the Yankee Clipper's ethnicity is Jack B. Moore, "Understanding Joe DiMaggio as an Italian American Hero," in *Italian Americans Celebrate Life: The Arts and Popular Culture,* ed. Paola A. Sensi Isolani and Anthony Julian Tamburri (American Italian Historical Association, 1990), pp. 169–178.

26. Donald Dewey and Nicholas Acocella, *The Biographical History of Baseball* (New York: Carroll and Graf, 1995), pp. 113–115.

27. Moore, "Joe DiMaggio," p. 171.

28. As quoted in Roy Blount, Jr., "Legend: How DiMaggio Made It Look Easy," in *The Ultimate Baseball Book,* ed. Daniel Okrent and Harris Lewine (Boston: Houghton-Mifflin Hilltown, 1984), p. 209.

29. Moore, "Joe DiMaggio," p. 177.

30. Allen, *Life Remembered,* p. 45.

31. Joseph Durso, *DiMaggio: The Last American Knight* (Boston: Little Brown, 1995), p. 260.

32. DiMaggio's heroic return, shades of Campbell, occurred on June 28, 1949. See Ward and Burns, *Baseball,* p. 315.

33. As discussed in Rudolf K. Haerle, Jr., "The Athlete as 'Moral' Leader," *Journal of Popular Culture* 8, no. 2 (Fall 1974), pp. 395/41.

34. Daniel Boorstin, "From Hero to Celebrity: Human Psuedo-Event," in *Heroes and Anti-Heroes,* ed. Harold Lubin (San Francisco: Chandler, 1969), pp. 325–340.

35. Spender, *I Think Continually,* p. 590.

14

Burt Shotton: The Crucible of 1947

Robert A. Moss

Introduction

On the fiftieth anniversary of Jackie Robinson's major league debut, it is also appropriate to remember Burt Shotton, recalled from retirement by Branch Rickey to manage Robinson and the 1947 Dodgers. Taking as our chronological boundaries Robinson's advent in 1947 and his retirement at the end of the 1956 season, the "Boys of Summer" held forth in Ebbets Field for exactly one decade, during which time they won six National League pennants and twice lost the pennant on the last day of the season (1950 and 1951). Four managers presided over this noontide of talent: Leo Durocher, Burt Shotton, Charlie Dressen, and Walter Alston. Of these, Shotton is arguably the least well remembered. Durocher and Alston are both in the Hall of Fame, while Dressen figures prominently in Roger Kahn's classic description of the 1952 Dodgers, *The Boys of Summer*.[1] Shotton has languished in comparative obscurity, although he is a major character in Red Barber's remarkable chronicle, *1947, When All Hell Broke Loose in Baseball*.[2]

Now David Gough has given us *Burt Shotton, Dodgers Manager*.[3] Subtitled *A Baseball Biography*, this brief work outlines the salient facts of Shotton's career as a player, coach, and manager. Gough succeeds in giving us a feeling for Shotton's honesty and integrity, the bedrock on which he built his approach to both baseball and life. Indeed, from the work of Gough (and especially Barber), a case can be made that Burt Shotton was the managerial father of the Boys of Summer; Dressen and Alston may have won with them, but it was Shotton who melded the team together in the crucible of 1947, and tempered the steel in 1949 and 1950.

Shortly before Gough's biography appeared, Roger Kahn published *The Era, 1947–1957: When the Yankees, the Giants, and the Dodgers Ruled the World.*[4] If *The Era* has a villain, it is Burt Shotton, who is time and again denigrated by Kahn as a kind of "American gothic of the diamond." The caricature of Shotton as an aged bumbler that emerges from Kahn's work is so at odds with the engaging portraits sketched by Barber and Gough that some comparison to clarify the record is useful. We will sample several areas of contention, and consider several highlights of the 1947 season. In order to understand Shotton's managerial style, it is first necessary to outline his career as a player, for it is clear that the way he directed the Dodgers between 1947 and 1950 followed from a perception of baseball strategy that had served him well in an earlier generation.

Shotton as a Player

Burton Edwin Shotton was born in 1884 in Brownhelm, Ohio, not far from Cleveland. Starting in 1908, at age twenty-three, Shotton began to play professional baseball as an outfielder with Erie of Ohio in the Penn League. By 1911, Shotton had become a major league center fielder on the St. Louis Browns, with whom he remained until 1918. The years 1912 and 1913 were career years for Shotton, with batting averages of .290 and .297 and stolen base totals of 35 and 43, respectively, as well as a league-leading 99 walks in 1913, when he also scored 105 runs.[5]

Here, we have a premonition of how good a fit Shotton would be as manager of the 1947 Dodgers, a team that featured Eddie Stanky, a past master at extracting bases on balls (103 in 1947, to go with 148 and 137 in the preceding two years), and Jackie Robinson, who led the league with 29 steals.[6]

But 1913 was a watershed year for Shotton for another reason; it was the year that Branch Rickey joined the Browns' front office, becoming field manager in 1914. Rickey and Shotton gradually established a deep friendship that, thirty-three years later, would result in Shotton becoming manager of the Dodgers. Rickey's religious scruples prevented him from managing or even attending games on Sundays; Shotton soon became Rickey's "Sunday manager." Additionally, his play continued to shine on a lackluster team. In 1915, Shotton batted .283, recording his personal highs of 118 walks and 43 stolen bases.[7]

By 1919, Rickey had become both field and general manager of the Cardinals, and he added Shotton to his team as a part-time player, Sunday manager, and prospective coach. Shotton ended his playing career in 1923, a lifetime .270 hitter, with 294 stolen bases, 747 runs scored, and 714 bases on balls over a thirteen-year career. These are the solid statistics of a proficient player.[8]

Shotton's Early Career as a Manager

Shotton began his managerial career in the Cardinal farm system with Syracuse in 1926. In 1927, with young players, he put together a 102-win season, finishing second and developing a reputation as a manager who was patient with raw talent. Moreover, this performance earned him a chance to manage at the major league level, though not with a strong team.[9]

From 1928 to 1933, Shotton managed the Philadelphia Phillies, a poor team that had finished 43 games out in 1927. Its deficiencies included a lack of pitching, a penurious owner, and an antiquated facility (Baker Bowl). Shotton did have some good hitters, however, including Chuck Klein, and he put together several decent seasons—at least by Phillies standards. The 1932 team finished fourth at 78–76; it was the *only* Phillies team to sport a winning record between 1918 and 1948.[10]

Shotton returned to the Cardinal system and Rickey in 1935 as manager of the Rochester Red Wings. In 1936, he moved to the Columbus Red Birds of the American Association. It was at Columbus that Shotton's reputation for nurturing young players was truly established. Some of the future stars who passed through Columbus included Mickey Owen, Enos Slaughter, Mort Cooper, Max Lanier, Murray Dickson, Harry Brecheen, and Preacher Roe, who would later star for the Dodgers.

Shotton molded some of these youngsters into American Association champions in 1937, only to lose the Little World Series to the Newark Bears. Rickey now called him "one of the best managers in the game," adding that Shotton was "a master in two fields—as a teacher and in maintaining a high standard of discipline among players, while at the same time possessing a marvelous way with his men."[11]

In 1941, the Red Birds won the American Association flag and went on to defeat the Montreal Royals in the Little World Series. The *Sporting News* named Shotton the Minor League Manager of the Year, and there were rumors that he would be made manager of the Cleveland Indians.

The Indians, however, opted for their popular shortstop, Lou Boudreau, who promptly selected the fifty-seven-year-old Shotton as his third base coach and pitching advisor. Shotton remained with Cleveland from 1942 until 1945, when he was sixty years old and suffering from painful sciatica. Vowing never to wear a uniform again, Shotton retired to Florida.[12] He accepted a part-time scouting position with the Dodgers, now run by Rickey. He was therefore on the Dodger payroll on April 9, 1947, when Commissioner Albert B. "Happy" Chandler suspended Leo Durocher for the 1947 season.

Brooklyn

On April 17, Rickey dispatched a masterfully precise but simultaneously vague telegram to Shotton in Florida: "Be in Brooklyn tomorrow morning. See nobody. Say nothing. Rickey."[13] Shotton, believing that he was going to discuss player acquisition, caught a plane to New York and had breakfast with Rickey. Installed as Dodger manager, that afternoon, he found himself at the Polo Grounds for a game against the Giants. He had neither a change of clothes nor a contract; the issue of salary was not discussed because, as he put it, "Rick has always been fair with me."[14]

Was a manager ever thrust into a more difficult situation? Here was the sixty-two-year-old "retired" Shotton assuming the leadership of a talented but disunited team that had lost a playoff for the 1946 pennant. He would be expected to make a good run for the 1947 flag, perhaps beat the Cardinals. At the same time, he was asked to preside over Jackie Robinson's rookie season and the breaking of organized baseball's color line. This was sure to provoke passionate resistance, both on the team itself and from bigots around the league. Gough tells us that, "if Robinson failed, opportunities for black athletes could be set back another decade. The weight of an entire race rested on one young man. But the weight of a nation of white critics rested squarely on the shoulders of Branch Rickey."[15] And now, by extension, that weight also descended onto the shoulders of Burt Shotton.

If this were not enough, Shotton, a reticent, conservative representative of the older generation, had to replace the colorful, voluble Leo Durocher, who had managed the Dodgers with potent showmanship since 1939. Durocher's departure, Robinson's advent, fan expectations, and curiosity but little support from the press all made Shotton's tenure suspect. That he went on to win the pennant and come within an ace of taking the World Series seems, in retrospect, a minor miracle.

What weapons could Shotton deploy against the difficulties facing him? Important was his long experience as a player, coach, and manager. Crucial were his character and integrity, rooted perhaps in the straightforward values of an earlier era. Shotton was an unusual man, with a number of eccentricities that have been examined by Barber, Gough, and Kahn. It is instructive to see the different refractions that appear in the lenses of these three observers.

Kahn tells us that "Shotton would manage from the dugout in civilian clothes. At sixty-two, Shotton said that he was too old to put on a uniform."[16] This is fairly accurate, but incomplete, and misses the opportunity to impart the flavor of the man. Barber is succinct and salty: Shotton, who wore a Dodger cap and warm-up jacket, "could have had a full-fledged Dodger uniform, but he had said when he quit coaching at Cleveland after the 1945 season that he'd never put on a uniform again. He didn't."[17] The emphasis here is on "He didn't." Shotton was nothing if not forthright.

Naturally, this disappointed the fans (and the sportswriters), accustomed as they were to the on-field, umpire-baiting antics of Durocher. But Shotton's calm managerial style was an appropriate part of the overall steadying influence he provided to this team of veterans and budding stars. Pee Wee Reese, the Dodgers' captain, said, "I know where he is. . . . He is in the dugout in full charge. The fans may not see him, but we see him. We know he is there."[18]

Shotton kept score of the games using his own notation. According to Kahn, Shotton would note in his "scruffy" scorebook "F for fly and O for making an out, hardly as precise as the accepted hieroglyphs. All game long, every day, Shotton made odd vague notes in his book."[19]

Barber, however, informs us that the purpose of Shotton's record was not to notate each play in the manner of an official scorer, but rather to follow the performance of his men. For example, a player who hit a hard liner that was, nevertheless, caught for an out, would be recorded by Shotton as having made a "hit"; he was putting good wood on the ball. In a story told by Reese, "Shotton would say when he came into the dugout, 'that's a hit in my book.' "[20] Aside from its tonic effect on the morale of a player just robbed of a hit, Shotton's method gave him "a record of every play. He knew what had happened. He never had to ask someone what so-and-so did in the first or in the eighth inning. He looked in his book. . . . Shotton was alert to every play. Just as he was to every one of his ball players."[21]

Kahn states that Shotton "simply ignored the terrible racial tension tormenting Jackie Robinson,"[22] but Barber's take on Shotton and Robinson is different: "Shotton was handed by Rickey and the fates the most upset, torn-apart ball club in history. The coming of Jackie Robinson brought a seething turbulence that was waiting to explode. Shotton saw to it that serious internal trouble didn't break loose."[23]

Shotton never stinted in his respect for Robinson's talents. His own career as a base stealer had taught him the value of speed, and he gave Robinson his head. "Robinson on base was always on his own."[24] Jackie, too, felt that Shotton supported him. During his first batting slump, Shotton left him in the lineup and made no comments. In her recent book on Jackie, Rachel Robinson quotes her husband on Shotton: "I liked and respected him. . . . I appreciated his patience and understanding as I struggled to get out of a slump."[25]

Manager of the Dodgers

In 1947, the Cardinals, victors over the Dodgers in the 1946 playoff, were the team to beat. And when, in mid-June, the Cards swept a four-game series with the Dodgers in St. Louis, Shotton needed to stem the incipient tides of defeatism. He decreed that there would be no further talk about how tough the Cardinals were. Barber reconstructs Shotton's remarks: "The Cardinals played under the same rules, they used only nine players at a time, they pulled their pants on one leg at a time."[26] And again, "let's get out and play this game today . . . we'll win some, St. Louis will lose some . . . play this one today . . . that's all you have to do. That series in St. Louis is gone. We'll see them again . . . in the meantime we play today."[27]

Here was a calming constancy of purpose and confidence to which his team could respond over the length of the season. Shotton wanted controlled emotion. When Barber asked him if he was going to get the team "fighting mad" to respond to a series of knockdowns by their opponents, Shotton responded, "They ain't going to be mad tonight, or at any other time. . . . I'm here to see they don't get mad. When a man gets mad he can't beat anybody doing anything. They are going out tonight and play their regular game and I expect them to win." Barber pithily adds: "They did."[28]

One of Shotton's strengths as a minor league manager had been as judge and nurturer of young talent. In Rickey's Cardinal organization many future stars flowed through Shotton's triple-A Red Birds. Shotton was therefore an appropriate pilot for the mix of established veterans and gifted rookies that constituted the 1947 Dodgers. In the former category were Dixie Walker, Pee Wee Reese, Peter Reiser, Eddie Stanky, and Hugh Casey. Among the rookies and developing stars were Ralph Branca, Robinson, Duke Snider, and Carl Furillo. An incident with Snider encapsulates Shotton's touch. The future slugger was asked to sacrifice in a crucial situation. Obviously nonplused, the Duke fouled off two pitches and then struck out swinging. Returning to the bench, he was heard to question Shotton's managerial acumen in asking a .300 hitter to bunt. According to Barber, Shotton said, "You'll find out tomorrow in Montreal." Snider was sent to triple-A Montreal for a week. When he returned to the Dodgers, "if that old so-and-so said 'Bunt,' Snider said, 'Yes, sir.' "[29]

Shotton also made personnel decisions that later proved crucial during the 1947 World Series. He kept Al Gionfriddo on the roster for his fielding and running skills. Gionfriddo had been a throw-in in a trade with the Pirates; 1947 would bring him his only moments of glory. A lesser Dodger manager would have sent him to Montreal, but Shotton saw potential that he wanted. Similarly with the veteran Cookie Lavagetto, Shotton convinced Rickey to keep him in Brooklyn; one could never have enough pinch-hitting.

In Gionfriddo and Lavagetto were the seeds of a harvest to be reaped in October. As Branch Rickey observed, "Luck is the residue of design."[30]

Shotton had good position players, good hitting, and a decent bench in 1947. What he didn't have was a first-place pitching staff. In Hugh Casey, Shotton had a world-class closer, and in Branca he had a near-rookie who would finish 21–12. The rest of the pitchers—Joe Hatten, Vic Lombardi, Hal Gregg, Harry Taylor, and Rex Barney—were rookies and question marks. They won and they lost, they never dominated. Shotton had to juggle them all season long. Under his direction, Branca and Hatten (17–8) enjoyed their career years, while Casey (10–4) compiled his entire record in relief. In Barber's memorable summary, "I have known two actual magicians—Blackstone and Shotton. Blackstone was on the stage. Shotton, with what passed for a pitching staff in 1947, was in the Brooklyn dugout."[31]

Under Shotton's patient control, the team came together: veterans and recruits, southerners and the black first baseman, journeymen pitchers and the nonpareil reliever. With Walker (.306), Reiser (.309), Robinson (.297), catcher Bruce Edwards (.295), Reese (.284), Furillo (.295), and reserves Arky Vaughan (.325) and Lavagetto (.261), there was enough hitting.[32] With Shotton perpetually juggling the pitchers, the Dodgers made do. "The only thing a manager can do," he said, "is know his men. There's no use bawling out a man because he tries to do something and can't. They're only human; they can't do it all the time."[33]

In mid-July, the Dodgers went on a thirteen-game winning streak that culminated in a three-game sweep of the Cardinals and a ten-game lead. They had slain the ghosts of 1942 and 1946. They held on through August and September, winning the crucial games and taking two of three from the Cards in their final confrontation, protecting a four-and-a-half game lead. They were headed for the World Series against the Yankees. "I'm happy for the boys," Shotton said, "they deserve a lot of credit for the way they hustled and fought against the odds all year. . . . I'm proud to be their manager."[34]

The 1947 World Series

Although Shotton was later to bring the Dodgers to the 1949 World Series, and to pilot them to within a game of the 1950 National League pennant, the 1947 season and championship series must rank as his finest performance. Called without warning from retirement to take over a race-riven team, Shotton smoothly assumed control, steadied his personnel, suppressed dissension, fostered Robinson's acceptance, instilled confidence, maximized the productivity of a mediocre pitching staff, defeated the arch-rival Cardinals, and brought the Dodgers to within a game of the World Championship. That he did not win that final game can be ultimately traced to a fatal lack of quality starting pitchers, but this in no way diminishes his accomplishment.

Here, we will focus on the ever-memorable fourth game, which the Dodgers, trailing two games to one, had to win.[35] Until Don Larsen's perfect game in the 1956 Yankees-Dodgers matchup, Bill Bevens' near no-hitter in this contest was the most famous pitching performance in series history. Its dramatic denouement signaled the summit of several careers, and Burt Shotton's finest moment as a manager.

The ninth inning of game four was the crisis. To set the scene: Bevens, a mediocre pitcher during the season, had gone eight innings without yielding a hit. No one had ever pitched a World Series no-hitter; Bevens was only an inning away, but he was also wild. He had walked eight batters, and the Dodgers had scored a run without a hit in the fifth inning on two walks, a sacrifice, and a fielder's choice. The Yankees, however, had scored twice (and missed several other chances). The Dodgers' Hal Gregg had relieved starting rookie pitcher Harry Taylor in the first inning with one run in, the bases loaded, and nobody out. Gregg retired the side on a pop-up and a double play, and proceeded to pitch a gutsy game through seven innings, surrendering only one run in the fourth inning. Hank Behrman relieved Gregg in the eighth and held the Yanks at bay, but in the ninth, Behrman faltered. A single, a bunt, and another single loaded the bases; Shotton called for Casey to face Tommy Henrich. How many spectators then recalled game four of the 1941 World Series? The Dodgers, similarly trailing the Yankees two games to one, had led 4–3 with two outs in the ninth inning, and the same confrontation had occurred; Casey against Henrich. Casey had struck him out on a razor-sharp curve (some say it was a spitter) that broke down and away, but catcher Mickey Owen couldn't hold on to the ball. Henrich reached first safely; Casey lost his poise and, shortly, the game, as the Yankees went on to score four runs.

Surely Casey and Henrich must have had it in mind. Now Casey threw one pitch—that same down-breaking curve—and Henrich tapped it back to Casey, who started a double play: Casey to Edwards to Robinson. Thus was history redeemed.

Let's imagine the situation as the crowd saw it. Bottom of the ninth, Bevens has only three outs to go. Bruce Edwards leads off with a long drive to left that backs Lindell up against the wall, but it is only a long out. Now Bevens issues his ninth walk to Furillo (matching a dubious series record). The tying run is aboard as rookie third baseman Spider Jorgensen comes to bat. Jorgensen, however, fouls out, and Bevens is only an out away.

Now, Shotton sends Gionfriddo in to run for Furillo. The Dodgers are *in extremis;* the runner on first must score or the game is over. From this point on, Shotton will make the incisive moves of a grandmaster. Gionfriddo is the throw-in utility man that he had kept on the roster; the first of Gionfriddo's two great moments has arrived. Shotton calls on Pete Reiser to bat for Casey. Reiser, had badly injured his ankle (broken it, in fact) the previous day. True to his ethic, Reiser had it taped and waited to do his part.

Reiser is the only left-handed batter remaining on Shotton's bench to hit against the right-handed Bevens; even if he can't run, he can hit, and it is only 297 feet down the right-field line in Ebbets Field. The count on Reiser goes to 2–1. Shotton brazenly calls for a steal, and Gionfriddo just manages to slide into second under Berra's high throw to Rizzuto.

All those years that Shotton stole bases for his livelihood in St. Louis culminate in this moment and daring call. We can easily imagine what would have been said if Gionfriddo were out. Shotton said only, "I wanted him on second base."[36]

The cogs are turning rapidly. The pitch to Reiser was ball three. Now a single will tie the game. First base is open. Bevens has still not allowed a hit, but he might groove a 3–1 pitch to Reiser. Stanky, the next batter, is right-handed, and Shotton has no remaining left-handed pinch hitters. Yankee manager Harris weighs the percentages and orders ball four thrown to Reiser. In so doing, he violates a cardinal rule—never put the winning run on base.

Shotton sends Eddie Miksis in to run for Reiser. The tying run is on second, the winning run on first; there are two outs and Shotton makes his final move. He recalls Stanky, only the second time all season that he has hit for his second baseman,[37] and sends up Lavagetto, the right-handed hitting veteran that Rickey kept on the team in April at Shotton's urging. Gionfriddo on second, Lavagetto at bat, Shotton's men, and Shotton's call.

Bevens suckers Lavagetto into swinging at a high and outside delivery; strike one. Bevens' second pitch is in the same place. This time Lavagetto crushes it high over Henrich's head and against the scoreboard in right field. Gionfriddo and Miksis, running with two out, score on Lavagetto's double. Bevens' no-hitter and the Yankees' victory are both gone; the series has been evened. Hugh Casey gets the win for a single pitch; Lavagetto gets the fame, Bevens the reverse. Shotton made it happen. Sure, he had luck, but Gionfriddo's steal was the key. I once had the opportunity to ask Gionfriddo if he was ordered to steal or if he had dared it on his own. "I was sent," he told me.[38] Indeed he was.

Conclusion

Although the Yankees recovered to win the series four games to three, the labors of this shining season were not in vain; the seeds of a great future

130   *Robert A. Moss*

had been well sown. Shotton would return to lead the Dodgers to another pennant in 1949, and would almost repeat in 1950. Robinson would go on to greatness. When we look at the personnel Shotton managed, and the team he left to Dressen in 1951, we recognize the Boys of Summer, assembled and in their proper positions: Campanella catching, Hodges at first, Robinson at second, Reese at short, Cox at third, Furillo in right, and Snider in center. The pitchers now included Don Newcombe, Preacher Roe, and Carl Erskine. These are names to conjure with; they are Shotton's legacy.

Burt Shotton died of a heart attack on July 29, 1962, at the age of seventy-seven. Of him, Branch Rickey once said, "He is a man of principle, a man of honor, honest and not afraid to work."[39] Reared in an earlier century, patient and steady, Shotton brought to his teams the "old-fashioned" virtues of loyalty, labor, and integrity. He had not been a star as a player; he was not a prima donna as a manager—but he far surmounted his limitations in both roles. His quiet confidence often inspired his men, regulars and role players, to perform in excess of their abilities.

Gough finds just the right epitaph: "He knew that triumph was transient and that defeat was neither fatal nor final. There would be another game tomorrow."[40]

Notes

1. Roger Kahn, *The Boys of Summer* (New York: Harper and Row, 1971).
2. Red Barber, *1947: When All Hell Broke Loose in Baseball* (New York: Da Capo Press, 1984).
3. David Gough, *Burt Shotton, Dodgers Manager: A Baseball Biography* (Jefferson, NC: McFarland, 1994).
4. Roger Kahn, *The Era, 1947–1957: When the Yankees, the Dodgers, and the Giants Ruled the World* (New York: Ticknor and Fields, 1993).
5. Gough, *Burt Shotton,* pp. 13–27, 131.
6. Joseph L. Reichler, ed., *The Baseball Encyclopedia,* 6th ed. (New York: Macmillan, 1985), pp. 1337–1338, 1421.
7. Gough, *Burt Shotton,* pp. 13–17, 131.
8. Reichler, *Baseball Encyclopedia,* p. 1390.
9. Gough, *Burt Shotton,* pp. 29–32.
10. Ibid., pp. 37–48.
11. Ibid., p. 62.
12. Ibid., p. 73.
13. Ibid., p. 77.
14. Barber, *1947,* p. 144.
15. Gough, *Burt Shotton,* p. 79.
16. Kahn, *The Era,* p. 40.
17. Barber, *1947,* p. 145.
18. Ibid., p. 146.
19. Kahn, *The Era,* p. 95.
20. Barber, *1947,* pp. 213–214.

21. Ibid., p. 214.
22. Kahn, *The Era,* p. 95.
23. Barber, *1947,* p. 214.
24. Ibid., p. 191.
25. Rachel Robinson with Lee Daniels, *Jackie Robinson: An Intimate Portrait* (New York: Harry N. Abrams, 1996), p. 73.
26. Barber, *1947,* p. 196.
27. Ibid., p. 222.
28. Ibid., p. 197.
29. Ibid., p. 156.
30. John J. Monteleone, ed., *Branch Rickey's Little Blue Book* (New York: Macmillan, 1995), p. 11.
31. Barber, *1947,* p. 193.
32. Reichler, *Baseball Encyclopedia,* p. 382.
33. Gough, *Burt Shotton,* p. 102.
34. Ibid., p. 87.
35. Barber, *1947,* pp. 314–329.
36. Ibid., p. 326.
37. Ibid., p. 327.
38. Al Gionfriddo, conversation with author, 1993.
39. Gough, *Burt Shotton,* p. 128.
40. Ibid.

15

Jackie Robinson on Opening Day, 1947–1956

Lyle Spatz

Jackie Robinson's major league debut was more than just the first step in righting a historical wrong. It was a crucial event in the history of the American civil rights movement, the importance of which went far beyond the insular world of baseball. Nevertheless, as powerful as his role was in that crusade, my intention in this chapter is to deal not with Jackie Robinson the social pioneer, but with Jackie Robinson the baseball player. Of course, dealing with Robinson the athlete without taking into consideration Robinson the man is not possible. More than any other player ever, his identity as a player was defined by his identity as a man—above all, a black man.

I have chosen to look at Robinson's major league career through the prism of Opening Day because of the special place that day has always had in the American psyche. Perhaps because it comes in the spring, the season of hope and renewal, Americans have always greeted the opening of a new baseball season with a euphoria that they give to no other sport. Moreover, Opening Day not only gives us our first look at the significant changes in baseball as a whole, but also in the fortunes of all of its players. In Robinson's case, it allows us to track him as he progresses from a twenty-eight-year-old rookie, duty bound to accept whatever vilification comes his way, to a controversy-ridden star, and finally to a fading veteran. Opening Day serves as a microcosm of his ten years in the game, including his on-field and off-field conflicts with opposing players and managers, and even his own managers and teammates.*

Because for so many fans Opening Day is the most exciting day on the baseball calendar, it seems only fitting that Jackie Robinson, the most exciting player of the last fifty years, should have excelled on that day. In his career with the Dodgers, which began on Opening Day 1947 and ended with the 1956 World Series, Robinson never missed an opener. Over those ten years, he was most often at second base and batting fourth, the position and place in the batting order we primarily associate with him. Yet, in addition to playing first base in his first opener, he also played at third base and in left field, while batting in five different spots in the order. And—unlike what happened in recent decades when only two men, Walter Alston and Tommy Lasorda, managed the Dodgers—Robinson played under five different Opening Day managers, four in his first five seasons.

The Dodgers signed Robinson to a major league contract just five days before the start of the 1947 season. Baseball people, especially those in Brooklyn, were still digesting the previous day's news of Manager Leo Durocher's one-year suspension (for conduct detrimental to baseball), when the story broke of Robinson's promotion from the Montreal Royals. He would be the first black American to play in the major leagues in the twentieth century, and the first since catcher Fleetwood Walker played for the Toledo Blue Stockings of the American Association back in 1884. Robinson had played second base for Montreal in 1946, but on orders from the Dodgers he had been working out at first all spring. He played first base in Brooklyn's final three exhibition games against the Yankees, and again two days later when they opened the season at Ebbets Field against Billy Southworth's Boston Braves. Rumors of a sellout may have discouraged some fans from attending, but whatever the reason, a crowd of only 26,623 saw Robinson's debut.[1]

Jack made the game's first putout, receiving the throw from fellow rookie Spider Jorgensen on Dick Culler's ground ball. Interim Manager Clyde Sukeforth had him batting second, so after Eddie Stanky grounded out, Robinson stepped in against Johnny Sain for his first major league at-bat. Sain, the National League's winningest right-hander in 1946 (20–14), retired him easily on a bouncer to third baseman Bob Elliott. After flying out to left fielder Danny Litwhiler in the third inning, Robinson

---

*Note: All attendance figures and game statistics in this chapter came from the *New York Times*. Descriptions of play-by-play for each game came from data furnished by Dr. David W. Smith of *Retrosheet*.

appeared to have gotten his first big-league hit in the fifth. But shortstop Culler made an outstanding play on his ground ball and turned it into a well-executed 6–4–3 double play.

When he next batted, in the seventh, Brooklyn was trailing 3–2. Stanky, who had opened the inning drawing Sain's fifth walk of the afternoon, was on first. It was an obvious bunt situation, and Robinson laid down a beauty, pushing the ball deftly up the right side. Boston's rookie first baseman, Earl Torgeson, fielded it, but with Robinson speeding down the line he was forced to hurry his throw. The ball hit Jack and caromed away, allowing him to take second and Stanky to reach third. Pete Reiser's double scored both runners and finished Sain. Reiser later scored on Gene Hermanski's fly ball off reliever Mort Cooper as the Dodgers won 5–3. Hal Gregg, in relief of starter Joe Hatten, got the win, and Hugh Casey got the first of his league-leading 18 saves. Of course nobody had ever heard of "saves" in 1947, and Casey would die never knowing that he had twice been the National League leader.

When the Dodgers took the field in the ninth inning, Robinson remained on the bench as veteran Howie Schultz took over at first base. Sukeforth had put him in as a defensive measure, but the Dodgers soon realized that Robinson needed no help. Schultz played in only one more game before Brooklyn sold him to the Phillies. Ed Stevens, the team's other first baseman, played in just five games before they sent him back to the minors.

Pete Reiser, a very popular player, coming back from yet another injury, clearly had been the star of the game and it was he, not Robinson, who was the focus of the story in the next day's *New York Times*. Roscoe McGowen's game account mentioned Robinson only in relation to his play,[2] leaving columnist Arthur Daley to take note of his debut, which he called uneventful.[3] In retrospect, it would be easy, and fashionable, to attribute the writers' casual treatment of this history-making game to racism. However, I prefer to think that they handled it in this way because it took place at a time when baseball reporters believed that that's what they were: baseball reporters, men who felt their sole duty was to report what took place on the field. Red Barber and Connie Desmond, the Dodgers' radio broadcasters, did the same. The mind boggles to think how the media would cover such an event today.

Although Robinson would not get his first major league hit until the Dodgers' second game, he would not go hitless on Opening Day again until 1956, his final season. His overall Opening Day batting average was a robust .368, and for the eight season openers between his first and his last (1948–1955), it was an extraordinary .438.[4] Moreover, his performances on Opening Day, particularly his propensity to be the game's focal point, mirrored his entire Dodger career.

Take 1948 for example. The Sunday finale to the traditional three-game series against the Yankees that preceded the opener drew a crowd of 62,369 tc Yankee Stadium. That was then the largest ever for an exhibition game, and Robinson, the Rookie of the Year in 1947 who had become a hero to millions of black Americans, was the big draw.[5] As *Daily News* sportswriter Hy Turkin phrased it in that less "politically correct" time, it was Robinson who was "largely responsible for that Harlem-studded record audience."[6]

Two days later Brooklyn opened against the Giants at the Polo Grounds. Robinson, batting in the leadoff spot, had only one hit in five at-bats, but it was the key blow in Brooklyn's 7–6 win. Actually, the hit was nothing more than a little pop fly to left, on which left fielder Whitey Lockman and shortstop Bobby Rhawn collided. Brooklyn had been trailing, 3–1, when they came to bat in the seventh—the Giants having scored single runs off Brooklyn starter Rex Barney in the second, third, and sixth innings. Larry Jansen had allowed just three hits to that point, but with one down, right fielder Dick Whitman and third baseman Billy Cox reached him for back-to-back singles. Whitman scored when Spider Jorgensen, batting for catcher Gil Hodges, doubled on a short fly ball to left that Lockman missed while attempting a shoestring catch. (Roy Campanella made his major league debut when he went in to replace Hodges behind the plate in the last of the seventh.) For Lockman, who had missed all but two games in 1947 because of a broken ankle, this was the second shoestring catch of the day that he had attempted and missed.

Jansen got pinch hitter Marv Rackley for the second out, as Cox and Jorgensen stayed put. Then Robinson, swinging on the 2–1 pitch, lifted another fly ball into short left. Rhawn, filling in for the Giants' regular shortstop, the injured Buddy Kerr, drifted back and made the catch. However, as he did it, Lockman came crashing into him, causing the ball to fall loose. Jack legged it into a double as Cox and Jorgensen raced home. Arky Vaughan followed with a single that scored Robinson and gave the Dodgers a 5–3 lead. They added two more runs in the eighth, just enough to hold off the Giants who bounced back to score three off reliever Hugh Casey.

Robinson was playing his first major league game at second base that afternoon. The Dodgers had opened the position for him a month earlier when they traded Eddie Stanky to the Braves. In doing so, they left a hole at first, which by Opening Day had not been satisfactorily filled. Returning Manager Leo Durocher used left-handed hitting Preston Ward in the opener, mainly because Jansen threw right-handed. Ward was a rookie who, except for one at-bat, had never played above the Class A level.

"He's my first baseman today," said Durocher before the game. "He will be my first baseman tomorrow. I hope."[7]

Yet Ward would not be the solution to the problem at first base, and his stay in Brooklyn would end at midseason. Durocher's would too, but before he left he made a major contribution to the Dodgers future success. He converted Gil Hodges from a catcher to a first baseman, a position Hodges would occupy for the next fourteen years.

Unlike Ward, the other newcomer to the Dodger lineup that day, third baseman Billy Cox, would stay with them well beyond midseason. He would join with Robinson, Hodges, and veteran shortstop Pee Wee Reese to form one of the game's great infields. Most everyone has heard the story of Dodger outfielder Dixie Walker's early opposition to Robinson and his wish to be traded. As the story goes, Walker later told Branch Rickey that he had changed his mind and wished to stay. Well, it was too late. Rickey had already decided to trade him, and that is how Cox got to Brooklyn. He and pitcher Preacher Roe came in the deal that sent Walker to Pittsburgh—a trade that remains arguably the best the Dodgers ever made.[8]

Rickey was at this game, observing the fruits of his labors. He sat in the Dodgers box with his wife and Laraine Day, Durocher's wife. Also in attendance at the refurbished Polo Grounds (the outfield walls were now painted green, with all the advertising signs removed) were National League President Ford Frick and Mr. and Mrs. Babe Ruth. This would be the last opener for the Babe, who was suffering from throat cancer and would die in August.

The Dodgers and Giants were back at it in the 1949 opener, this one at Ebbets Field. The standing-room-only crowd of 34,530 was the largest gathering ever for an Opening Day in Brooklyn, breaking the record, set in 1941, by more than 3,000.[9] And, according to police estimates, the Dodgers had to turn away an additional 10,000 fans who had tried to get into the park. Leo Durocher, who had stunned the city of New York the previous July by leaving the Dodgers to replace Mel Ott, was in his first full season as manager of the Giants. Burt Shotton, who had replaced Durocher during his suspension in 1947 and again the previous July, was managing his first opener for Brooklyn.

Larry Jansen was on the mound again for New York, pitching the first of the four openers he would pitch for Durocher. The Giants staked him to a quick 1–0 lead when second baseman Bill Rigney, after taking lefty Joe Hatten's first pitch for a strike, hit the next one into the seats in left. Rigney was playing only because rookie Bobby Hofman, who had won the second base job with an outstanding spring, had an injured finger.

Carl Furillo's home run tied the score in the second, but the Giants came back with two in the fourth to take a 3–1 lead. From then on, it was all Brooklyn. Robinson, who had batted second in the 1947 opener and first a year before, was batting fourth this afternoon. Although he would play all the infield positions at one time or another and bat in all nine spots in the order, Robinson would be the second baseman and cleanup hitter for more than half the games he would play for the Dodgers. He led off the fourth by blasting Jansen's 2–2 pitch for a long home run. Later in the inning, Roy Campanella followed with a three-run blast. The Dodgers added a run in the sixth and four more in the seventh off ex-teammate Hank Behrman. Robinson had three hits and scored two runs in Brooklyn's 10–3 victory. He also sparkled in the field, with six putouts and six assists, including the fielding play of the game. In the seventh, he grabbed a ball that had deflected off first baseman Gil Hodges and threw to Hatten covering to get the lumbering Johnny Mize. Robinson's spectacular opener set the stage for what would be his greatest season, one that culminated in his winning the league's Most Valuable Player award.

Due in large part to Robinson, the Dodgers were the league's best attraction throughout his career. In 1950, as the defending National League champions, they drew the largest opening-crowd (29,074) ever to see the Phillies at Shibe Park.[10] Philadelphia won, 9–1, behind Robin Roberts, with Robinson scoring the Dodgers' only run. Although Roberts had begun to show signs in 1949 of the great pitcher he would become, his record against Brooklyn that year was 0–5. That led to the supposition that the Phillies would open with Ken Heintzleman, their veteran left-hander. However, Manager Eddie Sawyer, disregarding Roberts' past troubles against the Dodgers, said the twenty-three-year-old right-hander had been his best pitcher all spring and deserved to start the opener.

Manager Burt Shotton's starting pitcher was Don Newcombe, the first black man ever to start a major league opener. Newcombe, last season's Rookie of the Year, would have an excellent sophomore season, but he was totally ineffective in this game. The Phillies, wearing their new red-striped uniforms (*Daily News* sportswriter Dick Young called them their "new gaudy peppermint-stick uniforms"),[11] pounded him and the four pitchers that followed for sixteen hits. Before he left, with nobody out in the second inning, Newcombe had given up four runs on five hits. Meanwhile, Roberts held Brooklyn to seven hits, with only Robinson getting more than one. The Dodgers were already down 8–0 when in the seventh inning they managed to push across their lone run. Robinson, who had an infield single earlier, led off with a long double to right center. When Phils' second baseman Mike Goliat mishandled the throw-in, he continued to third, and scored on Carl Furillo's single.

Newcombe and Roberts would meet again on the final day of the 1950 season, with the Dodgers needing a win to tie Philadelphia for the National

League pennant. In a game still bemoaned by old-time Dodger fans, Roberts again beat Newcombe, this time 4–1 on Dick Sisler's three-run homer in the tenth inning. Everyone remembers that Richie Ashburn threw out Cal Abrams (carrying the potential winning run) at the plate in the bottom of the ninth. But to force the game into extra innings, Roberts still had to get by a one-out, second and third situation. He did so by intentionally walking Robinson, although Jack hadn't had a hit in the game, and then getting Furillo on a pop-up and Gil Hodges on a long fly.

Roberts was back to face Brooklyn in the 1951 opener, but he had a different pitching opponent. Newcombe didn't want to risk further injuring his stiff shoulder on this 50°F day, so new Dodger Manager Charlie Dressen turned to twenty-four-year-old right-hander Carl Erskine. After a very lively pregame celebration, it was a most disappointing result for the crowd of 19,217, a low turnout for which the chilly temperatures were partially to blame. Philadelphia reached Erskine for two runs in the first inning and added a Mike Goliat homer in the second to take an early 3–0 lead. They extended it to 5–0 in the sixth on a two-run blast by Del Ennis, before the Dodgers scored their only two runs in the bottom of the sixth. Robinson accounted for both Brooklyn scores with a two-out drive into the left-field seats with Duke Snider aboard.

Jack had another hit in the eighth, a hard single to left that was part of a two-out threat that the Dodgers mounted. It was sandwiched between singles by Snider and Gil Hodges and loaded the bases for Roy Campanella. Roberts fell behind in the count, 2–0, but then ended Brooklyn's hopes by getting Campy to foul out to catcher Andy Seminick.

In 1952, the Dodgers opened at Boston in what would be the Braves' final year in that city. The game drew only 4,694 fans,[12] a turnout that would be indicative of that year's crowds at Braves Field. Later, team owner Lou Perini would cite the dismal 1952 home attendance of 281,278 as the major reason for moving the franchise to Milwaukee.[13] Though still haunted by the nightmarish end of the previous season, Brooklyn opened with a 3–2 victory behind veteran left-hander Preacher Roe. In doing so, they defeated Warren Spahn (like Roe a twenty-two-game winner in 1951), breaking Spahn's five-game Braves Field winning streak against them.

The Dodgers were a predominantly right-handed hitting team that did not face many left-handers. In an attempt to combat Spahn, the league's best, Manager Charlie Dressen rearranged his normal batting order. He moved Duke Snider, his only left-handed hitting regular, from the number 3 spot down to sixth, moved Robinson up one position to third and put Roy Campanella in the cleanup spot. As it happened, it was Campy who would provide the key hit of the game. His two-run single in Brooklyn's three-run

Left to right: Jackie Robinson (Brooklyn Dodgers); Sid Gordon (New York Giants); Joe DiMaggio (New York Yankees) in 1949 before a round-robin game to benefit local charities. They are emblematic of three major ethnic groups in New York: African American, Jewish, and Italian. Photo UPI/Corbis-Bettman.

Hank Greenberg in his year as a Pittsburgh Pirate. A man of conscience, Greenberg was the first player from an opposing team to encourage Jackie, which became the basis for a lifelong friendship. Photo from private collection, used with permission.

Jackie Robinson appearing before the House Un-American Activities Committee in Washington in July, 1949. Robinson later regretted his criticism of Paul Robeson. Photo UPI/Corbis-Bettman.

Robinson addressing students at a Cleveland high school in 1955, in connection with the National Conference of Christians and Jews. Never a one-dimensional athlete and always concerned with education, he preached the "Gospel of Brotherhood." Photo UPI/Corbis-Bettman.

Jackie with a young David Widensky (the photographer's son) on Camera Day at Ebbets Field in 1955. The boy's expression and Jackie's affectionately casual pose amply demonstrate his appeal across racial and ethnic lines, in this previously unpublished photograph. Photo by Irving Widensky, with permission.

MR. JACK R. ROBINSON
VICE PRESIDENT

After being traded to the New York Giants and denied an executive position with the Brooklyn Dodgers, Jackie retired from baseball and joined the Chock Full O'Nuts coffee company in 1957 as vice-president in charge of personnel. He is shown here with company president William Black, a renowned philanthropist. Photo UPI/Corbis-Bettman.

This striking undated photo was probably taken after Jackie's 1949 championship season, in which he hit .342 and stole 37 bases to lead the National League in both categories. He was also the first African American to win the MVP Award. National Archive photo.

Jackie appearing on local radio station WTL in 1970, shown here discussing the finer points of basketball with former Long Island University Athletic Director William "Buck" Lai. Photo courtesy Buck Lai.

Photos from the April, 1997, conference on Jackie Robinson at Long Island University. Paul Robeson, Jr., discusses the disagreement between his distinguished father and Jackie Robinson. Photography by Rodney K. Hurley.

Recently retired former All-Star Ozzie Smith, who replaced the legendary broadcaster Mel Allen on "This Week in Baseball," paying tribute to his childhood hero. Photography by Rodney K. Hurley.

Conference participants William Pickens and Evelyn Cunningham (background). Pickens is President of the Paul Robeson Foundation and a cousin of Robeson; Cunningham is a former assistant to Nelson Rockefeller, a reporter for the *Pittsburgh Courier*, and recent recipient of the Polk Award for career achievement. Photography by Rodney K. Hurley.

John "Buck" O'Neil, 85, responds to questions. He was a teammate of Jackie's on the old Kansas City Monarchs in 1945, and became the first African American to coach in the major leagues. Photography by Rodney K. Hurley.

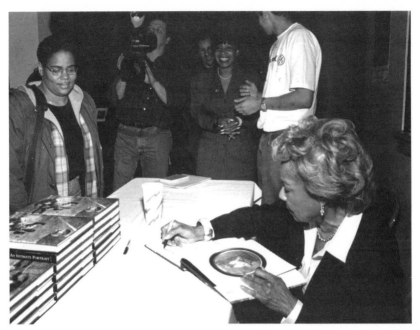

Jackie's widow Rachel Robinson signing copies of her book *Jackie Robinson: An Intimate Portrait* at the April conference. Photography by Rodney K. Hurley.

At the April conference, left to right: coeditor Joe Dorinson; retired Long Island University administrator William "Buck" Lai; Rachel Robinson; Gale Haynes, Provost of the Brooklyn Campus of LIU. Buck Lai is a former scout for the Brooklyn Dodgers, and managed a summer camp in Vero Beach, Florida, where the Dodgers still train. Photography by Rodney K. Hurley.

"Stan the Man" Musial, who defied a planned boycott of Jackie Robinson in 1947, at the April conference. His World Series ring is being examined by a slightly off-camera former Dodger pitcher Joe Black.

Buck O'Neil responds to questions from the audience at the April conference about his recent book, *I Was Right on Time: My Journey from the Negro Leagues to the Majors*, written with ESPN Magazine's Steve Wulf (pictured) and David Conrads.

A lineup of baseball greats. From left: Bobby Thomson (partially hidden); Enos Slaughter; Johnny Podres; Clem Labine; Joe Pignatano; Ralph Branca; Tommy Henrich.

fifth inning provided the margin of victory. Sam Jethroe's leadoff homer in the third had given Boston a 1–0 lead, but in the fifth, the Dodgers came back. Singles by Gil Hodges, Carl Furillo, and Billy Cox and a walk to Robinson had given them a run and left the bases loaded. Two men were out, and Campy was the batter. He had failed in a similar situation against Robin Roberts in the opener a year ago, but he did not fail today. Campy lined Spahn's first pitch into right field to score Furillo and Cox and put the Dodgers ahead to stay.

Besides his walk, Robinson had a fourth-inning single and a seventh-inning pop to shortstop Jack Cusick. In his first at-bat, as the game's third batter, Jack grounded out to twenty-year-old third baseman Eddie Mathews, the first major league chance for the future Hall of Famer. Oddly, the fifth-inning walk from Spahn would be the only Opening Day walk he would ever draw.

Robinson's major league career had been born amid controversy, and controversy would follow him the rest of his days. Opening Day was no different. If there was any kind of contentious issue on the field—or, for that matter, if there was any kind of contentious issue off the field—he was sure to be at the center of it. The arrival of Junior Gilliam in 1953 ended Robinson's days as Brooklyn's full-time second baseman. He had been the starter at that position for the National League in the four preceding All-Star games, but at thirty-four his range had noticeably begun to decrease. During spring training, Manager Dressen moved him to third base, and that's where he was in the opener. That meant, of course, that Billy Cox was without a regular position. Dressen claimed that he made the move to help the Dodger offense, but Cox was clearly unhappy and expressed his displeasure to the writers covering the team. Several hinted at racial problems resulting from the switch, and some went so far as to report that Cox was threatening to quit the game. He didn't, and before the year was out he had reclaimed his position, with Robinson moving to left field.

Brooklyn's opponent in the 1953 opener was the Pittsburgh Pirates, the first time in history that these longtime National League rivals had ever met on Opening Day. With the shift of the Boston franchise to Milwaukee (playing their first home game that day), Pittsburgh joined the Dodgers, Giants, and Phillies as the league's Eastern teams. While no "official" divisions existed in this more simple time, there was a tradition in both leagues that on Opening Day Eastern teams played against Eastern teams and Western teams against Western.

Pittsburgh had been by far baseball's weakest club in 1952, winning just forty-five games and finishing fifty-four and a half games behind the pennant-winning Dodgers. They had a new manager this season, Fred Haney, and some new players, but they would still finish a distant last, winning five more games but trailing the champion Dodgers by fifty-five games.

A chance to see the lowly Pirates, on a bitterly cold day no less, lured a crowd of just 12,433 to Ebbets Field. Still, fans who couldn't resist being at the ballpark on Opening Day got to see a most exciting game. The Dodgers won, 8–5, but Pittsburgh had the tying runs on in the ninth with two outs and home run king Ralph Kiner at the plate. Facing Joe Black, last season's rookie sensation, Kiner connected for what looked like a three-run homer. But he had hit the ball into a stiff wind blowing in from left field that held it up long enough for center fielder Duke Snider to make the game-ending catch. Black, who took over for starter Carl Erskine in Pittsburgh's four-run fourth, was the winner, and Pirates starter Murry Dickson was the loser. After scoring four runs of their own in the home fourth, the Dodgers drove Dickson out with four more runs in the fifth.

Roy Campanella, with a three-run homer, and Duke Snider with a two-run shot and a run-scoring double, led Brooklyn's thirteen-hit attack. Robinson contributed two hits, as did Carl Furillo. Jack singled in the fourth, coming home on Campy's homer, and singled again in the fifth. He scored his second run of the game on Don Thompson's fly ball to center fielder George Metkovich. Both of Robinson's hits came against Dickson, a pitcher whom he would face more times in his career than any other except Robin Roberts. Jack batted against Dickson 137 times, getting 43 hits, a .314 average. His mark against Roberts, whom he faced 160 times, was a very respectable .281.[14]

Cox replaced Robinson at third base in the seventh inning, but Dressen denied that he made the move for defensive reasons. He pointed out that Jack had pulled a muscle in his left side while racing out to his position during the sixth inning, and he didn't want to risk its getting worse in the cold weather.

Dressen would win a second consecutive National League pennant in 1953, but it was not enough to earn him what he wanted: a multiyear contract. When he insisted upon having one, Dodger owner Walter O'Malley simply replaced him. To lead the Dodgers in 1954, he chose Montreal's Walter Alston as his top minor league manager.[15]

Alston made his big-league debut at the Polo Grounds against a Giants club that would replace the Dodgers as National League champions and then sweep the Cleveland Indians in the World Series. They would be led all season, as they were today, by Willie Mays, back after a two-year hitch in the Army. Mays' sixth-inning home run, a 400-foot blast to the upper deck in left, broke a 3–3 tie as the Giants won 4–3 behind Sal Maglie and Marv Grissom.

Robinson was in left field, a position he had begun to play with regularity last season. Jim Gilliam, the National League Rookie of the Year in 1953 was at second base, and Billy Cox, in his final season in Brooklyn, was at third. Robinson would play in almost 200 games in the outfield over his final four seasons, and hit better in that position than in any other, a resounding .342.[16] Contrary to popular belief (and personal memory), he also hit very well against Maglie, batting a solid .310 against the Dodgers' chief tormentor.[17] And a tormentor he was; his victory this afternoon would be his nineteenth in twenty-five decisions against Brooklyn.

Robinson had one hit in three at-bats while Maglie was on the mound, a sixth-inning single that helped the Dodgers even the score at 3–3. His hit sent Duke Snider to third, which allowed Snider to score on Gil Hodges' sacrifice fly. That was the only run of the game that did not come as the result of a home run. Besides yielding Mays' solo shot, Dodgers' starter Carl Erskine gave up homers to Hank Thompson and Alvin Dark, Dark's with a man aboard. Roy Campanella furnished Brooklyn's first two runs with bases-empty home runs in the second and fourth innings.

Robinson's most critical at-bat of the day came in the seventh, after Mays' home run had again given New York a one-run lead. Brooklyn had loaded the bases on pinch hitter Sandy Amoros' double, and walks to Gilliam and Pee Wee Reese. With only one out, and Snider and Robinson due up, Giants Manager Leo Durocher made the right move, as he would do so often this season. He replaced Maglie with Grissom, a thirty-six-year-old right-hander picked up on waivers from the Red Sox in July 1953. After Grissom disposed of Snider on a pop to shortstop Dark, Robinson, a usually good clutch hitter, stepped in. Jack hit the ball sharply, but it was right at third baseman Thomson who tossed it to Davey Williams at second for the inning-ending force on Reese. The idea of "saves" was still fifteen years away, but by setting Brooklyn down over the final two innings, Grissom would earn one retroactively.

Not surprisingly, Robinson was involved in the game's only disputed play. With one out in the Giants eighth, he made an outstanding diving catch of Whitey Lockman's short liner to left. At least, third base umpire Bill Engeln ruled it a catch. The Giants and most observers in the press box thought he had trapped the ball. Robinson, who suffered a half-inch gash over his right eye and also did some damage to his lips on the play, was noncommital.

"I came up with the ball, didn't I? And I threw it in. The umpire called him out, didn't he?"[18]

Jack also was in the dark on how he had cut himself. "My sunglasses were down around my mouth when I got up, but they weren't broken," he said. "Must have been something else in the grass."[19]

While the 35-year-old Robinson stole only seven bases in 1954, the only time in his career he failed to reach double figures in steals, he did continue to hit well. His .311 average that season marked the sixth consecutive time he had batted above .300. It was also the last. He fell off to .256 in 1955 while playing in only 105 games. Most were at third base, where he shared duty with second-year man Don Hoak. Despite his own decline, Robinson contributed to and shared in the joy of that glorious season, which ended with Brooklyn winning its first and only World Series.

For even before defeating the hated Yankees in seven memorable games, the Dodgers had made a shambles of the National League pennant race. They began the 1955 season by winning their first ten games, and twenty-two of the first twenty-four. Carl Erskine, pitching the opener for the third consecutive year, got them off to a proper start with a 6–1 victory over the Pirates at Ebbets Field. Erskine went the distance for Brooklyn to collect his first Opening Day win after two losses and a no-decision. They played on a cold, rainy, foggy day that was only a slight improvement over the steady rain that had already caused a one-day postponement. Only 6,999 fans showed up, and while the club could blame the embarrassingly low attendance on the miserable weather, the foreboding fact remained that the Dodgers had not sold out a home opener since 1949.

Robinson had been involved in various personality disputes with Manager Walter Alston all spring; still, he was at third base and batting sixth in the opener. On his first swing of the season, leading off the second inning, he bounced what looked to be an extra-base hit down the third base line. However, veteran third baseman Sid Gordon, not known for his defense, made an excellent play to backhand the ball. His throw to first baseman Preston Ward beat Jack to the bag by a step, an outcome that might have been different a few years earlier. Robinson bounced to Gordon again in the fourth, but had hits in his next two at-bats.

Erskine and Pittsburgh's Max Surkont had kept the game scoreless until the home sixth when a leadoff double by Duke Snider and a single by Gil Hodges accounted for Brooklyn's first run. One out later, Robinson banged a double off the right-field wall, sending Hodges, who had singled, to third. Pirates' Manager Fred Haney then ordered Surkont to intentionally walk Carl Furillo, loading the bases. Haney chose to take his chances with the number 8 hitter, Roy Campanella. Campy would win his third Most Valuable Player award this season, but he was coming off an injury-ridden 1954 in which he batted a career-low .207, with just 51 runs batted in.

Baseball strategy dictated Haney's move, which appeared successful when Campy bounced Surkont's first pitch to shortstop Dick Groat. It looked like a sure inning-ending double play, but Robinson, running from second, allowed the ball to hit him. He was, of course, declared automatically out, but Campy was awarded a single and the bases remained loaded. Robinson's quick-thinking tactic went for nought as Surkont got out of the inning thanks to another fine play by Gordon on Erskine's slow roller.

The Pirates evened the score in the seventh, but Brooklyn broke it open with five runs in their half of the inning. Jim Gilliam opened with a homer against the foul screen in right. Two outs later, Robinson batted with Pee Wee Reese at third and Snider, who had a perfect afternoon, at first. Jack brought Reese home with a well-placed bunt single to the right side. His hit also served to keep the inning alive and allowed Furillo to apply the crushing blow: a three-run homer to the seats in left.

With the start of the 1956 season, Jackie Robinson, now thirty-seven, began his last year in Brooklyn. During the off-season, the Dodgers had acquired Randy Jackson from the Cubs specifically to play third base. Yet, when the club opened the season against Philadelphia at Ebbets Field, Jackson was on the bench and Robinson, who'd had a terrific spring, was the third baseman.

On the morning of the opener, the borough of Brooklyn held a victory parade down Flatbush Avenue to honor its world champions. The ceremonies, including musical entertainment and speech making, continued after the champs arrived at Ebbets Field. Finally, it was time for something that generations of Dodger fans had waited for all their lives: the raising of the World Championship flag atop the Ebbets Field scoreboard. It finally got done, but it took a while. True to the Dodger heritage of an earlier era, it seems that those in charge had failed to assign anyone the task of actually raising the flag.

Eventually they got around to the game, the final one to open a National League season in Brooklyn. It matched the league's only twenty-game winners from a year ago: Don Newcombe and Robin Roberts, facing each other for the eleventh time in their careers. Roberts had won five of the battles and lost three, while Newcombe, who had a decision in each of the previous ten meetings, was 3–7. Two of Newcombe's losses in his brilliant 20–5 season a year ago had come against Pitcher Roberts, and he would lose to him again today. The Phillies drove him out during a five-run third inning and behind a complete game by pitcher Roberts held on to win 8–6. Newcombe would recover from this afternoon's clobbering to win twenty-seven games, while losing only six more. At season's end, the sportswriters rewarded him with the league's Most Valuable Player award and the first-ever Cy Young award.

Robinson batted sixth in Alston's lineup and went 0–3, although he did drive in a run with a third-inning sacrifice fly. It was the first hitless opener for Jack since his first one back in 1947. He also committed his only opening-day error, throwing wildly on Andy Seminick's eighth-inning ground ball. Another error, this one by rookie second baseman Charlie Neal making his major league debut, led to the Phillies' eighth run, an unearned one. Neal had won the job in spring training as the versatile Jim Gilliam moved to left field. Robinson did contribute one of the game's better fielding plays. It was on a slow roller by Willie Jones and allowed nineteen-year-old Don Drysdale, also making his big-league debut, to pitch a hitless ninth inning.

This day had started out as one of the most glorious in Brooklyn baseball history. For in addition to the raising of the championship flag, Mayor Robert F. Wagner announced that New York Governor Averil Harriman had signed a bill authorizing a new stadium for the Dodgers in downtown Brooklyn. Called the Brooklyn Sports Center, it would have housed not only the new stadium, but also a new terminal for the Long Island Railroad. But Wagner, a Giants fan who was at their opener in the Polo Grounds, later confessed that there had been a mixup. Harriman had not signed the bill.[20]

Sadly, as we all know, no such bill was ever signed, and no Brooklyn Sports Center was ever built. By the next Opening Day, Jackie Robinson, the heart and soul of the Dodgers for the past ten years, was gone. And by Opening Day a year later, so were all the rest of them. All that remains are statistics. Table 15.1 demonstrates the contributions of Robinson to Dodger glory on Opening Day.

Much had changed in baseball since Jackie Robinson made his major league debut in 1947, when he was, of course, the only black player in either league. By 1956, his last Opening Day, five black players were in Brooklyn's starting lineup. The significance of that Opening Day lineup should not be overlooked. It was the first time the Dodgers had ever opened a season with more blacks on the field than whites. Yet, despite the progress toward the integration of baseball made in Brooklyn, in other cities much remained the same. While Robinson now had black teammates with him both on the field and in the Dodger dugout, the roster of the opposition Phillies on Opening Day 1956 contained as many blacks as did the roster of the opposition Braves on Opening Day 1947—none. Nine years after Robinson's debut, the Phillies remained an all-white team, and so too did two other clubs: the Detroit Tigers and the Boston Red Sox. A nondescript infielder named John Kennedy would integrate the Phillies in 1957, and with the addition of Pumpsie Green in 1959, the Red Sox would become the final team to field a black player.

Table 15.1

Jackie Robinson's Batting and Fielding Record on Opening Day, 1947–1956

				AB	H	2B	3B	HR	BB	SB	SAC	R	RBI	PO	A	E
April 15	1947	Vs. BOS	(1B)	3	0	0	0	0	0	0	1	1	0	11	0	0
April 20	1948	At NY	(2B)	5	1	1	0	0	0	0	0	1	2	2	3	0
April 19	1949	Vs. NY	(2B)	5	3	0	0	1	0	0	0	2	1	6	6	0
April 18	1950	At PHI	(2B)	4	2	1	0	0	0	0	0	1	0	2	1	0
April 17	1951	Vs. PHI	(2B)	4	2	0	0	1	0	0	0	1	2	8	1	0
April 15	1952	At BOS	(2B)	3	1	0	0	0	1	0	0	0	0	2	3	0
April 14	1953	Vs. PIT	(3B)	3	2	0	0	0	0	0	0	3	0	0	2	0
April 13	1954	At NY	(LF)	4	1	1	0	0	0	0	0	0	0	2	0	0
April 13	1955	Vs. PIT	(3B)	4	2	0	0	0	0	0	1	0	1	0	3	0
April 17	1956	Vs. PHI	(LF)	3	0	0	0	0	0	0	0	1	1	1	4	1
				38	14	3	0	2	1	0	2	9	7	34	23	1

Source: Compiled from data furnished by Dr. David W. Smith of *Retrosheet.*
BOS = Boston Braves; NY = New York Giants; PHI = Philadelphia Phillies; PIT = Pittsburgh Priates.

Notes

1. *New York Times,* 16 April 1947, p. 32.
2. Ibid., p. 32–33.
3. Ibid., p. 32.
4. Compiled from data furnished by Dr. David W. Smith of *Retrosheet.*
5. *New York Daily News,* 19 April 1948, p. 41.
6. Ibid.
7. *New York Times,* 21 April 1948, p. 36.
8. Harvey Frommer, *Rickey and Robinson* (New York: Macmillan, 1982), p. 151.
9. *New York Times,* 20 April 1949, p. 34.
10. *New York Daily News,* 19 April 1950, p. 88.
11. Ibid.
12. *New York Times,* 16 April 1952, p. 34.
13. *The Sporting News Baseball Guide* (1954), p. 97.
14. Compiled from data furnished by Dr. David W. Smith of *Retrosheet.*
15. Stanley Cohen, *Dodgers: The First 100 Years* (New York: Birch Lane Press, 1990), p. 108.
16. Compiled from data furnished by Dr. David W. Smith of *Retrosheet.*
17. Ibid.
18. *New York Times,* 14 April 1954, p. 40.
19. Ibid.
20. *New York Times,* 18 April 1956, p. 37.

Part V

Measuring the Impact on Baseball

The entry of Jackie Robinson into the major leagues had an ever-widening ripple effect on the sport and business of baseball and on American society itself. Perhaps one word best summarizes the effects of baseball integration: *expansion*—the broadening of opportunities to pools of playing talent previously not used; the increase of tactical options on the playing field; and the proliferation of new teams, new ball fields, and new markets across the nation. David Shiner, Samuel Regalado, and Lee Lowenfish each examine a component of this effect.

David Shiner illuminates Robinson's impact on the way the game was played. Robinson brought with him the style of the Negro Leagues, thereby transforming the game from a static, power-oriented one to the more dynamic mixture of speed with power. The social integration of baseball, Shiner argues, also brought with it a new tactical synthesis.

While the style of the game was changing, Samuel Regalado reminds us, the talent pool was also being widened, to include the large and largely untapped resource of South American and Caribbean ballplayers. There is a direct causal relationship between Jackie Robinson and the subsequent generations of Latin ballplayers in the major leagues. The ripples were expanding beyond the territorial boundaries of the United States, creating a symbiotic effect between Latin talent and the game itself.

By the late 1950s, major league baseball had changed from the "national pastime," psychologically and emotionally, to the "Pastime of the Nation." Teams were now established on both coasts, situated in the major markets and population regions of the country. This expansion of baseball involved the transference of teams from the East to the West. The Braves were already settled and thriving in Milwaukee when the Giants went to San Francisco and the Dodgers went to Los Angeles. Part II of this book reveals the unique interconnection that existed between Brooklynites and their Dodger team. The shift to Los Angeles was therefore not perceived as the transfer of a franchise from one market to another; it was seen as a desertion, the end of an era, a traumatic personal loss. The architect of this move was Walter O'Malley.

Lee Lowenfish examines the delicate interpersonal relationship of the Dodgers management. The move to Los Angeles was preceded by a change in leadership from Rickey to O'Malley. Holding the balance between these two "Titans" was a "mystery man" named John L. Smith. The causes of Rickey's defeat and O'Malley's victory in the corporate power struggle, and the corresponding shift in the organization's priorities, are still obscure. The effects of that shift, however, became evident in the later decision to go west. Lowenfish implies that one possible reason for the move may be traced back to O'Malley's subliminal desire to match his former foe, Branch Rickey, as a baseball pioneer. There is no doubt that the Dodgers as a business—and the business of baseball—had gained; but an age of innocent trust was lost. The symbiotic connection between the Brooklyn Dodgers and their loyal fans was cut, and the very fiber of the communities that had identified with the team was permanently severed.

Perhaps, the recent decline of baseball from an exclusive position as America's pastime may be connected with the sport's perceived conversion from a faithful expression of its communities to an impersonal business, competing not for people's hearts but for their entertainment dollars.

16

Jackie Robinson and the Third Age of Modern Baseball

David Shiner

Jackie Robinson's debut in the major leagues fifty years ago was a challenge to the apostles of racial segregation. It also challenged the dominant conception of offensive strategy in white baseball at that time. The segregation, so to speak, of power from speed was a major feature of the white game, but was notably absent from the Negro Leagues. In this essay, I will discuss the influence that the Negro Leagues in general and Jackie Robinson in particular had on the white major leagues. I will also show how the majors eventually and rightly came to adopt the more integrated offensive style that had long characterized the Negro Leagues.

Broadly speaking, modern (twentieth-century) major league baseball has featured three distinct ages. The first, which encompassed the first two decades of this century, has become known as the dead-ball era. It was the game of "inside baseball," featuring the bunt, the steal, the hit-and-run play, and opportunistic baserunning. The "base-to-base" game predominated, overshadowing long-ball hitting.

There are several reasons for the dominance of one-run strategies during the dead-ball era. The ball itself was soft—"a sponge," as old-time player Rube Bressler put it[1]—so that trying to hit it over a fence some 350 feet away was foolhardy for all but the most muscular of men. Only a few baseballs were used in each game, and they were usually dirty and discolored. Furthermore, any idea of converting to a predominantly long-ball–oriented game would have offended the sensibilities of most of the game's illuminati.

Table 16.1

Player	Team	G	AB	R	H	2B	3B	HR	RBI	BB	SB	Avg.
Daubert	Brooklyn	139	508	76	178	17	7	2	52	44	25	.350
Cravath	Philadelphia	147	525	78	179	34	14	19	128	55	10	.341

As Ty Cobb, the greatest practitioner of dead-ball–era baseball, put it, baseball was intended to be "an act of skill rather than simple power."[2] "Inside baseball," it was commonly believed, was the real thing; mere slugging, or "simple power," was seen by many as something of an affront to the game.

The lack of appreciation for home-run hitting during the dead-ball era can be shown in a variety of ways. In 1913, for example, first baseman Jake Daubert of the Brooklyn Dodgers led the National League with a batting average of .350, closely followed by Philadelphia Phillie right fielder Gavy Cravath at .341. Offensive statistics for the two players are shown in Table 16.1.

After the season a committee of baseball writers selected Daubert as the league's Most Valuable Player "for his good hitting and all-around work."[3] Such a decision can hardly seem credible to fans of the post–dead-ball period. Cravath's offensive statistics dwarf Daubert's in every category except batting average and stolen bases, completely dominating them in the power categories. Furthermore, Cravath's Phillies finished second in the National League, while Daubert's Dodgers were sixth. Still, Daubert had a better batting average, and he was a better bunter and base stealer. Cravath, for all his impressive slugging, was regarded as "a slow runner, a mediocre fielder, and an unknown quantity on inside baseball."[4] In the eyes of baseball people before 1920, this meant that he could not be as valuable a player as the punch-hitting but multitalented Daubert.

After 1920, it was a different story. Modern baseball's second age came quickly and unexpectedly in the wake of the Black Sox scandal and other sweeping changes. Various trick pitches were banned, and a clean baseball was kept in play at all times. The ball itself became more lively, possibly due to the better materials that became available after the First World War. Newly built major league ballparks usually had smaller dimensions than those they replaced. For these and perhaps other reasons, home-run hitting began to overshadow one-run strategies.

The resulting transformation of baseball was the most sudden and dramatic in baseball history. In the entire first decade of this century, no white major leaguer had hit as many as 100 home runs total. In the next decade, the 1910s, one did—Cravath, with 115. In the 1920s, Babe Ruth alone hit

467 homers. This was not only far more home runs than any player had hit before; it was more than any *team* had hit in either of the two previous decades.

With the increase in home runs throughout the white majors, stolen base totals began to decline. This decline, though stark, was not as abrupt as the rise in homers. In fact, the 1920s was the last decade to date in which more bases were stolen than home runs hit. There were several reasons for this. For one, the adjustment to the new long-ball game took some time to develop. In addition, many of the base-stealing superstars of the dead-ball era, such as Cobb, Eddie Collins, and Max Carey, were still considerable offensive forces well into the 1920s. As the dead-ball–era players faded and then retired, they were replaced by men who were not as skilled at baserunning but who could hit the ball out of the park with greater regularity. By the 1930s nearly all white baseball men agreed that one-run strategies could not overcome three-run homers, could barely even coexist with them. The strategies of the dead-ball era and the long-ball era had come to be viewed as almost polar opposites. Baseball during the dead-ball era, it was now thought, had been "a matter of manipulation, see, not power," according to Rube Bressler, whose career spanned both epochs. "All the great artists of the old days maneuvered. It was manipulation, then; today it's power. Manipulation and power, two entirely different things."[5]

The statistics of the day supported Bressler's view. Home-run totals in the white major leagues more than doubled in the 1920s from their previous level, while stolen base totals were cut in half. These trends continued, gradually but inexorably, in the years that followed. Thirty years later home-run totals were more than double the levels of the 1920s, while stolen base totals had again declined by half.

The following story is indicative of the perceived antagonism between speed and power in the white major leagues and the domination of the latter once the long-ball era was in full swing. In the 1940s Dom DiMaggio and Johnny Pesky hit just ahead of Ted Williams in the Boston Red Sox batting order. Both DiMaggio and Pesky were fast men and capable baserunners, but they were rarely allowed to attempt a steal. When Pesky asked for permission to try to steal bases more often, his manager, Joe Cronin responded, "You've got the best hitter in baseball coming up right behind you, and he hits the ball and you're going to score. You damn well won't run."[6] Not every team had a Ted Williams, but all had power hitters whose job was to blast the ball out of the park. Faster players were ordinarily expected to get on base and stay there until the next hit. This conception of offensive strategy was endorsed not only by Ted Williams' managers, but by almost all white baseball men during the long-ball era.

In the third age, which began with the arrival of Jackie Robinson, offensive strategies changed decisively for the third and final time this century. In essence, the approaches of the dead-ball era and the long-ball era became combined. Jackie Robinson and the Negro League alumni who followed him into the white major leagues proved that power and speed could be complementary rather than mutually exclusive, a fact Negro Leaguers had known and practiced since the days of Cobb and Ruth.

Like the white major leagues, the Negro Leaguers had had their own dead-ball era. Unlike the white major leagues, the Negro Leagues continued to employ the strategies of the dead-ball era even after 1920. Spitballs, emery balls, base stealing, trick plays, and all the rest were part of the Negro Leaguers' stock in trade. While white baseball aspired to a squeaky-clean image in the spirit of the "Marquis of Queensbury" rules, the Negro Leaguers, as Kansas City Monarchs star infielder Newt Allen put it, "played by the 'coonsbury' rules. That's any way you think you can win, any kind of play you think you could get by on."[7] The result was a multidimensional offensive display, one that was more exciting and productive than the game played by white major leaguers. Negro League teams characteristically combined speed and power in a manner unheard of in the white major leagues, and many individual players did so as well. In 1928, for instance, John Henry (Pop) Lloyd hit 11 homers and stole 10 bases in only 37 official games, which projects to an astonishing 46 home runs and 42 stolen bases over an 154-game season. And this was not even Lloyd's best year, which is hardly a surprise considering that he was forty-four years old at the time.

The magnitude of Lloyd's feat becomes clearer when we review the offensive figures posted in the white major leagues in 1928. Only three players matched or surpassed Lloyd in both categories that year, hitting at least 11 homers and stealing at least 10 bases: Kiki Cuyler, Goose Goslin, and Heinie Manush. These three men were all future Hall of Famers; each was in the prime of a long and brilliant career. Yet it took each of these players more than 130 games to match or exceed the totals posted by ancient Pop Lloyd in only 37.

Cuyler, Goslin, and Manush were far from the only future Hall of Famers active in the white major leagues in 1928. Ty Cobb was still playing, as was Eddie Collins. Babe Ruth was at the top of his game. So was his great teammate, Lou Gehrig. Rogers Hornsby, still regarded today as perhaps the greatest right-handed hitter of all time, was a major offensive force. Several of the greatest power-speed players of the long-ball era, including Charlie Gehringer and Frankie Frisch, were in their prime. In all, fifty-six future Hall of Famers were active in the white major leagues in 1928, the most of any year in baseball history. Hundreds of other talented players also appeared on the field that season. Still, only three of those hundreds equaled or exceeded Pop Lloyd's standard, although their official season was far longer than his.

The presence of power hitters such as Josh Gibson and Buck Leonard in the Negro Leagues, then, did not lead to a dramatic decline in the use of one-run strategies. Unlike their white counterparts, Negro Leaguers freely employed both types of offensive weapons, a point sometimes overlooked or underappreciated by baseball historians. For example, Donn Rogosin has written that "the central difference" between the Negro Leagues and the white majors during the long-ball era "stemmed from the Negro league's emphasis on speed and its rejection of the Babe Ruth-inspired long-ball game."[8] Such an account indicates a failure to appreciate the true distinction of players such as Lloyd, Oscar Charleston, Turkey Stearnes, and the newest member of the Hall of Fame, Willie Wells. These men were among the many Negro Leaguers who combined speed and power. So did the teams for which they played.

Jackie Robinson brought this multidimensional offensive approach to the Brooklyn Dodgers. Nowadays we speak respectfully of "30–30" men, players who have hit 30 home runs and stolen 30 bases in a single season. But this is a very recent phenomenon. Before Robinson's debut, no player in the history of the white major leagues had ever had more than six "12–12" seasons—that is, seasons in which he hit at least 12 home runs and stole at least 12 bases—in his entire career. Robinson broke that record by accomplishing this feat in each of his first seven years in the league. He demonstrated that power and speed were not mutually exclusive, and his example set the tone for the Dodgers. His double-play partner, Pee Wee Reese, had never stolen more than 15 bases in a season before Robinson's arrival. In 1948, the year he turned thirty, he stole 25. Pee Wee continued at that rate through age thirty-five–while compiling double-digit home run totals almost every year during that span. Duke Snider, who came up to the Dodgers a few months after Jackie, posted four 12–12 seasons in his first five full years in the big leagues, a feat no player had accomplished before Robinson. In short, the Dodgers were discovering what Negro Leaguers had always known, that power and speed were best regarded as complementary rather than contradictory.

Jackie Robinson's use of all his considerable offensive talents set the tone for a Dodger team that had had little conspicuous success before his arrival, winning only one pennant in the previous quarter-century. From 1949 through 1955 the Dodgers led the National League in both home runs and steals every year but one. In that one, 1954, they lost out in steals—and it was the only year of the seven that they did not either win the pennant or lose it on the final day of the regular season or in a playoff. This was an astonishing achievement. There had been only nine occasions in the previ-

Table 16.2

Player	Team	G	AB	R	H	2B	3B	HR	RBI	BB	SB	Avg.
Robinson	Brooklyn	149	510	104	157	17	3	19	75	106	24	.308
Sauer	Chicago	151	567	89	153	31	3	37	121	77	1	.270

ous half-century in which a team had led its league in both homers and steals in the same season. Now the Dodgers had accomplished this feat five years in a row and six out of seven, becoming the dominant team in the National League in the process. Surely this was ample evidence that power and speed could be profitably joined.

The integration of baseball strategies, like the integration of African-Americans into the major leagues, took time. Despite the example of Jackie Robinson's Dodgers, the 1950s continued to be an extension of the long-ball era. Home-run totals reached new highs during this decade, while stolen base totals sank to record lows. These trends continued to reflect the prevailing views of white baseball men.

These views were evident in other ways as well. In 1952 Robinson had a typical Jackie Robinson season, no better or worse than most of his others, while Chicago Cubs outfielder Hank Sauer had the best year of his career. Their respective offensive statistics are shown in Table 16.2.

Sauer could be described as a latter-day Gavy Cravath. A cleanup hitter, he hit twice as many homers as Robinson and drove in many more runs. Jackie dominated most of the other offensive categories. Defensively he played a key position, second base, excellently, while the slow-footed Sauer played a minor one, left field, adequately. Robinson's Dodgers won the National League pennant; Sauer's Cubs finished fifth, nineteen and a half games off the pace. But Sauer won the Most Valuable Player award, while Robinson finished a distant seventh. Just as the Daubert-Cravath vote four decades earlier had represented the views of white baseball men during the dead-ball era, this decision exemplified those of the era of the long ball.

Despite such anomalies, or perhaps because of them, the attitudes and assumptions of the long-ball era soon began to fade. The feats of young Negro League alumni like Willie Mays and Henry Aaron lent further evidence to the argument that power and speed could be beneficially combined. This evidence continued to mount through the 1950s.

By 1960 every major league team was integrated. For the first time this century, stolen base totals began to rise. Significantly, this shift was not accompanied by a decline in homers. Baseball men were no longer using the stolen base to the exclusion of the long ball; rather, they were beginning to follow the lead of Jackie Robinson's Dodgers in combining the two. Within a few years after Robinson's retirement, as Jules Tygiel has aptly put it, "The national pastime more closely resembled the well-balanced offensive structure of the Negro Leagues than the unidimensional power-oriented attack that had typified the all-white majors."[9] By the 1970s, the average major league team was hitting more than a hundred homers and stealing more than a hundred bases per season, a trend that continues to the present day.

Does it work? The results tell the tale. In 1956, Jackie Robinson's last year in the National League, the league batting average was just under .260. Last year, 1996, it was just over .260. The on-base average and the slugging percentage for the entire National League in 1956 were also extremely comparable to last year, again just a tiny bit lower. In 1956 the average National League team hit 152 homers in 154 games; in 1996 it was 159 homers in 162 games, a nearly identical percentage. Based solely on these statistics and given that major league teams play eight more regular-season games now than they did forty years ago, the average National League team of 1996 should have scored 30 or 40 more runs than its 1956 counterpart. The actual difference was 100 runs. The average National League team scored 759 runs in 1996, compared with 659 forty years earlier. The difference is baserunning. Last year the average National League team stole 128 bases, nearly three times its 1956 counterpart.

During the first half of this century, black and white touring teams often met on the baseball diamond, and some of their games have become legendary. Pitching and defense were normally excellent, and both sides had abundant power. However, time and again we hear of the Negro Leaguers winning games through daring on the basepaths. That same baserunning prowess is the major difference between major league offenses at the end of the long-ball era and those we see today, fifty years after Jackie Robinson's debut and twenty-five years after his death.

Nowadays the home run and the stolen base are both considered key elements to winning baseball. This multidimensional offensive approach is far more indebted to the legacy of the Negro Leagues than to either the dead-ball era or the long-ball era. Beginning with Jackie Robinson, then, racial integration brought in its wake a synthesis of offensive strategies. Like racial integration, this synthesis was long overdue, and it too has served baseball magnificently.

Notes

1. Lawrence Ritter, *The Glory of Their Times* (New York: Morrow, 1992), p. 196.
2. Ty Cobb with Al Stump, *My Life in Baseball: The True Record* (Lincoln: University of Nebraska Press, 1993), p. 145.

3. Roach ed. *Official American League Base Ball Guide for 1914* (Philadelphia: A.J. Roach Co. 1914), p. 124.

4. *Baseball Magazine,* July 1914, quoted in Bill James, *Whatever Happened to the Hall of Fame?* (Edgarton, MA: S and S Trade, 1995), p. 328.

5. Ritter, *Glory,* p. 196.

6. David Halberstam, *Summer of '49* (New York: Avon, 1990), p. 230.

7. John Holway, *Voices from the Great Black Baseball Leagues* (New York: Da Capo Press, 1992), p. 96.

8. Donn Rogosin, *Invisible Men: Life in Baseball's Negro Leagues* (New York: Kodansha, 1995), p. 80.

9. Jules Tygiel, "Black Ball," in John Thorn and Pete Palmer, eds., *Total Baseball: The Official Encylopedia of Major League Baseball* (New York: Viking Penguin, 1995), p. 560.

17

Jackie Robinson and the Emancipation of Latin American Baseball Players

Samuel O. Regalado

Dominican Felipe Alou was only twelve years old when, in 1948, the Dodgers paid a visit to his homeland. Excited about the prospects of seeing big leaguers in action, Alou's young eyes focused on the team's star second baseman. "It was a proud moment. To see [Jackie] Robinson in the Brooklyn lineup gave us hope. . . . [T]here was a black man out there with a major league uniform on," he recalled.[1] Indeed, Robinson's appearance throughout Latin America inspired others as well. "When I see Jackie Robinson play in my country, I say, 'if he can do it, I can do it too,' " Edmundo "Sandy" Amoros vowed to himself when Robinson played in Cuba.[2]

While Jackie Robinson's monumental career gave much-needed attention to the issue of race relations in the United States, the international ramifications of his achievement have been lost in the historical discussion. Yet, the long shadow of baseball's "great experiment" also reached into Latin America, where Robinson's stature was of great importance to generations of Latins. Until 1947, Latin baseball players made up only a tiny percentage of those who competed as big leaguers. And those who did participate in the majors were considered white. Racial considerations aside, however, most big-league operations did little business south of the United States border. Though Clark Griffith initiated scouting campaigns in the Caribbean a decade into the twentieth century, and again in the 1930s through the pioneering of scout Joe Cambria, none of the players who signed with his Cincinnati Reds and, later, Washington Senators ever blossomed into stars. Hence, other owners could not justify the time and expense to put into a campaign for the sake of Latin American recruitment. There was, of course, ample talent in that region, but little that major league owners wanted to pursue.

Latins, of course, had been part of American baseball's saga since the late nineteenth century. A Cuban student, Esteban Bellan, adopted the game while attending Fordham University. Proficient as an infielder, he signed on to play with the Troy Haymakers of the American Association in 1871. Bellan's place on the roster earned him a spot in history as the first Latin to play big-league baseball. Later, the Cuban played a major role in expanding baseball's popularity in his homeland.

Esteban Bellan's entry, however, did not lead to an avalanche of recruits from Latin America. Indeed, between 1871 and 1911 only one Latino, Louis Castro from Colombia, played in the big leagues. However, between 1911 and 1947, fifty-four players from Latin America joined major league rosters. Forty-five were Cuban and all were deemed to be white. Though most competed in relative obscurity to mainstream American baseball aficionados, one, pitcher Adolpho Luque, rose to stardom. Luque's major league career, which spanned from 1914 to 1935, was impressive. During those years he won 194 games and lost 179. He also finished with a 3.24 earned run average and one World Series victory.

But Luque and his white peers represented only a small portion of Latinos who played professional baseball in the United States. Many more black Latins toiled in the world of the Negro Leagues. Approximately 190 players from Spanish-speaking regions wore the uniforms of black clubs at one time or another. Moreover, their reputations in the Latin world sometimes exceeded that of their white counterparts in the majors.

Jose Mendez, a sterling right-hander, was, for instance, among the earliest of the Latin superstars who only played black baseball. Called the "Black Diamond," Mendez was considered by his contemporaries to be one of the finest hurlers in the early twentieth century. Tales of Mendez's skills captivated even major league players. This was, in large part, due to the success he had against big-league clubs who barnstormed the Caribbean during the winter months. "If [John] McGraw did not think he would raise too much of a racket he would sign Mendez today," reported one newspaper back in 1911.[3] Moreover, "John McGraw placed a value of $50,000 on Mendez if he could play in the big leagues," said writer Robert Peterson.[4] Chronicler John Holway also credits the Cuban with a no-hitter against the barnstorming Detroit Tigers in 1909. Prevented from playing in the majors, however, Mendez could only achieve fame in the Caribbean and black leagues.

Cristobal Torrienti was another of the Latino baseball treasures whose notoriety, much like Mendez's, lay only in Latin America and the American Negro Leagues. Between 1913 and 1934, the Cuban slugger hit for a .339 average between the two leagues. Though his fame was somewhat embellished in black baseball lore, Torrienti was a bona fide star who played primarily for the Chicago American Giants. Indeed, C.I. Taylor, manager of the Indianapolis ABCs, once remarked, "If I should see Torrienti walking on the other side of the street, I would say, 'There walks a ballclub.' "[5]

But fame and high salaries remained distant to Latin blacks who toiled in the black leagues, as elusive to them as to their American counterparts. While several stars from the majors routinely evaluated their winter league Spanish-speaking opponents as players of high caliber, American owners wanted no part of any possible controversy that might involve race. The enlistment of Latinos, most worried, always invited suspicion. "With the admission of Cubans of a darker hue in the two big leagues it would then be easy for colored players who are citizens of this country to get into fast company," wrote a journalist at the beginning of the twentieth century.[6] On occasion, managers and owners dabbled with the thought of recruiting mulatto-toned Latins. Several clubs, for instance, scouted slugger Cristobal Torrienti. But the coffee-colored Torrienti's kinky hair overshadowed his propensity to routinely hit line drives off outfield walls.

During the period of segregation in the United States, racial controversies were, of course, serious issues that often held deadly consequences. Lynchings were common. And each time blacks attempted to expand their limited citizenship, the response was usually accompanied with violence. In 1919, for instance, some twenty-five cities experienced race riots during what John Hope Franklin called "the greatest period of interracial strife the nation had ever witnessed." "Mobs took over cities for days at a time, flogging, burning, shooting, and torturing at will," claimed historian C. Vann Woodward.[7] Ironically, black achievement in sports sometimes fueled the flames of racist attitudes. Jack Johnson's prominence as boxing's heavyweight champion in the early twentieth century, for instance, exacerbated the racial tensions of the period. Indeed, in 1910, following Johnson's victory over former champion James Jeffries in the so-called fight of the century, whites, disgruntled over the loss, "expressed their displeasure in spontaneous outbursts of violence."[8] Blacks were murdered and beaten in several regions of the United States amid the general chaos that came about as a result of the fight.

Hence, media suggestions that a roster player might be "tainted" with black blood did not amuse baseball administrators. Thoughts of losing fan support, or worse, motivated administrators to extinguish potential fires concerning race. In 1911, for example, the Cincinnati Reds quickly provided affidavits for proof of "whiteness" after rumors circulated that Rafael Almeida and Armando Marsans were not Caucasian. Convinced of the legitimacy of the certificates, one local journalist dubbed the Cubans as "two of the purest bars of Castillian soap [that] ever floated to these shores."[9] Adolpho Luque and Mike Gonzalez also fell under scrutiny after they donned big-league uniforms. But a Gonzalez defender wrote that, "His people were of pure Spanish blood, not of the mongrel Indian or negro mixture that has barred many a star of 'The Pearl of the Antilles' from major league company."[10]

Latins likewise posed an especially complicated problem for proponents of "racial purity." Generations of miscegenation made it virtually impossible for investigators to accurately assess one's racial background. Census reports and church baptismal records were loosely kept and often lost. Oral backgrounds, usually employed as "evidence," were rarely legitimate or reliable. This, of course, made life difficult for Latinos and other ethnics whose goals were to make the big leagues. Always concerned that black blood permeated the veins of Latins, bigoted fans often responded to rumors concerning race by becoming more suspicious. Ultimately, Latinos whose racial background might prove controversial ended up in the Negro Leagues.

These and the other Latins of the preintegration period were baseball's real "invisible men." Overlooked by both the black and the white presses, often mocked for their broken English, they toiled in obscurity as professional baseball players in the United States. Moreover, they represented only a small allotment of the many talented players who were well suited to play at the major league level. Hence, Robinson's appearance and ultimate success became a transitional event for Latinos as well as American blacks. For the generation of Latins already playing professional baseball in the Caribbean and/or the black leagues, Robinson's entry proved to be their emancipation.

Among the beneficiaries was Orestes "Minnie" Minoso, a talented black player from the Pearl of the Antilles who played with the New York Cubans during Robinson's historic rookie season. Having come to the United States in 1946, the young Cuban was thrilled to be "mingling with the great players in the Negro Leagues."[11] Though Minoso played well for the Cubans, his goal was to play in the big leagues. To that end, in 1947, he participated in a St. Louis Cardinals' tryout. But his hopes were dashed on the same afternoon following a brief workout. "I want[ed] no bonus. I just wanted to play in the big leagues." He added, "My style of play at third base was criticized: They said I shouldn't throw so hard to first. I couldn't understand why they wanted to cramp my style."[12] The Cardinals, unbeknownst to the Cuban, had, at that point, no real intention to integrate and did not do so until 1953. Minoso, however, did get his opportunity with the Cleveland Indians. Signed by the tribe in 1948, Minoso took one year to climb through the minor league system before a 1949 debut with the Indians' parent team. His appearance marked the first time a Latin black had joined a major league club. Though he appeared little with Cleveland that year, his fame was forthcoming. In 1951, following a trade that sent him to the White Sox, the Cuban joined a club that needed him and, with his appearance, broke the color barrier in Chicago. During the early 1950s Minnie Minoso captivated American League fans with his skill and flamboyance. Indeed, in his first full year, the "Cuban Comet," as he came to be known, hit .326, drove in 76 runs, and stole 31 bases. For his efforts, he won the *Sporting News* Rookie of the Year award.

Vic Power also was another Latin black who came with the Latino surge in the 1950s. Signed to his first professional contract with Caguas in the Caribbean winter league in 1947, the Puerto Rican, two years later, competed in the Canadian Provincial League. In 1950, the New York Yankees purchased his contract and sent the infielder into their minor league chain. Between 1951 and 1953, he exhibited all the tools characteristic of potential stardom in the major leagues. Unlike Minoso, however, as Power's impressive statistics in the minors drew him closer to a deserved promotion to the Yankees, the Puerto Rican's achievements fell under a cloud of controversy. The legendary club, it appeared, did not want Power on its roster. The debates reached a crescendo in 1953, as critics charged that the Yankees purposely detained Power's elevation to the majors.

Though his .331 average with the Yankees' top farm club offered sound credentials, the top brass balked at his promotion, based on the contention that he did not possess the "right attitude." Power was at a loss. "I wasn't outspoken. I never had any trouble with my managers or my white teammates. I was never drunk or late to the ballpark. I never missed a sign," he later recalled.[13] That Power supposedly dated white women also was of major concern to the club. The Yankees never did promote the flamboyant infielder. Instead, in 1954 they sent him to the Kansas City Athletics. It was there that his impressive major league career commenced. But the memory of his trials with the Yankees lingered many years later. "I wish someone would have explained to me about the racial problem because it was confusing. They just let me find out for myself. I gained so much respect for Jackie Robinson, Willie Mays, and the other blacks who came before me," Power stated.[14]

Younger Latins of color also revered Jackie Robinson. That many of these baseball hopefuls adopted the Dodgers as their favorite team was not surprising. "Not many people know this, but I was a Dodgers fan for a while when I was a kid," said Juan Marichal, who, ironically, became a Dodgers' nemesis during his big-league days. "They came to Santo Domingo in 1948 during spring training, with Jackie Robinson, Pee Wee Reese, Gil Hodges, and Duke Snider. I was nine then and it made an impression."[15]

Puerto Rican Roberto Clemente was another who came of age during the Robinson era. Born in 1934, Clemente was a thirteen-year-old youth when Robinson and others broke the color barrier. Originally signed by the Dodgers in 1954, Clemente, instead, ended up with the Pirates, where he spent his entire star-laden big-league career. A big leaguer during the traumatic years of the civil rights struggles, Clemente encountered the travails of racism throughout his American odyssey. Additionally, he endured the trauma of acculturation into United States culture. Nonetheless, during his eighteen-year career, he overcame these barriers to win four batting titles, the 1966 Most Valuable Player trophy, and twelve Gold Glove awards. Shortly after his untimely death in 1972, he entered the United States Baseball Hall of Fame as the first representative from Latin America.

Clemente's early career also took place during a period of great significance with respect to baseball's business. Branch Rickey, baseball's architect for integration, joined the growing movement which sought talent in Latin America. Prodded by Clemente's tremendous potential in 1954, the Mahatma, who by then was with the Pirates, instructed scout Howie Haak to explore the Caribbean for talent, and said, "If there's anymore of those creatures [like Clemente] down there, I want 'em." Haak, who came to be one of the most well-traveled scouts in Latin America, recalled, "I went to Venezuela and Panama, and then I started to spend three or four months a year in Latin America. I was the first scout who went to all the countries."[16]

Prior to the 1950s, however, the Caribbean had been solely Joe Cambria's beat. After the late 1930s, the former laundry owner came to dominate the area on behalf of the Washington Senators. "Papa Joe" came to be one of the most popular men in the area. And though he remained a fixture in Cuba primarily during the immediate postintegration period, competitors soon appeared in his "domain." Indeed, baseball's movement to integrate made it considerably easier for scouts to round up talent in that region. Moreover, not only did Latino blacks benefit from the expanded scouting, but their white counterparts also profited from the added exposure. Scouts like Howie Haak, Al Campanis, and George Genovese explored baseball's expanded horizons and came away with far more valuable booty than had their predecessors of an earlier era. During the 1950s alone, sixty-nine Latin players debuted in the big leagues. This number represented fifteen more players than had debuted during the entire first half of the twentieth century.

Additionally, scouts ventured into regions other than Cuba far more often than before Robinson's 1947 season. As a result, black, mulatto, and white players from Puerto Rico, the Dominican Republic, Mexico, and Venezuela could exhibit their skills before the eyes of major league recruiters. No longer concerned with controversy, several teams such as the Pittsburgh Pirates, the Washington Senators, and the New York Giants made strong efforts to sign players from Latin America. Not surprisingly, the ultimate success of the Giants and the Pirates, in particular, encouraged other clubs to follow suit during the 1960s.

Jackie Robinson's 1947 season did not mark the beginning of Latin baseball interests in the United States. Nor did it serve to temper the trauma associated with their cultural transitions. The era of club orientations and academies came much later. But baseball's integration period marked an important turning point in the fortunes of Latin players. Latinos became a fixture in the big leagues, and their success spawned expanded avenues by which baseball pursued the recruitment of talent. And not lost to those, like Minnie Minoso, who also pioneered in this era, was the importance of Robinson himself. In reflection, Minoso later concluded that "Every black baseball player, every black athlete for that matter, owes Jackie Robinson a genuine debt of gratitude. He showed the way."[17]

Notes

1. *Newsday,* 8 Septemeber 1971.
2. Jules Tygiel, *Baseball's Great Experiment: Jackie Robinson and His Legacy* (New York: Oxford University Press, 1983), p. 343.
3. Robert Peterson, *Only the Ball Was White: A History of Legendary Black Players and All-Black Professional Teams Before Black Men Played in the Major Leagues* (New York: McGraw-Hill, 1984), p. 62.
4. Ibid., p. 212.
5. Peterson, *Only the Ball Was White,* p. 245.
6. Ibid., p. 62.
7. C. Vann Woodward, *The Strange Career of Jim Crow* (New York: Oxford University Press, 1966), p. 114.
8. Randy Roberts, *Papa Jack: Jack Johnson and the Era of White Hopes* (New York: Free Press, 1983), pp. 107–108.
9. Peterson, *Only the Ball Was White,* p. 245.
10. Harold Seymour, *Baseball: The Golden Age* (New York: Oxford University Press, 1971), p. 85.
11. Minnie Minoso, Fernando Fernandez, and Robert Kleinfelder, *Minoso: Extra Innings: My Life in Baseball* (Chicago: Regnery Gateway, 1983), p. 36.

12. Minoso et al., *Minoso: Extra Innings,* pp. 37–38.

13. Danny Peary, ed., *Cult Baseball Players: The Great, the Flakes, the Weird, and the Wonderful* (New York: Simon and Schuster, 1990), p. 355.

14. Ibid.

15. Rob Ruck, *The Tropic of Baseball: Baseball in the Dominican Republic* (New York: Carroll and Graf/Richard Gallen, 1993), p. 84.

16. Kevin Kerrane, *Dollar Sign on the Muscle: The World of Baseball Scouting* (New York: Avon Books, 1985), p. 81.

17. Minoso et al., *Minoso: Extra Innings,* p. 39.

18

The Two Titans and The Mystery Man: Branch Rickey, Walter O'Malley, and John L. Smith as Brooklyn Dodgers Partners, 1944–1950

Lee Lowenfish

It was Thursday afternoon, October 26, 1950, and a conference room in the Bossert Hotel in downtown Brooklyn was packed to overflowing with New York City sportswriters. "Comest thou here to see the reed driven in the wind?" quipped Branch Rickey, the Brooklyn Dodgers president and general manager, who was expected momentarily to announce his resignation after eight very event-filled and largely successful years.[1] Rickey always liked to pepper his conversation with folksy homilies and biblical parables, to the bewilderment of the New York scribes. Only Milton Gross, sportswriter for the *New York Post,* could identify the source for the "reed driven in the wind" as the Book of Matthew. Rickey frowned in mock dismay when some other ink-stained wretches suggested *Gone with the Wind.*[2]

The New York writers had coined many nicknames for this amazingly complex and fascinating man, whom John J. Monteleone in the introduction to the recent collection *Branch Rickey's Little Blue Book: Wit and Strategy from Baseball's Last Wise Man,* has accurately called "a capitalist/moralist/competitor/do-gooder/reactionary/visionary all rolled into one."[3] He was the "Mahatma," because he reminded sportswriter Tom Meany of a combination of "India's independence leader Mahatma Gandhi, your father, and a machine politician."[4] Another nickname was the "Brain," and Harold Burr,

Dodger beat reporter for the *Brooklyn Eagle,* dubbed Rickey the "Great White Father" and called his office the "Cave of the Winds."[5] The most virulent moniker was "El Cheapo," coined and incessantly used by Jimmy Powers, sports editor of the widely read *New York Daily News.*[6]

Yet there was no doubting that Wesley Branch Rickey was very good at what he did for a living, building championship baseball organizations. At the helm of the St. Louis Cardinals from 1917 until 1942, he pioneered with his first baseball revolution, the farm system of growing and nurturing one's own talent, and the Cardinals became a dynasty second only to the New York Yankees. When he came to Brooklyn after the 1942 season, Rickey built another great farm system and pioneered a second baseball revolution, signing Negro ballplayers hitherto banned by baseball's so-called gentleman's agreement against racial integration. By 1947, the Dodgers had supplanted the Cardinals as the National League's reigning dynasty, and Branch Rickey seemed content to spend the rest of his working career in Brooklyn.

But all was not calm within the Dodger organization. For years, there had been a rarely reported but raging internal power struggle between Rickey and Walter O'Malley, an ambitious engineer and attorney who had become a force on the Dodger board of directors and since 1943 had served as the Dodger's chief legal counsel (replacing Wendell Willkie, the 1940 Republican presidential candidate).[7] According to Murray Polner, Rickey's admiring but thorough biographer, O'Malley had been involved from the outset in Rickey's top-secret search for Negro ballplayers. During World War II, for instance, O'Malley had even carried to Cuba a $25,000 letter of credit from Rickey to sign a Cuban Negro ballplayer, who it turned out was unavailable because he had been drafted by the Cuban army.[8]

But as their partnership developed in the post–World War II years, Walter O'Malley had become increasingly critical of the cost of Rickey's baseball administration. It included a far-flung farm system of twenty-five teams; an expensive new spring training headquarters, Dodgertown, opened in Vero Beach, Florida, for 1949 spring training; and, not least, a five-year contract for Rickey which earned the canny baseball executive over $100,000 a year, making him the highest-paid individual in baseball, when salary, attendance bonuses, and percentage of sales of player contracts were combined.[9]

Walter O'Malley and Branch Rickey also presented dramatic contrasts in backgrounds and personalities. O'Malley was an Irish Catholic Tammany Hall Democrat, born in the Bronx in 1903, the son of Edwin O'Malley, a dry goods merchant who had once been a New York City commissioner of markets. A graduate of Culver Military Academy in Indiana (the same school, incidentally, which George Steinbrenner attended) and the Ivy

League University of Pennsylvania, Walter O'Malley switched careers from engineering to law just before the start of the Great Depression. "A lot of people were selling apples on streets at the time," he once recalled. "I was fortunate in building up an active practice, mostly in bankruptcies."[10]

On the other hand, Branch Rickey was a fervent Methodist, born into the rural poverty of southern Ohio in 1881. He was a teetotaler, who supported the prohibition of alcohol movement, who fought vigorous if unsuccessful battles against beer sponsorship of baseball broadcasts, and who obeyed a deathbed promise to his mother never to work on the Sabbath (although Rickey's critics never failed to mention that he was not averse to earning profits on the Sabbath).[11] Rickey was also trained as a lawyer—a graduate of the University of Michigan Law School, which he completed in two years while also serving as the baseball coach![12]—but the abiding passions of his life were family, God, and baseball—and not necessarily in that order.

If anything in a baseball history that has been dominated by strong personalities can ever be deemed inevitable, it is that these two strong personalities, Branch Rickey and Walter O'Malley, would not coexist indefinitely. In fact, the major reason that this uneasy partnership lasted as long as six years was the presence of a third, equal but largely silent, partner on the Dodgers' governing syndicate, John L. Smith. Smith was a multimillionaire executive of the old Brooklyn firm, the Charles Pfizer Chemical Company, and he was the chief shareholder and vice-president and treasurer of the Dodgers. It was Smith's death in July 1950 after a long battle with lung cancer, O'Malley's long and successful courting of the support of Smith's widow, and the expiration of Rickey's contract at the end of the 1950 season that led inexorably to the announcement on this late October afternoon.

Dodger officials tried to make the transition in power appear nothing out of the ordinary. Branch Rickey played along at first, introducing Walter O'Malley, his successor as team president, as "a man of youth, courage, enterprise, and desire." For his part, O'Malley said, "I have developed the warmest possible feelings of affection for Mr. Rickey as a man. . . . I do not know of anyone who can approach Mr. Rickey in the realm of executive ability in baseball. . . . I am terribly sorry and hurt personally that we now have to face this resignation," he concluded, obviously having tongue-kissed the Blarney Stone on his way to the conference.[13]

Upon hearing O'Malley's comments, Rickey decided to tear asunder the facade of the day's fake bonhomie. "I have just received a telegram," he said, pausing dramatically, raising and lowering his eyebrows for effect, and chomping on an unlit cigar—all part of a standard Rickey public performance—"from a man who is shipping me a prize bull to my farm in

Chestertown [Maryland]. I contemplate studying a new tangent in handling the bull."[14]

Walter O'Malley's ouster of Branch Rickey did not come cheaply. A clause in their ownership agreement allowed any partner to offer his shares to an outside bidder, subject to a matching offer by an existing partner. Rickey had recently informed O'Malley of an offer for Rickey's shares of almost a million dollars from William Zeckendorf, a powerful New York real estate developer. The amount was almost three times the price that Rickey had paid in 1945 and that O'Malley was offering now. O'Malley thought Rickey and Zeckendorf might be bluffing, but he could not be absolutely certain. So to be rid of Branch Rickey's presence forever, Walter O'Malley arranged for a payment of almost a million dollars. Then, swallowing hard because he did not like to be outfoxed in anything, Walter O'Malley wrote out a check for $50,000 to Zeckendorf, honoring a clause in the Zeckendorf-Rickey agreement that provided a fee to Zeckendorf for the "tying up" of his capital while his bid was being considered. O'Malley suspected that Zeckendorf and Rickey were in cahoots on this $50,000 fee, a fact that he verified when he received the canceled check and noted that Zeckendorf had endorsed the $50,000 over to Rickey.[15]

From October 26, 1950, onward, Walter O'Malley decreed that the name of Branch Rickey not ever be spoken again in Dodger offices, subject to a $1 fine. He pledged that no one ever again in the Dodger front office would hold Rickey's title of general manager,[16] and when Rickey shortly took over the general manager position of the Pittsburgh Pirates, O'Malley arranged that henceforth the Dodgers would not play the Pirates in spring training exhibition games.[17]

It is easy to demonize Walter O'Malley, especially here in Brooklyn from where O'Malley uprooted the Dodgers just seven years after assuming total control. "The three greatest villains of the twentieth century are Adolf Hitler, Joseph Stalin, and Walter O'Malley" goes a line which is generally attributed to Brooklyn-born New York writers Pete Hamill and Jack Newfield.[18] I have found that one-liner irresistible on many occasions, but I believe that the job of the historian is to go beyond the witty phrases, to dig beneath the labels and stereotypes, and to try to recreate the actual context of the times. I do not think it was inevitable that, once Walter O'Malley drove Branch Rickey out of Brooklyn, the move to the West Coast would occur. At the same time, I disagree with what Neil Sullivan suggests in his important book, *The Dodgers Move West,* that Branch Rickey might have moved the Dodgers if the opportunity was presented him.[19] Everything we know about Rickey's sense of history and his belief in baseball's positive role in the community makes me doubt that Rickey would ever have let the

National League abandon both Brooklyn and Manhattan (as they did for four seasons after 1957), but these thoughts are in the realm of speculation. I prefer to deal with what actually happened, so for the remainder of this paper I want to explore why, in the words of his biographer Murray Polner, Branch Rickey "seems to have deluded himself into believing he might overpower the formidable O'Malley."[20] I also want to explore the key issue of how silent partner John L. Smith was slowly "weaned away" from Rickey toward O'Malley.[21]

I must state that this paper is a work in progress because of the difficulty of obtaining hard information on the inner workings of the baseball business. Baseball officials have always talked about their patriotic calling, but they are blessed with a federal antitrust exemption, which keeps most of their operations free of detailed scrutiny. There are well over a hundred boxes of loosely organized Branch Rickey papers at the Library of Congress, but in the words of historians John Thorn and Jules Tygiel, these papers are "strangely silent" regarding the key years 1944–1948. Thorn and Tygiel add that the National League does not open its archives to outsiders, and the Dodgers claim that they cannot find the records from this period.[22] But there are many ways to get to the bottom of a story: interviews with surviving participants, rummaging in clipping files in local historical societies, and scrolling through microfilms of the national sports weekly, the *Sporting News*. It was during an afternoon of perusing old *Sporting News* microfilm through the almost blinding sunlight in the main reading room of the 42d Street Library in New York City that I began to unearth some clues about the mystery man in the Dodger internal struggle, John L. Smith.

Just who was John (L. for Lawrence) Smith? He was one of the most unknown figures in Brooklyn Dodger history, let alone baseball history, in large part because he wanted it that way. The May 20, 1946, issue of *Time* magazine described Smith as "a shy man with an intense dislike for publicity."[23] The reason Smith made the national news weekly was that, in the Pfizer Brooklyn laboratories, Scottish chemist Sir Alexander Fleming began to mass-produce the miracle drug penicillin, which saved thousands of lives and won for Fleming the Nobel Peace Prize in 1945. Fleming was also quite a baseball fan and was often seen with Smith in the owner's box at Ebbets Field.[24]

Smith's life was a genuine Horatio Alger, American "rags-to-riches" story. He was born February 10, 1889, in Krefeld, Germany, to Johanna Dollbaum and Gottfried Damian Schmitz, a weaver and textile worker. In 1892, the family moved to Stonington, Connecticut, where young John developed an interest in chemistry. While still a teenager he moved to Brooklyn to start work as a laboratory assistant at the Charles Pfizer factory. One of Smith's hobbies was track and field—he ran the quarter-mile for the Eastern District YMCA—but mainly he was bound by a strong work ethic.[25] Over eight years he earned degrees in chemistry at Cooper Union night school in Manhattan. He spent virtually his entire adult working life at Pfizer, rising to become president and later chairman of the board.[26]

John L. Smith was a rarity in the manufacturing business, a man equally at home in the laboratory and in the board room. With Smith playing a major role in the leadership, Pfizer rose to become a major player in the chemical business. It mass marketed vitamin C in the 1920s, citric acid in the 1930s (thereby breaking the monopoly of Italian dictator Benito Mussolini), and during the early 1940s the company became a leading manufacturer of penicillin.[27]

Smith was brought into the baseball business by his close friend George V. McLaughlin, president of the Brooklyn Trust Company bank, which had essentially operated the Dodgers since the bleak days of the Great Depression. A former New York City police commissioner, McLaughlin was also the man who hired Walter O'Malley to oversee Dodger finances, and he was instrumental in having O'Malley named to the Dodger board of directors.[28] Since the death of Charles Ebbets and one of his partners, Ed McKeever, within ten days of each other in 1925, Dodger ownership had been a messy tangle of warring heirs, and McLaughlin was always looking for ways to streamline the operation. When he learned early in 1944 that the heirs of Ed McKeever, who controlled 25 percent of Dodger stock, wanted to sell, McLaughlin came up with the idea of a tripartite syndicate consisting of Branch Rickey, John L. Smith, and Walter O'Malley, the latter's stake guaranteed by the bank; O'Malley would not have to invest any money until the team started turning a profit.[29] With the formation of the unusual three-part syndicate, "for the first time since 1924, the ownership of the club passed from the hands of executors of estates into the control of living, breathing people," sportswriter Tommy Holmes wrote in his excellent team history, *Dodger Daze and Knights.*[30]

In 1945, the Ebbets heirs, who controlled 50 percent of the team, sold out to the syndicate which now controlled 75 percent of the team. Only Ann McKeever "Dearie" Mulvey, daughter of Judge Steve McKeever and benefactor of hundreds of fans, to whom she gave free tickets for every game at Ebbets Field, held out, holding on to her 25 percent share of the team, along with her husband, Jim Mulvey, a movie executive with the Samuel Goldwyn company.[31]

At first glance it seemed that self-made man and observant Christian John L. Smith was cut from the same cloth as Branch Rickey. Murray

Polner tells us that Smith's long work hours and passionate concern for the lives of his employees really impressed Rickey. "Each year [Smith] dictated individual letters to employees evaluating and grading their work," Polner writes. "One year [Smith] stopped the sale of beer during work hours not because he was a 'dry' —as was Rickey—but because someone made off with the beer money."[32] While Smith's meticulous Germanic appearance and dress code contrasted greatly with Rickey's remarkable slovenliness ("everything the Boss had for dinner looks good on him," one of Rickey's aides once said jokingly),[33] Smith and Rickey shared an almost obsessive frugality. "It was said of John L. Smith that he personally scrutinized every request for supplies and ruled it with an iron hand," Samuel Mines writes in the official Pfizer Company history. "If you wanted a new pencil you had to bring him the stub of the old one to prove you really needed it."[34] Another shared interest of Rickey and Smith, according to Murray Polner, was a concern for improved relations between the races. Polner tells us that Smith had racially integrated the company athletic teams at Pfizer and told an impressed Rickey in one of their early meetings that he wanted "to do something for blacks."[35]

What John L. Smith had in common with Walter O'Malley was a mutual desire to enjoy the luxuries coming to them as a result of their capitalist success. Smith and O'Malley were both avid sailors and fishermen. O'Malley loved to entertain on his eight-seat cabin cruiser, and Smith liked to sail his 60-foot motor yacht down the Atlantic coast to Florida for spring training, where he would meet up with O'Malley and local Brooklyn Judge Henry Ughetta, an unswerving O'Malley ally on the Dodger board of directors. Smith, O'Malley, and Ughetta were often seen together enjoying the comforts and perks of ownership. "The three crony directors went every place the Dodgers went [in 1947]," Harold Burr wrote in the *Brooklyn Eagle*, "spring training at Havana, Venezuela and Panama and even took a Western trip together."[36]

In the same article, Harold Burr gave a description of a postseason directors' party that gives a rare look into what the dynamics of the O'Malley-Rickey-Smith relationship may have been. One burning question of the post-1947 hot stove league was: would combative Leo Durocher return from his year-long suspension to manage the Dodgers in 1948, or would Burt Shotton be rehired? Durocher had been suspended just before the start of the 1947 season by baseball commissioner A.B. "Happy" Chandler because of Leo's unrepentant association with gamblers and also because his marriage to actress Laraine Day before her American divorce was official outraged many conservative Brooklyn members of the Catholic Youth Organization.[37]

Burr reported that Branch Rickey rose at the dinner and "gravely announced . . . that he had decided on the 1948 manager. It isn't Leo Durocher, it isn't Burt Shotton." As Burr recounted the moment, "The great white father of the Flock threw the table into an uproar by announcing, 'Gentlemen, it's John L. Smith.'" Twenty minutes of cheering led by O'Malley and Judge Ughetta followed, according to Burr. Later at this same dinner, John L. Smith, rarely voluble in public, told the gathering what went on at a typical Dodger board of directors meeting. With Rickey chuckling up front and O'Malley and Ughetta heckling from the back, Smith explained, "We sit around and informally discuss everything. We even keep minutes. Nothing is done in a hurry." Regarding the plans for the Dodgers to hold 1948 spring training in Santo Domingo, Burr quoted Smith, "I told Mr. Rickey that I wasn't ready to fall in with the Santo Domingo idea. 'But what about the contract we've signed with the hotel, John?' he [Rickey] asked. 'Oh, don't let's pay any attention to a contract,' I advised. 'We never do in the chemical business.' That broke up the party," Harold Burr concluded his story.[38]

It is very likely that the mirth and good feeling at that dinner in October 1947, however much it was put on for public consumption, was never again shared by the Rickey-O'Malley-Smith syndicate. A sense of Smith's growing disagreements with Rickey can be found in a March 1948 story of sportswriter Michael Gaven of the *New York Journal American* who had visited the chemical mogul at the Pfizer offices in the Williamsburg section of Brooklyn. After donning a white coat and joining the Pfizer kingpin on his daily visit to the factory, the journalist sat down with the manufacturer for a rare interview. Gaven mentioned that, when he covered Dodger spring training in Daytona Beach in 1946, he had seen Smith, not even knowing that he was the chief Dodger stockholder. Smith replied, "Certainly Rickey talks as if he owned the whole works." He later added, "I have heard that Rickey is cheap. As treasurer of the Brooklyn club I think he is extravagant. He makes financial gambles you wouldn't dare make in any other business. But that's baseball, they say."[39]

Among the "financial gambles" Smith was evidently questioning were Rickey's approval of increased investment in the Dodger farm system; a new private plane for team and executive travel; and the Vero Beach spring training complex, Dodgertown, which was due to open in 1949 at a cost ten times more than previous spring training headquarters.[40] It was not uncommon for Rickey to fly 2,000 miles to a farm club in Texas, for instance, to see firsthand how a blister on the pitching hand of a prospect was healing.[41] The most profligate investment that Rickey had made with Brooklyn Dodger money was taking on in 1948 financial responsibility for a Brooklyn football Dodger franchise at Ebbets Field, which, though in existence since the early 1930s, had never caught on. It disbanded by the end of 1949, suffering losses of nearly half a million dollars. Murray Polner, Rickey's biographer, admits that Rickey could only "lamely" explain away the football losses to Smith, O'Malley, and other members of the board of directors as "regrettable."[42]

Another item in the growing dossier against Rickey was his unilateral decision to rehire Leo Durocher in 1948. The fiery and incorrigible Durocher was Rickey's "pet reclamation project,"[43] according to his son, baseball executive Branch Rickey, Jr. (inevitably nicknamed "The Twig"), but by the conservative Brooklyn constituency of the Catholic Youth Organization, Durocher was considered "box office poison."[44] It hardly helped Rickey's standing when the Dodgers got off to a terrible start in 1948 and were in the league basement by the end of May. With attendance falling and even television sets reportedly being turned off in disgust, Rickey fired Durocher in mid-July and brought Burt Shotton back as Dodger manager.[45] In one of the amazing twists of the soap opera, or perhaps grand opera, that was New York City baseball in this period, Rickey arranged for New York Giants owner Horace Stoneham to sign Durocher as the manager of the Dodgers' arch-rival.

It is a mistake to believe, however, that John L. Smith was passively in O'Malley's corner on every issue, at least in 1948. In the same interview with Mike Gaven in which he was critical of Rickey's spending, he uttered some thoughts very rare for an owner in any period of baseball history: "I am not in baseball to make money, I just don't want to lose any money." He also said he wished that he had more time to debate the question of a new stadium because he felt that Ebbets Field, double-decked in the 1930s, could not be expanded again. He offered the common-sensical opinion that a new ballpark, like a new chemical plant, does not have to look the same as one built thirty-five years ago.[46]

While Smith's name rarely made the sporting pages of the 1940s, and he was happy with that anonymity, he is remembered fondly by survivors of that period. "He used to come to the clubhouse every Sunday that there was a game at Ebbets Field," Dodger pitcher Rex Barney recalled in July 1997, only weeks before Barney died. "We autographed baseballs for him, you would see him carrying caps and team pennants, and he always had an encouraging word to say to the players," Barney recalled.[47] *New York Herald Tribune* sportswriter Harold Rosenthal remembered fascinating conversations he used to have with Smith about the science of immunology and the discovery of penicillin.[48]

We will never know, of course, whether Branch Rickey's career in

Brooklyn might have been salvaged had John L. Smith lived. We do know that Smith agreed with O'Malley that Rickey's spending practices were detrimental to the profitability of the ball club. And John L. Smith could not have been pleased that during the final stages of Branch Rickey's career as Brooklyn Dodger president and general manager, the ardent baseball capitalist, dubbed the "Great White Father," took on the additional mantle of the "Great White Cold Warrior Against Godless Communism." "We should be made aware of the fact that Communist forces intend the overthrow of our Democratic government by force," Rickey told a Rotary Club group in West Palm Beach, Florida, in October 1947. He added a cautionary note to Floridians that they had better watch out for their Democratic U.S. Senator, Claude Pepper, sometimes known as "Red" Pepper, who was traveling the country with former Secretary of Agriculture Henry A. Wallace.[49] (The next year, Wallace would run for president on a Progressive third-party ticket, and would be vilified as being "soft on communism.")

In February 1948 Rickey continued his anticommunist theme in a speech at the Negro Wilberforce University in Rickey's home state of Ohio. "There is a Communistic effort to get credit 'forcing' us to sign Robinson," he declared. "But I warn you to be on guard against that thing. Everything will be for the best if we follow our time-honored democratic practices."[50] As the Cold War heated up internationally, so did Branch Rickey's domestic anticommunist fervor, and by the late 1940s any critic of the baseball system in Rickey's mind had to be tarred with the "red" brush. On April 13, 1949, Rickey made a speech at the Advertising Club in Baltimore, Maryland, in which he denounced the "avowed Communistic tendencies" of John L. Flynn,[51] the lawyer for St. Louis Cardinals pitchers Max Lanier and Fred Martin, who had just sued baseball because they had been banned for five years for playing in the so-called outlaw Mexican League. When Flynn threatened to file a million-dollar suit for slander against Rickey, the Dodger executive knew he had been intemperate, and quietly sought the advice of the Dodgers' legal counsel, none other than Walter O'Malley. O'Malley was just as anticommunist as Rickey, of course, but he did not go around indiscriminately attacking any critic of the baseball system, a lawyer no less. "Rickey lost his cool, and I showed I could act in a bad situation," Murray Polner writes perceptively of how O'Malley viewed the fallout from John Flynn's threatened suit and how Rickey was inexorably losing ground on the Dodger board of directors.[52]

Near the end of the 1950 season, less than a month before Rickey's ouster became official, Jackie Robinson was asked by Harold Rosenthal, Dodger beat writer for the *New York Herald Tribune,* for his opinion on the power struggle. Robinson claimed, "It means nothing to me. I just play ball," adding that it would not surprise him if he were traded soon.[53] But Robinson knew full well that the departure of Branch Rickey from Brooklyn in October 1950 would cost him his best friend and supporter in the front office. When an exodus of Rickey supporters in the front office began almost immediately to his new post in Pittsburgh, it was not long before Walter O'Malley's criticisms of Robinson as "a prima donna and a Rickey man"[54] were widely known.

Hindsight always brings with it 20–20 vision, so the triumph of the younger, cunning ambitious urban attorney over the aging, middlewestern cracker-barrel baseball philosopher may seem inevitable. It should be noted that Rickey was hospitalized at least twice during the course of his difficult partnership with O'Malley: in late 1945, not long after his initial signing of Jackie Robinson, with what was diagnosed as the nervous condition of Meniere's disease, and then in June 1948, not long before the ouster of Leo Durocher, with a bladder infection.[55] We can only guess what the role of his stressful relationship with O'Malley played in Rickey's illnesses. But, on the other hand, Rickey rebounded quickly from his hospitalizations, never wanting to be far from the firing line of action in the baseball business. John L. Smith, for that matter, was hospitalized in mid-1946 with what may have been early symptoms of lung cancer, but he too recuperated from his illness, and until he required an operation in February 1950, his health was not considered a problem.[56] But once Smith died in July 1950, Walter O'Malley's carefully cultivated support of Smith's wife paid immediate dividends in the form of the voting rights to Smith's shares on the board of directors, thereby setting into motion the end game that terminated Branch Rickey's services.[57]

While it was not inevitable from the day O'Malley took control that the Brooklyn Dodgers would no longer exist seven years later, it is certainly an intriguing idea that at least subconsciously Walter O'Malley would come to desire to engrave his name in baseball history as a pioneer western expansionist to match the pioneer achievements of his arch-rival, Branch Rickey, the creator of the first farm system and the man who racially integrated professional baseball.

Notes

1. Tommy Holmes, *Dodger Daze and Knights* (New York: David McKay, 1953), p. 249.

2. Harold Rosenthal, *New York Herald Tribune*, Sports Section, 27 October 1950, p. 1, "Rickey treated newspapermen with condescending flattery, as one might treat stepchildren, recognizing them as an inescapable price one pays for other delights." See also Roger Kahn, *The Boys of Summer* (New York: Harper and Row, 1972), p. 97.

3. John J. Monteleone, ed., *Branch Rickey's Little Blue Book: Wit and Strategy from Baseball's Last Wise Man* (New York: Macmillan, 1995), p. xvi.

4. Murray Polner, *Branch Rickey: A Biography* (New York: Atheneum, 1982), p. 122. See also Lee Lowenfish, "Sport, Race and the Baseball Business: The Jackie Robinson Story Revisited," *Arena Review* (Spring 1978): 3.

5. Holmes, *Dodger Daze,* pp. 180–181.

6. Polner, *Branch Rickey,* pp. 128–130. See also Kahn, *Boys of Summer,* p. 426.

7. Walter O'Malley entry in *Current Biography 1954* (New York: H.W. Wilson, 1954), p. 494. Journalist and author Andy McCue, who is writing a biography of Walter O'Malley, has informed me that there is probably an error in this capsule biography of O'Malley. It lists O'Malley's arrival on the board of directors as 1932 whereas, in fact, it was probably ten years later, because O'Malley never mentioned an earlier arrival in any other source (letter of McCue to Lowenfish, 27 May 1997). I want to thank McCue for sharing his research and for several helpful and continuing conversations. For O'Malley's arrival on the Dodgers scene, see also Roger Kahn, *Good Enough to Dream* (New York: New American Library Signet, paperback edition, 1986), pp. 61–63.

8. Polner, *Branch Rickey,* p. 147.

9. Robert Rice, "Thoughts on Baseball—I," *New Yorker,* 27 May 1950, p. 32. It is interesting to note that in this laudatory two-part piece about Rickey (the second one appeared 3 June 1950), there is no mention by name of either O'Malley or John L. Smith. They are only referred to as "two silent partners."

10. *Current Biography,* p. 494.

11. John Lardner, *It Beats Working* (Philadelphia: Lippincott, 1947), p. 131.

12. Polner, *Branch Rickey,* p. 55.

13. Holmes, *Dodger Daze,* p. 250.

14. Roscoe McGowen, *New York Times,* 27 October 1950, p. 32.

15. Harold Parrott, *The Lords of Baseball* (New York: Praeger, 1976), pp. 30–32.

16. Harvey Frommer, *Rickey and Robinson* (New York: Macmillan, 1982), p. 175.

17. Polner, *Branch Rickey,* p. 227. See also Frank Graham, Jr. *A Farewell to Hero* (New York: Viking, 1981), p. 234; and Kahn, *Boys of Summer,* p. 426.

18. Peter Golenbock, *Bums: An Oral History of the Brooklyn Dodgers* (New York: Villard, 1984), p. 261.

19. Neil J. Sullivan, *The Dodgers Move West* (New York: Oxford University Press, 1987), p. 28.

20. Polner, *Branch Rickey,* p. 220.

21. The phrase "weaned away" is from Polner, *Branch Rickey,* p. 153.

22. Jules Tygiel, ed., *The Jackie Robinson Reader* (New York: Dutton, 1997), University Press, Lexington, K.Y., p. 93. Fortunately, during the summer of 1997, professional organization of the over one hundred boxes of the Branch Rickey Papers began at the Library of Congress in Washington, D.C. They are a mine of information and insight into Rickey's long career in (and out of) baseball. The Papers of Arthur Mann (1901–1961), the sportswriter who served for many years after 1946 as Rickey's trusted but perhaps overbearing assistant, are also at the Library of Congress and are a well-organized and valuable source.

23. "Penicillin Grows in Brooklyn," *Time,* 20 May 1946, p. 78.

24. Polner, *Branch Rickey,* p. 153.

25. Obituary of John L. Smith, *Sporting News,* 19 July 1950, p. 20.

26. Samuel Mines, *Pfizer: An Informal History* (Brooklyn, NY: Pfizer, 1978), pp. 21–22, 53, 81. A new 150th anniversary history of Pfizer is in preparation, but no new material on John L. Smith as baseball owner will be included. According to John Vanzile, chief researcher for *The Write Stuff* (a Florida-based company overseeing the

new Pfizer history project), telephone conversation with the author, 11 July 1997.

27. "Penicillin Grows in Brooklyn," *Time*, p. 78.

28. Smith obituary, *Sporting News*, p. 20.

29. *Current Biography*, p. 494.

30. Holmes, *Dodger Daze*, p. 187.

31. Obituary of James Mulvey, *New York Times*, 4 December 1973, p. 48.

32. Polner, *Branch Rickey*, p. 153.

33. Golenbock, *Bums*, p. 85.

34. Mines, *Pfizer*, p. 19.

35. Polner, *Branch Rickey*, p. 154. It must be said that neither fact is confirmed or even mentioned in Mines' official company history of Pfizer.

36. Harold Burr, *Brooklyn Eagle*, 16 November 1947. O'Malley also claimed an early association with John L. Smith when the pharmaceutical kingpin served on the board of an athletic club to which O'Malley belonged. See *Long Island Press* article on Smith, 19 November 1950. Once again, I am indebted to Andy McCue for this information.

37. I am grateful to Bill Marshall for letting me read, in manuscript, part of his forthcoming book, *When Baseball Was the National Pastime: 1945–1951* (Lexington, KY: University of Kentucky Press), due in 1998. See also Red Barber, *1947: The Year All Hell Broke Loose in Baseball* (New York: Doubleday, 1982).

38. Burr, *Brooklyn Eagle*, 16 November 1947.

39. Mike Gaven, *Sporting News*, 10 March 1948.

40. Rice, "Thoughts on Baseball—I," p. 40.

41. Rosenthal, *New York Herald Tribune*, p. 1.

42. Polner, *Branch Rickey*, p. 217. Associated Press sportswriter Frank Eck maintained that, although Smith was very upset at the pro football losses, he never would have allowed Rickey to be replaced if he had lived. See *Sporting News*, 4 October 1950. The minutes of the Brooklyn Dodger board meeting of 21 December 1947 indicate that Smith was the only board member to vote against taking on the fiscal responsibility for the Brooklyn football Dodgers. Walter O'Malley had his reservations about the project, but he did vote for it. Clearly, however, Branch Rickey was leading the way and he was going to take the credit for its success, or, as matters turned out, the full blame for its failure. Minutes in the Rickey Papers, Library of Congress.

43. Polner, *Branch Rickey*, p. 123.

44. Arthur Mann, *Branch Rickey: American in Action* (Cambridge: Riverside Press; and Boston: Houghton Mifflin, 1957), p. 267.

45. "Boycott in Brooklyn," *Time*, 31 May 1948, p. 51.

46. Gaven, *Sporting News*, 10 March 1948.

47. Rex Barney, conversation with the author, 7 July 1997, Washington, D.C.

48. Harold Rosenthal, conversation with the author, 10 March 1997, Boca Raton, Florida.

49. *Sporting News*, 5 November 1947.

50. *Sporting News*, 25 February 1948, p. 2. This is the same speech in which Rickey charged that the owners had voted secretly, 15–1, in mid-1946 to deny Jackie Robinson's right to sign with the Dodgers, but then, according to Rickey, destroyed the evidence. To this day, no one knows (or is saying) whether a vote was taken. But clearly another reason for destroying evidence of the meeting was that Larry MacPhail had warned the owners that some changes in the reserve system would be necessary if they wanted to maintain their antitrust exemption. See Marshall, *When Baseball Was the National Pastime*; book cited in footnote 37, and Lee Lowenfish and Tony Lupien, *The Imperfect Diamond: The Story of Baseball's Reserve System and the Men Who Fought to Change It* (Briarcliff Manor, NY: Stein and Day, 1980), pp. 148–150.

51. *New York Post,* 14 April 1949, p. 57; see also Polner, *Branch Rickey,* p. 217.

52. Polner, *Branch Rickey,* p. 217. In the winter of 1948–1949, Arthur Mann, Rickey's former special assistant and very sympathetic biographer, noted that Rickey also avidly extolled Dwight Eisenhower's memoirs, *Crusade in Europe,* and became convinced that "a whole team ... could be taught to 'take charge' on the ball field as they had for Eisenhower on the battlefield" Mann, *American,* p. 277.

53. Harold Rosenthal, *New York Herald Tribune,* 24 September 1950, Sports Section, p. 1.

54. Rachel Robinson, *Jackie Robinson: An Intimate Portrait* (New York: Harry Abrams, 1996), pp. 37, 139.

55. Polner, *Branch Rickey,* p. 178; Mann, *American,* pp. 230–233, 268.

56. Smith obituary, *Sporting News,* p. 20.

57. Harold Rosenthal, conversation with the author, March 1997. "Mrs. Smith looked at Walter O'Malley as if he were God," Rosenthal remembered. "He seemed to score points with Mrs. Smith by ridiculing Rickey for being a midwestern farmer." But up until the last month of Rickey's Brooklyn employment, he put on a good front about being the main man in charge. See, for instance, Robert Rice's two-part interview in the *New Yorker* ("Thoughts on Baseball), in which Smith and O'Malley are never mentioned by name but just in passing as Rickey's "silent partners." A recent family memory of Rickey's last days in Brooklyn describes his leaving the Dodgers as "an unanticipated departure." See Branch Rickey III, "A Tip of the Cap from a Grandson," *New York Times,* 3 August 1997, Sunday Sports Section. Rickey III has served as the president of the Triple-A minor league American Association, and in 1998 he began serving as the president of the expanded Pacific Coast League, which had merged with the American Association.

Part VI

Measuring the Impact on Society

The four authors in this section raise profound questions and offer new perspectives on the social legacy of Jackie Robinson and the integration of baseball.

Henry Fetter cites hard attendance figures to challenge the oft-repeated assertion that Robinson was a financial magnet who drew crowds, particularly black crowds—that he made the "turnstiles click." National League and Dodger attendance figures in the 1940s declined precisely at the time when baseball was integrating. This raises disturbing questions concerning the uniqueness and special receptivity of Brooklyn for the "great experiment," and the relationship between white and black baseball audiences, if indeed the black audience increased during a time of decline in overall attendance figures. The statistics also invite a reevaluation of Walter O'Malley's motivation to relocate the team. An alternative interpretation of that decision might argue that working-class Brooklynites were attaining their upward mobility and becoming part of the middle-class migration to the suburbs—that the relocation of the team was preceded by the exodus of its former fan base.

Fetter relies on quantitative data to question some of "the starry-eyed myths that have flourished since." By revising previous assessments of Robinson's impact on the business of baseball, Fetter refocuses attention on what he perceives to have been the real consequences of the integration of the major leagues.

Ron Briley introduces a reconsideration of the extent of baseball's influence beyond the ballpark, pointing out that, even by the mid-1960s, baseball's integration remained limited to the playing field. Not even—or, possibly, especially not—for Jackie Robinson. Yes, upon retirement, Jackie Robinson gained a good job, but it paled in comparison with the opportunities made available to Bob Feller, who had retired at the same time. Briley juxtaposes the opportunities and fortunes of these contemporary Hall of Famers. Briley suggests that the "great racial divide" had not yet been eliminated by the early 1970s, and indeed may still prevail in contemporary America.

Patrick Henry introduces considerations of ethnic self-perception, arguing that how modern African-Americans perceive themselves is connected to their choice of role models and heroes. Even Kareem Abdul Jabbar's *Black Profiles in Courage,* Henry points out, seems strangely limited on Robinson, as the book is devoted primarily to black American heroes in fields other than sports. Henry reminds us that Robinson transcended sports. He was a civil rights advocate and a symbol of black pride and dignity. Perhaps most important of all, Henry cites Rachel Robinson's assessment that her husband enabled white America to root for a black man. Thus, Robinson became a credit to his race—the human race. Patrick Henry's study may be read in conjunction with the presentations in Part II, to gain further insight into the development and processes of personal and communal self-definition.

Robert Cherry expands the field of study to the marketplace. The business of baseball is connected to bottom-line considerations. Cherry provides detailed graphs to illuminate the balance between discriminatory hiring practices and productivity results. These data pinpoint the degree to which an organization can accept discrimination before it harms the productivity of the enterprise. They also reveal the dangers of preferential hiring practices to the effectiveness of an organization. However, the imperatives of business, if pegged exclusively to the marketplace, do not guarantee integration or an end to discrimination. There is a tolerance level for discriminatory hiring before such practices impact negatively on productivity. So, Cherry suggests that the marketplace by itself, though a formidable influence on policy, does not by itself overcome bigotry.

Cherry's economic paradigm invites the reader to draw several interrelated inferences: since baseball was a virtual sports monopoly, and since monopolies have no need to integrate because they are not impelled to do so by considerations of competition or productivity, what other than marketplace considerations prompted it to integrate? Cogent counterpoints may be found in chapters in Parts I and III of this book.

The Cherry model also connects with the Marxist perception of ballplayers as workers. Cherry indicates that corporate management can manipulate bigotry to keep the workforce divided. One may then conclude that integration would have the opposite effect of unifying labor. Is it therefore a coincidence that the first major leaguer to insist on freedom from arbitrary management decisions was Curt Flood, a black man? Is there a connection between integration and today's free agency? Finally, as is alluded to in other sections of this book, baseball damaged the special affiliation it enjoyed with its traditional communities precisely at a time when it was undergoing integration and accepting the mega-corporate model of organization. One might well speculate on what has been lost or gained by this metamorphosis.

Each of the authors in this section examines one special area of social significance. Together they provide us with a new mosaic—often a revisionist interpretation—of the impact of baseball's integration on society. Their collective verdict, and that of other writers in this book, would indicate that the American dream is still not equally attainable; social justice and economic opportunities have improved, but there is still more work that needs to be done.

19

Robinson in 1947: Measuring an Uncertain Impact

Henry D. Fetter

On April 15, 1947, Jackie Robinson took his position at first base for Brooklyn as the Dodgers opened the 1947 season before 26,623 fans at Ebbets Field.[1] Neither the national pastime nor the nation would ever be the same. The breaking of the color line in major league baseball, by far the dominant spectator sport of the time, counts as the one event in sports history that merits inclusion in any American history text.

But if, in retrospect, there can be no question about Jackie Robinson's ultimate impact on both baseball and society at large, measuring that "impact" can be an elusive task, and one inevitably burdened by our knowledge of what came next. History, it has been said, although written backward, is lived forward. In thinking about the 1947 season it is necessary, but exceedingly difficult, to remember that the place held today by Robinson in both baseball history and American history is largely dependent on events that lay in a then-uncertain future. That the Dodgers, led by Robinson and the other black stars who soon joined him, would go on to win six National League pennants over the next decade (and lose two more only on the last days of the seasons), could not, of course, be known on April 15, 1947. Nor could the breaking of baseball's color barrier then be seen as a milestone in race relations that foreshadowed, and indeed contributed to, the dismantling, within twenty years, of the long-established structures of legal and customary segregation. Precisely because they loom so large in retrospect, it is hard to recapture the events of 1947 as they happened—and without the knowledge of what was to follow.

Is there a way to measure how contemporaries actually responded to the unprecedented happenings on National League ball fields that season? One common way of doing so has been to look at attendance figures for the 1947 season. These figures, we are told, are entirely commensurate with the history that we now take for granted was being made. In his recent book on baseball's struggle to adapt itself to the changes in twentieth-century American life, G. Edward White writes that, in 1947, "the Dodgers had also drawn over a million fans for the first time in their history, and National League attendance had set an all-time record."[2] Jules Tygiel's oft-cited account similarly sums up Robinson's impact at the gate: "Throughout the season fans continued to watch him in record numbers. . . . Thanks to Robinson National League attendance in 1947 increased by more than three-quarters of a million people above the record set in 1946. Five teams set new season records, including the Dodgers, who attracted over 1.8 million fans for the first, and last, time in the club's Brooklyn history."[3] Red Barber recalled that "wherever Jackie played, he drew large crowds. He became the biggest attraction in baseball since Babe Ruth. Robinson put serious money into the pockets of every National League owner."[4] This consensus was indeed summed up, during the 1947 season, by Wendell Smith, who wrote, "Jackie's nimble/ Jackie's quick/ Jackie's making the turnstiles click."[5]

But simple errors in these accounts aside (the Dodgers had drawn over one million in five previous seasons, and National League attendance increased by about one and one-half million),[6] do the 1947 attendance figures actually support such sweeping statements, no matter how charmingly rhymed, about Robinson's impact at the box office? In fact, close study of attendance in 1947, in the context of seasons before and after, reveals a more complicated picture of how baseball's paying customers responded to Robinson's debut. Indeed, these accounts, by overstating Robinson's impact on attendance, and glossing over some troubling issues raised by the numbers, thereby—unintentionally to be sure—tend to minimize the challenges and limits which even so great an athlete as Jackie Robinson faced, in what proved to be difficult years for the business of baseball.

How to get at a more accurate perspective on attendance and fan reaction to Robinson in 1947? To begin with, it needs to be recognized that, even before Robinson became a Dodger, Brooklyn was the top gate attraction in the National League, leading the league in both home and road attendance in 1946.[7] And, although it is true that National League paid attendance increased in 1947 by 1,500,000 over 1946, reaching 10,388,470, a league record which stood until 1960, any assessment of Robinson's role in stimulating that increase must start with the inconvenient fact that, as Table 19.1 (National League Attendance by City, 1946–1947) shows, the 1947 atten-

Table 19.1

National League Attendance by City, 1946–1947

City	1946	1947
Boston	969,673	1,277,361
Brooklyn	1,796,824	1,807,526
Chicago	1,342,970	1,364,039
Cincinnati	715,751	899,975
New York	1,219,873	1,600,793
Philadelphia	1,045,247	907,332
Pittsburgh	749,962	1,283,531
St. Louis	1,061,807	1,247,913

dance gain over 1946 was *not* attributable to increased crowds at Ebbets Field.[8] Brooklyn home paid attendance was a league-leading 1,796,000 in 1946. In 1947 Dodger home attendance did increase, but only by 11,000, for a total of 1,807,000. *The Flatbush faithful thereby made virtually no contribution to the increase in National League attendance.* Indeed, Dodger home game attendance as a percentage of total National League attendance actually declined from 20.18 percent in 1946 to 17.40 percent in 1947—in both cases a sharp decrease from 1941, when fully 25.4 percent of all National League fans attended games at Ebbets Field.[9]

In fact, Robinson's arrival in Brooklyn was conspicuous for the absence of hometown reaction it generated. Robinson's formal transfer to the Dodgers from the minor league Royals was announced in a brief press release, passed around the Ebbets Field press box during the late innings of the Dodgers-Royals exhibition game on April 10, 1947. Rather than dominating the news (even the baseball news), Robinson's call-up yielded top billing on the city's sports pages to the continuing furor generated by the stunning suspension, the day before, of Leo Durocher as Dodger manager for the season.[10]

Ebbets Field had been barely one-third full on April 10 when Robinson made his first Brooklyn appearance, in a Montreal uniform, in a Royals-Dodgers exhibition game.[11] (Robinson's local debut, the year before in a Montreal-Jersey City game, by contrast, had drawn over 25,000 to Roosevelt Stadium.)[12] The season opener crowd at Ebbets Field on April 15, 1947, was the *smallest* at any National League ballpark that day, and 5,000 below the turnout at the *1946* opener.[13] The 26,000 fans at Ebbets Field that day fell far short of the 39,000 who turned out that same afternoon to see the Yankees open the season in the Bronx.[14] (Not to mention the 27,306 fans attending the races at Jamaica Race Track that afternoon.)[15] In their second home game that spring, two days later, Dodger attendance fell to 10,252—a smaller turnout than for that day's Newark-Rochester minor league game in Newark, which drew 13,779.[16] Rather than generate unprecedented excitement at the gate, after 50 home games in 1947, Dodger attendance trailed behind 1946 levels.[17]

If Brooklyn is not the place to look for any increased 1947 attendance that can be attributed to Robinson's debut, can the attendance increase that season be credited to fans in other cities turning out to see Robinson on the road? It is true that Dodger road attendance increased from 1,534,000 in 1946 to 1,863,000 in 1947—an increase of 329,000.[18] And, it is also true that local attendance records were set in a number of cities around the league when the Dodgers came to town, although it should be noted that, in each of those cases, crowds that were almost as large turned out during the season to see opponents other than the Dodgers. However, as a direct factor in driving attendance to a record level, Robinson's appearances in Dodger blue cannot be assigned preponderant weight.

In 1946, 7,106,000 fans attended National League games outside of Brooklyn. That number rose to 8,581,000 in 1947—an increase of 1,475,000, of which Dodger games accounted for some 325,000 (less than one quarter of the increase).[19] In 1946, 21.4 percent of National League attendance outside Brooklyn had been generated by Dodger games (a tribute to the drawing power of the Dodgers even before Robinson). In 1947, that percentage did increase, but only slightly, to 21.7 percent. Amid the overall increase in attendance, Dodger home attendance did no more than hold its own in 1947.[20]

Furthermore, in 1947 the Dodgers simply played more road dates than in 1946—a total of 69 road games in 1947 as compared to 62 in 1946 (they played only 5 doubleheaders in 1947, down from 14 the year before).[21] The increase in the number of dates alone accounts for about half the overall increase in Dodger road attendance. In fact, *average* attendance at Dodger games at the Polo Grounds and St. Louis actually decreased significantly in 1947, and was no better than even with the 1946 average in Boston.[22] In Boston, in St. Louis, and even at the Polo Grounds the largest single game crowds drawn by the Dodgers in 1947 were smaller than the top attendance marks reached by the Dodgers the year before.[23]

It is true that, by starting at a higher base, the potential range for further increases in Dodger attendance was limited, especially at a time when weekday afternoon games were common, so that potential attendance increases were limited as a result. But the fact remains that by far the greater part of the substantial increase in National League attendance in 1947 cannot be directly attributed to fans turning out to see Robinson play, whether in Brooklyn or on the road. Adding together the paid attendance at Dodger games at home and on the road, 3,330,000 fans watched the Dodgers in 1946, and 3,670,000 in 1947. In 1946, 5,616,000 fans turned out for games *not* involving the Dodgers. In 1947 that number increased by over one million, to 6,720,000, which accounts for almost three-quarters of the overall increase in attendance. *By definition, this increase owed nothing directly to any desire to see Robinson and the Dodgers play.* In fact, total Dodger attendance (home and away) actually declined from 1946 to 1947 as a proportion of total National League attendance. In 1946, fully 37 percent of the fans attending National League games came out to watch the Dodgers. In 1947 only 35.3 percent did so. It is true that the total number of fans watching the Dodgers increased by 10 percent in 1947 from the prior year (almost entirely attributable to the increase on the road). But the total numbers of fans watching all games was up by 16 percent and attendance at games *not* involving the Dodgers increased by 22 percent.[24]

The excitement generated by Robinson's debut may well have spilled over into heightened interest in baseball generally around the league in 1947. But to reduce the attendance boom of that season to the impact of Robinson alone does not do justice to reality. Of the forces that drove National League attendance to a record high in 1947, Robinson can be counted as only one, and not, on the evidence, the predominant one.

Moreover, in assessing the impact on attendance of either Robinson's pioneering efforts, or the broader racial integration of teams that followed, it has to be recognized that the attendance gains of 1947 were short-lived. Table 19.2 (National League Attendance, 1946–1960) tells the story.[25] In 1948, attendance fell by 600,000 from the 1947 record. By 1950, National League attendance had actually fallen below 1946 levels. Thereafter, league attendance continued to decline, until the Braves' move to Milwaukee in 1953 reversed the downward trend. However, after 1950, the 1946 attendance total of 8,946,000 was not exceeded again until 1958—after the Dodgers and Giants moved to the West Coast.

Of course, the great social trends of the postwar years, suburbanization and the coming of television above all, posed an overwhelming challenge to the prospects for sustaining the attendance surge, which had followed the end of the war. Perhaps attendance would have fallen even further, and faster, without integration. Such speculation aside, the fact is that the novelty of integrated baseball proved an inadequate counterforce to those trends.

What about the role of increased attendance by black fans as a force in driving attendance up in 1947, a set piece in most accounts of that revolutionary year? There are too many contemporaneous, if anecdotal, reports about an unprecedented 1947 influx of black fans into the grandstands of

Table 19.2

National League Attendance, 1946–1960

1946	8,902,107
1947	10,388,470
1948	9,770,743
1949	9,484,718
1950	8,320,616
1951	7,244,002
1952	6,339,148
1953	7,416,716
1954	8,013,519
1955	7,674,412
1956	8,634,000
1957	8,819,601
1958	10,164,596
1959	9,994,525
1960	10,684,085

the previously segregated sport to be entirely dismissed. But from the perspective of half a century, the significance of that factor in driving attendance up appears to have been exaggerated. As Figures 19.1 and 19.2 show, the greatest increases in 1947 attendance tended to occur in those National League cities with the smallest (in both percentage and absolute terms) black populations.[26] The four teams registering the greatest percentage attendance gains in 1947 (Pittsburgh, Boston, New York [Giants], and Cincinnati, in that order) included the three cities in the league with the smallest black populations. In fact, as illustrated in Figures 19.1 and 19.2, there is a slight negative correlation between the size of a city's black population and the increase in attendance in 1947. Perhaps the fact that any noticeable numbers of blacks were in attendance at all was so novel an experience that it registered disproportionately on contemporary observers. Such has, for example, been true recently in golf, where the sight of any measurable number of blacks at all in the galleries in the year of Tiger Woods's professional debut has led to an exaggeration (at least to judge from my observations at the 1997 Los Angeles Open) of the actual numbers of such spectators.

Moreover, consideration of the significance of an increase in black attendance in response to the coming of Robinson raises a disturbing question that cuts to the heart of one key component of the Robinson-Rickey myth—that Brooklyn provided a fortuitously welcoming setting for this tale of racial tolerance. For, given the static Brooklyn attendance figures between 1946 and 1947, if it is true that Robinson generated a dramatic

Figure 19.1

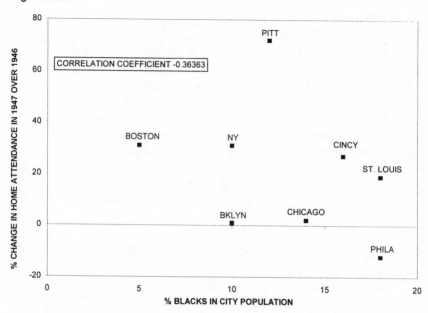

Note: New York City % used for Brooklyn.

Figure 19.2

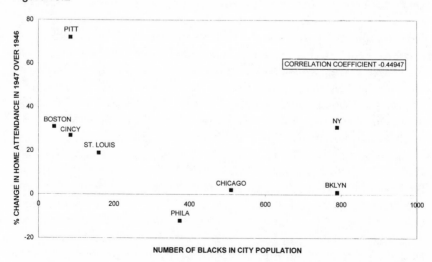

Note: New York City % used for Brooklyn.

increase in black attendance at Ebbets Field in 1947, the necessary (and unmentioned) corollary is a heavy decline in white attendance—a disturbing loss of support that was never recouped as Dodger attendance declined from 1,807,000 in 1947 to 1,033,000 in the World Championship season of 1955, as shown in Table 19.3 (Dodger Home Attendance, 1946–1957).[27]

But, if Robinson's impact appears to have been overstated in the traditional accountings for the increase in attendance in 1947, it is certainly true that Robinson's impact on Brooklyn—and National League—baseball was profound. Robinson's debut had immediate consequences for the game on the field. The Dodgers leveraged their readiness to sign up black ballplayers into a decade of unprecedented success. Together with the Giants, who were similarly in the forefront of baseball integration, this advantageous tolerance secured National League pennants for New York City in eight of the ten years after 1947. That edge was reinforced by the fact that the Dodgers' great rival, the St. Louis Cardinals—the dominant team in the National League from the mid-1920s to the mid-1940s (and indeed the only National League team to win a World Series from the Yankees between 1923 and 1955)—moved slowly in signing black players and did not integrate until the 1954 season. After 1949, the Cards faded swiftly from contention, and would not again make a serious run for the pennant until 1963. From 1947 through 1956, winning National League baseball was virtually a New York City monopoly.

In the American League, as well, the integration of baseball had important consequences for the standings of the clubs. Unfortunately for the competitive balance of a league that was hard pressed at best to match the well financed and brilliantly managed Yankees, the Yankees' prime adversaries stumbled badly on the integration issue. The Tigers and the Red Sox, the only Yankee rivals with deep pockets, refused to integrate for over a decade after 1947, and thereby turned their backs on the best way to cut into the edge that the Yankees already held over them. This allowed the Yankees to drag their feet on integration without sacrificing their dominance, and ensured dull mediocrity throughout the 1950s.

In these ways, by the early 1950s competition had largely vanished from both leagues, in unprecedented fashion. What the people of Brooklyn and New York celebrated—and still celebrate—as a golden age held ever-decreasing interest for those fans in the thirteen other Major League cities, shut out of the festivities. As competition declined, attendance fell everywhere, including in Brooklyn and New York, where it was abetted by the unparalleled proliferation of free baseball on television. The Dodgers' great success generated growing television revenues; but as more and more baseball was broadcast, the live gate at Ebbets Field (as

Table 19.3

Dodger Home Attendance, 1946–1957

1946	1,796,824
1947	1,807,526
1948	1,398,967
1949	1,633,747
1950	1,185,896
1951	1,282,628
1952	1,088,704
1953	1,163,419
1954	1,020,531
1955	1,033,589
1956	1,213,562
1957	1,026,158

Table 19.3 shows) fell sharply. In 1955, the World Champion Dodgers shared one distinction with the last-place (by 38 games) Pirates—they were the only teams in the National League drawing fewer fans than in the last prewar season of 1941.[28]

By the mid-fifties, moreover, a new challenge emerged to the Dodger dynasty, both on the field and, even more seriously, at the box office. Hurriedly transplanted to Milwaukee just days before the start of the 1953 season, the Braves aggressively followed on the pioneering heels of the Dodgers and Giants and built up a contending, racially integrated team. The Braves steadily rose in the standings from seventh place in their last season in Boston, to second place, a game behind the Dodgers, in 1956. Aided by a strict no-television policy for both home and road games, the Braves were also breaking all National League attendance records. By the mid-1950s they were outdrawing the Dodgers by about a million fans per season.[29] More than anything else, it was those midwestern throngs, and the prospect of duplicating such crowds, and of breaking loose from the stranglehold that free television had established in Brooklyn, that provided the proximate cause of Walter O'Malley's decision to move to Los Angeles.

If the primary measure of a professional athlete is to help his team win, Robinson's impact in that regard can hardly be overstated, and that record on the field was surely an important element in the success of the "great experiment" in overturning baseball's color line. But Robinson's impact on the business of National League baseball is not as sharply drawn, and does not, in important respects, fulfill the somewhat starry-eyed myths that have flourished since. In the end, stemming the declining fortunes of major league baseball as a business in Brooklyn was one burden that was too great even for Robinson to bear. What Robinson did ensure was that, when the end came for major league baseball in Brooklyn—just one year after his retirement—an imperishable legacy had been left, which players and fans alike can still draw on fifty years later.

Notes

1. *New York Times,* 16 April 1947, p. 32.
2. G. Edward White, *Creating the National Pastime: Baseball Transforms Itself, 1903–1953* (Princeton: Princeton University Press, 1996), p. 157.
3. Jules Tygiel, *Baseball's Great Experiment* (New York: Oxford University Press, 1983), p. 105.
4. Red Barber, *1947: When All Hell Broke Loose in Baseball* (Garden City: Da Capo, 1982), p. 155.
5. As quoted in Tygiel, *Great Experiment,* p. 189.
6. Attendance figures from U.S. Congress, House of Representatives, *Study of Monopoly Power: Part VI, Organized Baseball,* 82d Cong. 1 Sess. 1952, p. 1617.
7. Ibid.
8. Ibid.
9. Ibid., p. 1619.
10. *New York Times,* 11 April 1947, p. 20.
11. Ibid.
12. *New York Times,* 19 April 1946, p. 22.
13. *New York Times,* 16 April 1947, p. 32; 19 April 1946, p. 21.
14. *New York Times,* 16 April 1947, p. 31.
15. Ibid., p. 34.
16. *New York Times,* 18 April 1947, p. 28.
17. Calculations based on author's study of game-by-game National League paid attendance figures for 1946 and 1947 from box scores published in the *New York Times.*
18. Ibid.
19. Ibid.
20. For source of calculations, see notes 6 and 17.
21. Ibid.
22. Ibid.
23. Ibid.
24. Ibid.
25. For 1946–1951, attendance figures from U.S. Congress, House of Representatives, *Study of Monopoly Power,* p. 1617; 1952–1960 attendance figures from annual editions of *The World Almanac* and *Book of Facts.*
26. Population data in Figures 19.1 and 19.2 from U.S. Department of Commerce, Bureau of the Census, *1950 Census of Population, Vol. II,* Table 86 (Summary of Population Characteristics for Cities of 100,000 or More), pp. 139–140. I am indebted to Robert Fetter for preparing the graphs, performing the regression analysis, and calculating the correlation coefficients.
27. Table 19.3 derived from sources cited in note 25.
28. *1957 World Almanac and Book of Facts* (New York: World Almanac, 1956), p. 806.
29. Ibid.

20

"Do Not Go Gently into That Good Night": Race, the Baseball Establishment, and the Retirements of Bob Feller and Jackie Robinson

Ron Briley

On July 22, 1969, organized baseball officially celebrated its centennial with the All-Star Game in Washington, D.C., and a White House reception hosted by President Richard Nixon. The controversial Nixon was not the focal point of political fireworks that day, as prior to the White House reception, Hall of Fame players Bob Feller and Jackie Robinson squared off at a press conference in the Sheraton Park Hotel.

Irritated by Afro-American charges of racism in baseball and American society, the conservative Feller lashed out at Robinson for his criticism of baseball hiring practices. The former Cleveland pitcher asserted, "Robinson has always been bush. He's always been a professional agitator more than anything else. He's just ticked off because baseball never rolled out the red carpet when he quit playing and offered him a soft front office job." Feller argued that there had been no discrimination in the sport since Robinson integrated the game, and, furthermore, that baseball contributed more to minority groups than almost any other institution in the country. Feller ended his diatribe by concluding, "Ability alone is what should count in the front office, too. I think there will be a Negro with that ability." Obviously Feller did not believe that Afro-Americans in 1969 were yet ready for the responsibilities of management.

An angry Robinson retorted that Feller had grown little since 1947, Robinson's rookie season, continuing to bury "his head in the sand." Perhaps expressing some resentment that he was employed as a fast-food-chain executive rather than in baseball management following his playing days, Robinson proclaimed, "My big thing is I don't believe that the black players are getting an equal opportunity with the whites after their playing days are through."[1]

The 1969 exchange was not the first time that the two stars had crossed swords. In 1946, Feller, who was considered somewhat of an expert on the Negro Leagues due to his postseason barnstorming tours against black competition, told reporters that he could see no future for Jackie Robinson in the major leagues. The Cleveland pitching star maintained that Robinson had "football shoulders and couldn't hit an inside pitch to save his neck. If he were a white man, I doubt they would consider him big league material."[2] While Robinson took exception to these remarks and interpreted them as being racially biased, Feller insisted that he bore no racial animosity toward the former UCLA football player. He was simply basing his opinion on professional observations. According to his memoirs, Feller easily retired Robinson the six times he faced him during a 1946 West Coast barnstorming tour, striking him out three times on ten pitches in San Diego. Feller stood by his assertion that Robinson could not hit the high fast ball.[3] Whether Feller's comments were professionally based or tinged with racial superiority, there were certainly hard feelings between the two players, and, according to Robinson biographer David Falkner, Feller had initially asked not to share the same platform during their 1962 inauguration into the Baseball Hall of Fame.[4]

Although their Cooperstown plaques are placed side by side, suggesting that personal antagonism did not interfere with baseball integration, the reactions of the baseball establishment and press to the retirements of Robinson and Feller provide evidence that considerable racism remained in the sport and in American society, probably continuing to fuel Robinson's resentment toward Feller.

As far as baseball's self-proclaimed "bible," the *Sporting News,* was concerned, the sport, a decade after the breaking of baseball's color barrier, was a model for racial integration and toleration. In an editorial commentary, the paper reminded readers, "The Negro in Organized Ball is so completely taken-for-granted these days that it must be difficult for younger fans to recall the time little more than a decade ago, when both majors and minors raised an invisible but effective barrier on the color line."[5] Yet, the story of the Robinson and Feller retirements casts a very different light on the baseball establishment's racial enlightenment. Following his announcement that he was leaving the playing field, Feller was awarded a job as a spokesman for the Motorola Corporation and toured the country as a goodwill ambassador for baseball. On the other hand, Robinson's retirement was controversial, with allegations that he had betrayed his baseball employers by first breaking his decision in a *Look* magazine exclusive. Robinson accepted a position as personnel director for the Chock Full o' Nuts company, and reporters questioned whether Robinson possessed the proper qualifications for personnel supervision, although no one seemed to question Feller's capabilities to speak for Motorola. In addition, Robinson commenced on a speaking tour for the NAACP which was not covered by the baseball press with the reverential tones reserved for Feller's engagements. The differing treatment given Feller's and Robinson's departures from the game indicates the amount of institutional racism remaining within the baseball establishment and exposes as a sham the *Sporting News* editorial claiming that baseball had solved its racial problems. After ten years baseball still did not understand Robinson, as the former Dodger star challenged racism in the nation and in its self-proclaimed pastime.

The Feller retirement story broke first, but was not unexpected. During the 1956 baseball campaign, the former ace of the Cleveland staff appeared in only nineteen games, winning none and losing four, striking out only eighteen, and compiling an earned run average of almost five runs per game.[6] Feller reportedly wanted to come back for one more season and conclude his career on a more positive note. Cleveland management made it clear that they would be willing to give him his release so that he could hook up with another club, but the right-hander was not in the Indians' plans for 1957.[7]

Accordingly, at a December 28, 1956, luncheon at Municipal Stadium in Cleveland, Feller announced his departure from the game he loved. The proud athlete maintained that he could still pitch, but he did not wish to leave his Cleveland home. Feller turned down the offer of an administrative position with the Indians, stating, "I expect to devote all my energies to the insurance business, to civic activities, and to my job as president of the Baseball Players' Association."[8] Although he was sometimes a thorn in the side of management, Feller was given permission by the owners to continue his service as president of the Players' Association through the completion of a new pension plan, which Feller the insurance executive may have understood better than many baseball owners did.

Reactions to the retirement announcement poured in from across the country, praising the Cleveland star's accomplishments on and off the playing field. Arthur Daley of the *New York Times* wrote a piece on Feller's career, while storm clouds were beginning to break over the end of

Robinson's playing days. The key to Feller's success, according to Daley, was that the Cleveland hurler never became "swell-headed." During the peak of his career, Feller lost three years to the U.S. Navy and World War II, denying him the opportunity to garner 300 wins in his twenty-year major league tenure. Yet, Daley observed that Rapid Robert Feller "never uttered a complaint nor let himself grow wistful at the might-have-been."[9]

The *Sporting News* treated the Feller retirement story in a similar fashion. After noting his three no-hitters and twelve one-hitters, the "bible" of baseball extolled Feller's achievements off the field of play, calling him "one of the outstanding individuals of our time." The paper concluded,

> As the years passed, it became evident that here was no run-of-the-mill citizen of baseball, content to win as many games as possible and earn as much as he could. Feller became a smart businessman, but he also interested himself in the welfare of others—including his colleagues on the diamond.[10]

In fact, *Newsweek* carried this theme so far as to argue, "In a business-minded age, he was probably the best businessman that baseball's player ranks ever produced." The *Newsweek* profile described Feller as the quintessential corporate organizational man of the 1950s. With outside business investments in General Mills, Gillette, Wilson, and others, he was incorporated into R-Fel, Inc. According to *Newsweek,*

> If you wanted a ball game pitched, some insurance sold, a newspaper column written, a radio or banquet speech made, or even a new luxury gimmick thought up for a car, Feller was your man.[11]

And like the great philanthropists of the late nineteenth century, he was perceived as a man who worked for the benefit of his community, giving speeches for civic clubs, churches, and schools. His climb from the cornfields of Iowa to the pinnacle of athletic and financial success epitomized the American dream of social mobility contained in the stories of Horatio Alger. Thus, Feller seemed well suited to assume the mantle of an ambassador for baseball and a corporate spokesman for the radio and television firm Motorola.

Following negotiation of a new pension plan, which Feller lauded as making baseball more attractive to the youngsters of America, he was off on a baseball promotional tour sponsored by Motorola. Feller's speaking engagements enjoyed detailed coverage by the *Sporting News,* which saw no conflict of interest between corporate sponsorship and the free publicity provided by the paper's features on Feller, Motorola, and baseball. In fact, the paper made its editorial position quite clear, writing,

His sponsorship is commercial, but far from considering this a reason to withhold publicity, the *Sporting News* salutes the Motorola people for their recognition of Feller as an ideal ambassador and for their confidence in baseball as a medium of appeal to their prospective customers.[12]

As Motorola's Youth Baseball Counselor, Feller visited fifty-four cities during the summer of 1957. A typical Feller schedule, such as an August visit to Bangor, Maine, called for a morning arrival and meeting with city officials. After changing into his uniform, Feller was taken via motorcade to the local ballpark, where enthusiastic youngsters were treated to a baseball clinic and a Feller lecture. Feller's talks usually consisted of baseball adaptations of Ben Franklin's *Poor Richard's Almanack,* emphasizing the value of hard work. A favorite Feller saying was, "It takes a lot of practice to be a good bunter."[13]

Also included on Feller's itinerary was a visit to Texas League Park in Shreveport, Louisiana. In 1956, the Louisiana state legislature passed a law barring interracial athletic contests in the state. Texas League clubs complied with the law by withholding black players in Shreveport. Evidently, Feller and Motorola had no problems with legitimizing segregation by scheduling Shreveport on the tour. Feller told approximately one thousand youngsters in Shreveport that the keys to baseball success were: listening to your coaches, finding the right playing position, practicing, and displaying enthusiasm. Feller failed to acknowledge that these qualities still did not allow a black youngster in Louisiana to compete with white players.[14]

While organized baseball did not protest Feller's Shreveport appearance, his testimony before the House Subcommittee on Monopolies, investigating baseball's financial and legal structure, did evoke controversy. After Feller suggested that the owners were arrogant and that the players should have a role in selecting the commissioner, his promotional appearance at the Brooklyn Dodgers–owned Los Angeles Wrigley Field was canceled. Nonetheless, these disputes with management did little to change Feller's image as an ambassador for the game. The *Sporting News* concluded that with his promotional work and service as a player representative, Feller placed baseball "in a position to compete with industry for the service of young people."[15] The paper encouraged other players to follow in Feller's path and to become involved in the work of promoting baseball. His spectacular pitching career, business acumen, and enthusiasm for the game continued to make Bob Feller a promotional fixture in minor and major league baseball parks for the next forty years. However, Jackie Robinson's retirement would not go so smoothly, raising questions about racial attitudes within the baseball establishment.

By the conclusion of the 1956 season, in which the New York Yankees edged Brooklyn for the World Series championship, it was apparent that the illustrious career of Jackie Robinson was winding down. Battling injuries and health problems, Robinson had a playing time in 1956 that was limited to 117 games. However, his games played, batting average, home runs, and runs batted in were all improvements over his 1955 marks.[16] Thus, many in baseball were shocked to learn on the morning of December 13, 1956, that Brooklyn had traded Robinson to the team's fierce National League rivals, the New York Giants, for cash and journeyman pitcher, Dick Littlefield. In an official statement, Robinson stated that he was disappointed in having to comfort his crying son, Jackie, Jr. However, trades were part of baseball, and he spoke of his relationship with the Brooklyn club in diplomatic terms, stating, "There are no hard feelings. The Brooklyn club had to protect its own best interests. I thought I helped Brooklyn last year and didn't figure to be traded." Robinson concluded that he would wait until January 10, 1957, to inform Giants owner Horace Stoneham whether he would retire or play for the Giants.[17]

Dodger fans were outraged. The *New York Times* quoted one Brooklyn partisan as proclaiming, "I'm shocked to the core. This is like selling the Brooklyn-Battery Tunnel. Jackie Robinson is a synonym for the Dodgers. They can't do this to us." Of course, this fan did not realize the Robinson trade was only the beginning of Dodger management's betrayal of Brooklyn. Despite outrage among the Dodger faithful and Robinson's hint that he might retire, the baseball establishment's assumption was that business would go on as usual. Giants owner Stoneham did not believe Robinson would retire. Instead, Robinson, whom Stoneham labeled the "greatest competitor I've ever seen in baseball," would play first base for the Giants in 1957. Referring to Jackie Robinson, Jr.'s tearful reaction to the trade, the *Sporting News* insisted,

> Jackie, Sr., being an adult, recognizes the expediency that exists in this world with which he must cope and has displayed no tear-stained-face to the public. He is now a Giant and will play ball for the Giants with the same fiercely competitive spirit he displayed for so long as a Dodger. That is the only way Robinson knows how to play.[18]

However, when Robinson engaged in a bit of his own expediency regarding the announcement of his retirement, the *Sporting News* and baseball establishment yelled foul.

While Brooklyn fans were dismayed with the trade, Robinson was less surprised and was already making plans for his departure from the game. Robinson did not get along well with Dodger manager Walter Alston, and his relationship with the Dodgers' front office deteriorated when Walter O'Malley maneuvered to force Branch Rickey out of Brooklyn. From a peak figure of $39,000, Robinson's salary suffered slight reductions for each of his last three seasons in Brooklyn. In his memoirs, Robinson commented unfavorably on the racial views of O'Malley, alleging that the Dodger president perceived him as an "uppity Nigger."[19]

Accordingly, on December 10, 1956, Robinson met with William Black, president of Chock Full o' Nuts, a fast-food restaurant chain in the New York City area. Black, whose employees were predominantly Afro-American, offered Robinson a position as vice-president in charge of personnel at an annual salary of $50,000. That evening Robinson attempted to reach the Dodgers' general manager, "Buzzy" Bavasi, to inform him of his intentions. However, Bavasi, who was negotiating with the Giants, was unavailable. The next day, Robinson signed a contract with Black. That same evening, Robinson was told that he had been traded to the Giants. He did not advise Dodger officials that he had decided to retire from baseball and accept a position with Chock Full o' Nuts. The reason for Robinson's apparent duplicity was an exclusive contract for $50,000 which he had signed with *Look* magazine. That contract stipulated that Robinson's retirement would first be announced in a magazine exclusive.[20]

Yet, the story broke early before the magazine hit the newsstands. A few *Look* subscribers received advance copies, and *Look* executives scrambled to call a press conference for Robinson. When asked why he had chosen to work through a magazine deal and not keep his employer informed of his intentions, Robinson replied, "I had given my best to Brooklyn for eleven years and my debt to baseball has been paid." Buzzy Bavasi did not agree, insisting that Robinson owed an obligation to the Dodgers as well as the sportswriters of New York. Bavasi told reporters, "And this is the way he repays the newspapermen for what they've done for him. He tells you one thing and then writes another for money. You fellows will find out that you've been blowing the horn for the wrong guy." An angry Robinson retorted, "After what Bavasi said, I wouldn't play ball again for a million dollars."[21]

The New York press immediately weighed into the Robinson-Bavasi debate. Red Smith of the *New York Herald Tribune* rebuked Robinson for his lack of loyalty to the Dodgers, asserting,

> But for the Dodgers, the Jackie Robinson of this last decade would not have existed. The fact that he gave them full value on the field and the fact that after eleven years they sold his contract without consulting him, these do not alter the fact that everything he has he owes to the club. His debt to the

Dodgers had precedence over any agreement to sell a story to *Look,* and with his mind already made up at the time of the trade he was honor bound to speak up.[22]

Dick Young of the *New York Daily News,* who often chastised Robinson, maintained that the Brooklyn great did not owe anything to reporters or the Dodgers. Young was more upset that Robinson, in his *Look* press conference of January 6, had criticized baseball for lacking sentiment. Rallying to the defense of the national pastime, Young argued,

> So Robinson should have quit, which certainly is his privilege, without smearing the game that has earned him $500,000 in ten years. Baseball has as much sentiment as any business he can name, much more than the cream cheese sandwich business, for one.[23]

On the other hand, Joe Williams of the *New York World Telegram* insisted that Robinson would be a "dope" to not take *Look*'s lucrative offer. Seeking to take a more neutral position, the *Sporting News* editorialized that while Robinson had every right to sell his story, the "bible" of baseball preferred the "outstanding example" of dignified retirement established by Bob Feller.[24]

In the much maligned *Look* article, Robinson simply maintained that his decision to leave the game was based on financial security for his family. He concluded the article by noting, "I know I'll miss the excitement of baseball, but I'm looking forward to new kinds of satisfaction. I'll be able to spend more time with my family. My kids and I will get to know each other better. . . . They won't have to look for me on TV."[25] However, shortly after his retirement, Robinson agreed to postpone assuming his duties with Chock Full o' Nuts while he commenced on a speaking and fund-raising tour on behalf of the NAACP. Perhaps, as biographer David Falkner suggests, Robinson's retirement was also related to the athlete's decision to make a larger commitment and contribution to the burgeoning civil rights movement.

On December 8, 1956, two days before he met with William Black, Robinson received the prestigious Spingarn Medal, awarded annually "for the highest achievement of an American Negro." Ed Sullivan, columnist and television celebrity, presented the gold medal at a New York dinner sponsored by the NAACP. Among the previous recipients present were Ralph Bunche, W.E.B. DuBois, and Thurgood Marshall. The award citation placed Robinson's contributions in historical perspective, proclaiming,

> The entire nation is indebted to him for his pioneer role in breaking the color line in Organized Baseball. Through sheer ability and exceptional competitive zeal, he won popular acclaim of sports lovers of all races and demon-

strated that there were no fore-ordained racial restrictions upon the ability to play the National Game. He opened the doors of the major leagues for Negro stars whose skill, zest, and stamina have entered the national sport.[26]

Perceived as a symbol of opportunity and struggle for Afro-Americans, Robinson could hardly refuse when NAACP Executive Secretary Roy Wilkins asked Robinson to chair the organization's 1957 Freedom Fund drive. While a novice as a public speaker, under the tutelage of veteran NAACP organizer Franklin Williams, Robinson became a successful orator and fund raiser, proudly pointing out that the 1957 tour was able to garner $1 million for the NAACP coffers. Echoing the sentiments of Martin Luther King, Jr., Robinson argued that Afro-Americans were out of patience and could no longer wait for equal rights. He told a Chicago audience, "We have waited almost one hundred years for these rights. In my view, now is the time for Negroes to ask for all of the rights which are theirs."[27]

It is worth noting the courage which Robinson displayed in embracing the cause of the NAACP. In the late 1950s, opponents of racial integration attempted to brand the civil rights organization as a subversive tool of the Communist Party and the Soviet Union. For example, appearing before the Louisiana Joint Legislative Committee on Segregation, Afro-American Manning Johnson, who had been a minor Communist Party official in New York, attacked Martin Luther King, Jr., and the NAACP. The vitriolic Johnson described King as a "dastardly misleader who is taking his race down the road of violence, bloodshed, revolution, and possible communism in the South." In concluding his testimony, Johnson denounced the NAACP as a "communist vehicle designed to initiate the overthrow of the government."[28]

However, sports coverage of the Robinson speaking tour failed to acknowledge his courage and determination. Instead, publications such as the *Sporting News* focused upon baseball questions Robinson fielded during press conferences. The Robinson image projected by the *Sporting News* was not the crusader for racial equality, but rather a hot-headed commentator who antagonized fellow players and baseball executives. For example, at a speaking engagement in Wauhegan, Illinois, Robinson stated that too much night life cost the Milwaukee Braves the 1956 National League pennant. Braves players replied to the criticism by labeling Robinson a "rumor monger." Braves shortstop Johnny Logan maintained that Robinson was "just popping off to keep his name in the headlines."[29]

On a more serious note, Robinson was quoted as describing former teammate Roy Campanella as "washed up." An angry Campanella retorted that he was tired of Robinson's "popping off." The burly catcher criticized Robinson for demonstrating a negative attitude toward baseball, asserting,

"Instead of being grateful to baseball, he's criticizing it. Everything he has he owes to baseball. That beautiful house of his, and this new job of his, too. Does he think those people would have had anything to do with him if he had never played baseball?"[30] The two men initially quarreled over Campanella's failure to join Robinson in challenging segregated housing for the black Brooklyn ballplayers. The antagonism between Campanella and Robinson reflected a debate within the Afro-American community about the necessity of pushing for racial integration going back to the days of Booker T. Washington and W.E.B. DuBois.

But Campanella's complaints failed to silence Robinson, who observed that it was "strange" that no Afro-American players could make the major league rosters of Detroit, Philadelphia, and Boston. While speaking in Detroit, the former Brooklyn star further acknowledged that he was puzzled by the fact that "for some reason there are no Negro players on the fields of Detroit. Detroit is a great sports town. But you can't help but wonder about the absence of Negro players in both football and baseball."[31]

While Robinson insisted that he was speaking honestly, seeking a better nation for all Americans, former playing field opponents of Robinson continued to label the Dodger great a troublemaker. Giants pitcher Sal Maglie, no stranger to baseball rhubarbs, was quoted as saying Robinson was unpopular with the players due to self-promotion. Maglie believed Robinson, who had expressed interest in managing, would never be given the reins of a major league club. Maglie concluded, "I don't think any ball club would take a chance on Jackie, because you just couldn't get anybody to play for him after the way he's been rapping other players."[32]

Though he achieved business success, valued his political involvement, and played a respected role in the civil rights movement, Robinson was greatly disappointed that he was never allowed to try his hand at piloting a major league franchise. Writing in 1972, Robinson observed,

> I felt that any chance I might have had of moving up to an administrative job with the Dodgers or any other team was mighty slim. Had I been easy going, willing to be meek and humble, I might have had a chance. But this fact has not changed much even today There are many capable black athletes in the game who could contribute greatly as managers or in other positions of responsibility, but it just isn't happening.[33]

In fact, Robinson never lived to see his dream of an Afro-American manager, for Frank Robinson was not named to manage the Cleveland Indians until 1975, three years after the death of the pioneering Dodger great.

Baseball's reluctance to provide opportunities for black managerial experience on the playing field and in the executive suite demonstrated that the sport had serious problems with institutional racism long after the playing career of Jackie Robinson had supposedly erased racial barriers in the sport. In addition, an examination of the retirement stories of Bob Feller and Jackie Robinson suggests a lack of racial understanding if not overt racism. Despite some criticism of management, Bob Feller was welcomed into the baseball establishment and into corporate America. Feller was extolled as the embodiment of the American success epic, a farm boy who rose from the cornfields of Iowa to athletic and corporate success. Robinson was also a good fit for the Horatio Alger imagery so dear to the American mythology of success and social mobility. Through hard work and a fierce competitive spirit, Robinson surmounted racial barriers to become one of the nation's outstanding athletes and role models. And although Chock Full o' Nuts lacked the executive pedigree of the Motorola Corporation, Robinson also found success within the economic and business spheres. Yet he was never embraced by the baseball establishment. Feller became an ambassador for baseball, citing clichés about the value of hard work, while failing to challenge racial segregation in a city such as Shreveport. Robinson, on the other hand, left the playing field to champion the standard of racial equality. Nevertheless, the baseball press viewed him as a troublemaker when he drew attention to continuing racial segregation in cities such as Philadelphia, Boston, and Detroit. Although only two weeks separated the officially announced retirements of Robinson and Feller, the reaction of the baseball world to their departures reveals much about the great racial divide within American society.

Notes

1. For the Feller and Robinson confrontation during the centennial ceremonies, see *Sporting News,* 9 August 1969.
2. For Feller's 1946 comments on Robinson, see Jules Tygiel, *Baseball's Great Experiment: Jackie Robinson and His Legacy* (New York: Random House, 1983), p. 76; and Jackie Robinson, *I Never Had It Made* (New York: G. P. Putnam's Sons, 1972), p. 48.
3. Bob Feller with Bill Gilbert, *Now Pitching: Bob Feller* (New York: HarperPerennial, 1990), pp. 140–141.
4. David Falkner, *Great Time Coming: The Life of Jackie Robinson from Baseball to Birmingham* (New York: Simon and Schuster, 1995), p. 294.
5. *Sporting News,* 22 May 1957.
6. For statistics, see John Thorn and Pete Palmer, eds., *Total Baseball: The Ultimate Encyclopedia of Baseball* (New York: HarperPerennial, 1993), p. 1491.
7. For a management perspective on the Feller retirement, see Ira Berkow, ed., *Hank Greenberg: The Story of My Life* (New York: Times Books, 1989), pp. 221–222. For Feller's thoughts on retirement, see Bob Feller, "I'll Never Quit Baseball," *Look* 20 (20 March 1956), p. 53–54.

8. *Sporting News,* 2 January 1957; and *New York Times,* 29 December 1956.

9. *New York Times,* 7 January 1957.

10. *Sporting News,* 9 January 1957.

11. "R-Fel, Inc.," *Newsweek* 49 (7 January 1957), p. 44.

12. *Sporting News,* 13 February and 15 May 1957.

13. *Sporting News,* 14 August 1957.

14. *Sporting News,* 1 May 1957.

15. *Sporting News,* 3 and 17 July; 6 November 1957.

16. Thorn and Palmer, eds., *Total Baseball,* pp. 1, 182.

17. *Sporting News,* 19 December 1956; *New York Times,* 14 December 1956; and "If You Can't Beat Him," *Time* 68 (24 December 1956), p. 42.

18. *New York Times,* 14 December 1956; *Sporting News,* 19 and 26 December 1956; and "After Ten Years," *Newsweek* 48 (24 December 1956), p. 49.

19. For Robinson's perspective of O'Malley, see Robinson, *I Never Had It Made,* pp. 110–115.

20. For Robinson's negotiations with William Black, see Falkner, *Great Time Coming,* pp. 249–251; and Robinson, *I Never Had It Made,* pp. 130–134.

21. *Sporting News,* 16 January 1957; and *New York Times,* 7 January 1957.

22. Quotations from *New York Herald Tribune,* as cited by *Sporting News,* 16 January 1957.

23. Quotations from *New York Daily News,* as cited by *Sporting News,* 16 January 1957.

24. Quotations from *New York World Telegram,* as cited by *Sporting News,* 16 January 1957.

25. Jackie Robinson, "Why I'm Quitting Baseball," *Look* 21 (22 January 1957), pp. 99–102.

26. *New York Times,* 9 December 1956; and *Sporting News,* 19 December 1956.

27. For Robinson's Freedom Foundation tour, see Robinson, *I Never Had It Made,* pp. 137–146; and Falkner, *A Great Time Coming,* pp. 253–262.

28. For the public hearings of the Louisiana Joint Legislative Committee on Segregation, see *Shreveport Times,* 7–10 March 1957. For background information on Manning Johnson, see Harvey Klehr, *The Heyday of American Communism* (New York: Basic Books, 1984), pp. 400–401 and 471–472.

29. *Sporting News,* 23 January 1957.

30. *Sporting News,* 6 February 1957. For the Robinson-Campanella relationship, see Robinson, *I Never Had It Made,* pp. 110–111. For additional background information on Campanella, see "Big Man from Nicetown: Roy Campanella," *Time* 66 (8 August 1955), pp. 50–55; and Roy Campanella, *It's Good to Be Alive* (Boston: Little, Brown, 1959).

31. *Sporting News,* 6 and 27 February 1957.

32. *Sporting News,* 6 February 1957. For the temperamental Maglie, see Robert W. Creamer, "An Angel of Darkness Named Sal the Barber," *Sports Illustrated* 2 (6 June 1955), pp. 43–44; and Millan J. Shapiro, *The Sal Maglie Story* (New York: Julian Messner, 1957).

33. Robinson, *I Never Had It Made,* p. 130.

21

Kareem's Omission? Jackie Robinson, Black Profile in Courage*

Patrick Henry

In 1996, with a definite nod toward John Kennedy, whose courage during the Cuban missile crisis he greatly admired, Kareem Abdul-Jabbar published *Black Profiles in Courage: A Legacy of African-American Achievement*. In this, his third book, "dedicated to all Americans who seek to embrace their heritage . . . [but] especially dedicated to young Americans, who most need a heritage to embrace,"[1] Kareem tells the stories of a group of black Americans, some better known than others, "whose sacrifices," as Henry Louis Gates, Jr., writes in the Foreword, "were for the common good, whose will was unbending . . . [in] the triumph over slavery and over antiblack racist segregation . . . [in short] in the triumph of the human spirit over seemingly insurmountable odds" (pp. xii-xiii).

Here we learn of Estevanico, the first black mentioned by name in American history, a true pioneer and only black in the first party to cross the North American continent; of Crispus Attucks, "the most significant African American hero in the eighteenth century, (p. 35), who began the Boston Massacre and was the first to die in it; of Joseph Cinque, who led a revolt on a slave ship and was of extreme importance to the abolitionist movement; of Frederick Douglass, "the most visible, persuasive, influential African American of the nineteenth century" (p. 73), who escaped slavery to

---

*Portions of this article appeared in "Jackie Robinson: Athlete and American Par Excellence," *The Virginia Quarterly Review*, Spring 1997.

become the founding father of the first civil rights and black protest movements and who, anticipating speeches of Martin Luther King, Jr., and Malcolm X, urged his listeners to "make character, and not color, the criteria of respectability" (p. 90); of Harriet Tubman, the illiterate heroine of the Underground Railroad who courageously returned nineteen times into slave territory to liberate at least three hundred slaves; of Bass Reeves, the first black deputy U.S. marshal west of the Mississippi, who arrested over three thousand outlaws while killing only fourteen, and who was never wounded; of Lewis Latimer, a seminal figure in the work of Thomas Edison on the incandescent light bulb and in the development of the telephone with Alexander Graham Bell; and of Rosa Parks, the local secretary of the NAACP whose sense of pride triggered the bus boycott in Montgomery, Alabama.

Other black figures mentioned in passing are W.E.B. DuBois, the writer and founder of the original NAACP; Benjamin O. Davis, the first African-American general; Lieutenant Henry Ossian Flipper, the first black to graduate from West Point; Richard Theodore Greener, the first black to graduate from Harvard; Colin Powell, the chairman of the Joint Chiefs of Staff; Thurgood Marshall, the pioneer of school desegregation and the first Afro-American Supreme Court Justice; and the great civil rights leader, Dr. Martin Luther King, Jr. In addition to specific individual black people central to the founding and the development of our country, Kareem paints the roles of unnamed masses of Afro-Americans played in the defense of this country from its inception, particularly stressing the five thousand Afro-Americans in the Continental Army and the enormous contribution of black soldiers in the Civil War and the two world wars of the twentieth century.

Kareem's obvious purpose in writing *Black Profiles in Courage* was to demonstrate the roles African-Americans have played in the founding, development, and defense of our country. Many of these important black figures have been marginalized in traditional textbooks, thereby depriving black and white children of key black models of achievement. "If people think of me as a hero," writes Kareem, "how can I influence their character in some positive way, other than just teaching them basketball?" (p. xxiii). Certainly he must have concluded that to tell young blacks what other blacks have achieved in America is to teach them what they too can accomplish in their country.

Throughout the book, as the title indicates, the notion of courage is central and the author consistently highlights the importance of individual acts of courage. Courage itself is loosely defined as "recognizing when something needs to be done and doing it, even when there are easier choices. [It] should also be motivated by intelligence and moral understanding. The attempt to do the right thing," Kareem adds, "despite adverse consequences ... is the measure of character" (p. xxiv). Abdul-Jabbar, who says he writes "to inform, encourage, [and] inspire" (p. 5), doesn't hesitate to speak directly and didactically: "Never underestimate the power of an individual act of courage," he writes, "it may one day affect many other lives" (p. 67).

After reading this inspirational and informative book, I decided to invite Kareem to Whitman College to speak during Black History Month. Following his exceptionally well-received talk on important black figures in American history, I had an opportunity to talk with him about *Black Profiles in Courage*. By this time, I had clearly anticipated his response to my first question: Why is there no chapter on Jackie Robinson? "I didn't want to write about athletes or entertainers," he replied. I went on to remind him, however, that despite the fact that there is no chapter on Jackie Robinson, Robinson is often mentioned in the text. The book begins, for example, with an epigraph taken from Jackie's tombstone: "A life is not important except in the impact it has on other lives" (p. vii). Then, in the introduction, Kareem notes: "I also learned important lessons from my other personal heroes. . . . Jackie's pride, courage, and fierce determination left an imprint on my soul. One way or another, with his bat or his glove, or his legs, or his mind, he kept trying to beat you. I wanted a touch of that in me" (p. xxiii). Finally, in the very last paragraph of the book, we read: "If anyone epitomizes Jackie Robinson's inspiring statement that 'a life is not important except in the impact it has on other lives,' it is Rosa Parks" (p. 222). Kareem nodded agreement as he brought the fingers of his right hand together and began tapping the left side of his chest. "Jackie's in there," he said, meaning the book, "because he's always been in here," meaning his heart.

Although, surprisingly, Robinson makes no appearance in Kareem's autobiography,[2] which takes us from his childhood in Harlem through the 1982 NBA finals, Jackie is again a real presence in Abdul-Jabbar's second book, entitled *Kareem,* a diary written during his final 1988–1989 NBA season. Here again the epigraph—"Athletes die twice"—is taken from Robinson and, much more importantly, the four-page April 16 diary entry is dedicated to him. Here are the first six sentences of that entry:

Sunday, April 16 [1989]

My thoughts are on Jackie Robinson today, my birthday. I was born in Harlem the day after Jackie's first major league game across the river in Brooklyn's Ebbets Field. It was forty-two years ago that I was born and that Jackie Robinson, in 1947, at age twenty-eight, crossed baseball's color line. I have always considered it a gift that I slipped into the world just at that moment.

> All the courage and competitiveness of Jackie Robinson affects me to this day. If I patterned my life after anyone, it was him.[3]

There can be no doubt that, before Martin Luther King, Jr., before Malcolm X, and before Nelson Mandela, Jackie Robinson was for Kareem, as he was for all of us born in New York City in the late 1930s and 1940s, our first and unquestionably most formative black profile in courage. Now, at a distance of fifty years, we can place Jackie in proper perspective and see how his courage displayed itself in what he did before, during, and after his baseball career.

Several years before playing baseball for the Dodgers, and long before anyone knew it had begun, Robinson was making his mark in the civil rights movement. Shortly after the attack on Pearl Harbor, he entered the Army. After completing his basic training at Fort Riley, Kansas, despite his college background, he was denied admission to Officers Candidate School. Robinson complained to black heavyweight champion, Joe Louis, who also happened to be stationed at Fort Riley. Louis contacted the Department of War and a representative was sent to Fort Riley. Immediately, the policy toward black recruits was reversed. Jackie completed Officers Candidate School and was made a second lieutenant in the cavalry. Named morale officer, he began by trying to change Jim Crow policies on the base. Robinson fought and succeeded, for example, in increasing the number of seats provided for black soldiers at the segregated PX at Fort Riley. Shortly after doing so, he was transferred to Fort Hood, Texas, a particularly difficult assignment for a black officer. In July 1944, in the isolation of a heavily racist army camp and eleven years before Rosa Parks, Robinson refused to sit in the back of a post bus. He was court-martialed but eventually acquitted of all charges and "honorably relieved from active duty" in the same year.

Robinson's entire baseball career was a centerpiece of the civil rights movement. During their years together on the Dodgers, wherever the team went, the double-play combination of Harold "Pee Wee" Reese and Jackie Robinson also served metaphorically as the twin killing of bigotry and segregation. The desegregation of baseball that Robinson pioneered proved that integration could work in America and inspired others to try and make it work in different areas. Jackie never ceased to push for full equality for blacks in the game he loved, not only as players, but in all managerial and front office positions. As a player he spoke out often against racism in baseball. In 1952, for example, he denounced the Yankees as prejudiced since they had not yet fielded a black player, and in 1956 he charged that advances were not being made fast enough and that baseball needed to bring economic pressure on the South to help remedy a still intolerable situation. The abuses he cited, the lack of equal accommodations and services to all players, black and white, would continue for another ten years in various spring training sites.

Jackie Robinson came to symbolize the new American black—proud, defiant, articulate, no longer patiently waiting to receive civil rights, and no longer willing to reinforce an image of inferiority by expressing gratitude for getting his or her due. In July 1949, for example, Robinson took advantage of his appearance before the House Un-American Activities Committee to denounce racism in America: "White people must realize," he told the audience, "that the more a Negro hates Communism because it opposes democracy, the more he is going to hate the other influences that kill off democracy in this county—and that goes for racial discrimination in the Army, segregation on trains and buses, and job discrimination."[4]

After his baseball days, Robinson demonstrated the same pioneering spirit his career on the diamond came to symbolize. This began immediately after his retirement from baseball, when he became vice-president in charge of personnel in the white-owned corporation Chock Full o' Nuts. He pioneered again when he served as chairman of the board of Freedom National Bank in Harlem, which would become the nation's largest black-owned bank.

In the main, during the last twelve years of his life, Jackie Robinson was destined to be as much a loner in his political affairs as he had been during his playing days. Caught between young black militants who dubbed him an "Uncle Tom" because he persisted in trying to work through the system and an older generation that wasn't activist enough to suit him, arguing publicly with figures as politically opposed as Malcolm X and Roy Wilkins, he would act independently and courageously, stubbornly forging his own path through these turbulent years. Each of his actions seemed to alienate someone: when he denounced anti-Semitism among blacks; when he attacked Adam Clayton Powell for urging blacks to abandon the NAACP and support the Black Muslims; when he resigned from the NAACP in 1967 because it opposed his connection with Nelson Rockefeller and because he resented the fact that it hadn't given more voice to younger, more aggressive black leaders; when he denounced police brutality in the treatment of the arrested Black Panthers in New York City in 1968; and in 1971 when he publicly criticized his friend Nelson Rockefeller for authorizing the assault on rioting prisoners in the Attica penitentiary, most of whom were black. Jackie was uninterested in adhering to any inflexible political perspective; his sole commitment was to integration and improved social conditions for black Americans.

If Robinson felt close to one black leader during the civil rights movement, it was Martin Luther King, Jr. Although the two would disagree publicly over the war in Vietnam, Robinson never doubted that he and King were working for the same goal: integration, and not separation, of the races in America. With a hostile white crowd outside the building, Robinson spoke in Jackson, Mississippi, on February 16, 1958, urging his listeners to press on peacefully for their rights. In the fall of the same year, he took part in the Youth March for Integrated Schools in Washington, D.C. In 1962 King picked Robinson to lead a fund-raising drive to help rebuild churches in the South. Jackie would go on to raise money to support King's work and to help voter registration in the South. In May 1963, Jackie went to Birmingham, just after the hotel where King had been staying was bombed, and spoke to a packed church with King at his side. In August 1964, in typical Robinson fashion, after the discovery of the bodies of slain white civil rights workers, Jackie co-chaired the campaign to raise $25,000 to build a memorial center in Meridian, Mississippi, in their honor.

Up to this point, I have defined Jackie's courage in terms of *doing*, stressing all that he did before, during, and after his career in baseball. But, to my mind, the most striking and significant aspect of his courage had to do with *nondoing*. How did this powerful, volatile, proud, deeply sensitive man refrain from retaliating to the abuse he suffered on the baseball diamond during two key years, 1947 and 1948, in the desegregation of baseball? For those who might be tempted to think that he was thick-skinned, listen to what went through his mind when Ben Chapman and other Philadelphia Phillies launched a barrage of filth and racial slurs in his direction in April 1947: "All of a sudden I thought, the hell with this. This isn't me. They're making me be some crazy pacifist black freak. Hell, no. I'm going back to being myself. Right now. I'm going to the Phillie dugout and grab one of those white sons of bitches and smash his fucking teeth and walk away. Walk away from this ballpark. Walk away from baseball."[5]

In late August 1947, to choose one other example, Robinson singled in his next at-bat after Enos Slaughter had deliberately spiked him and opened up a gash eight inches above his ankle. While standing at first base, Jackie told Stan Musial: "I don't care what happens, but when I get to second base, I'm gonna kill somebody. I'm gonna knock him into center field. I don't care what kind of play it is, he's going down." Musial's response disarmed Robinson, and, once again, he did nothing. "I don't blame you," Musial said. "You have every right to do it."[6]

It should have come as no surprise in 1960, when former President Harry Truman denounced the students staging sit-ins in the South, that Jackie would defend those students in his column in the *New York Post* and justify their nonviolent actions to end injustices. A good decade earlier, Jackie had already been practicing his own ethic of nonviolence, a particularly difficult one for him to enact since his natural impulse was retaliation. Drawing on his deep spiritual reserve, Jackie had the strength of character not to do what most certainly would have, at least temporarily, undone all that he had already done for the advancement of African-Americans in the national pastime. Indeed, Jackie's ethic of nonviolence was so powerful that, as Rickey had predicted, it knit the team together and brought even opponents of integration to Robinson's defense.

Jackie knew, whether he liked it or not, from the very beginning, that he was an individual ball player, a symbol of black people, and part of an experiment with immense social ramifications for the advancement of blacks in America. He accomplished what he did because he practiced daily acts of courage, real courage, born of his deep awareness of community and his profound sense of responsibility—not only toward black America but toward that segment of white America that supported him. "Then, I thought of Mr. Rickey," he wrote about a particularly trying moment, "how his family and friends had begged him not to fight for me and my people. I thought of all his predictions, which had come true. Mr. Rickey had come to a crossroads and made a lonely decision. I was at a crossroads. I would make mine."[7]

At the crossroads, Jackie knew which road to take, the road that led to Hank Aaron and Martin Luther King, Jr. Both men have recorded their gratitude. Aaron called Robinson "the Dr. King of baseball," and King told his aide, Wyatt Tee Walker, "Jackie Robinson made it possible for me in the first place. Without him, I would never have been able to do what I did."[8] Transforming "stumbling block into stepping stone," as Jesse Jackson worded it in his eulogy on this great American hero—two years before the desegregation of the armed forces, seven years before *Brown vs. Board of Education* declared public school segregation illegal, more than a decade before the sit-ins and the efforts of Martin Luther King, Jr.—Jackie Robinson changed the way blacks thought about themselves, among other things, giving them a new sense of pride and reason to hope for genuine fulfillment in America.[9]

As much as Robinson did for blacks, however, he did far more for white America. By appealing to the national consciousness, he compelled white Americans to confront the reality of racial prejudice and to redefine their values. I know of no more moving account of this influence than that noted by Red Barber in his autobiography. Barber, the announcer of Dodger games in Brooklyn who had been born and raised in the South, did not easily accept the desegregation of baseball. "It tortured me," he writes. "I set out to do a deep self-examination. I attempted to find out who I was. I know that if I have achieved any understanding and tolerance in my life . . . it all stems from this." Barber, whose daughter became a teacher in Harlem, concluded: "I thank Jackie Robinson. He did far more for me than I did for him."[10]

I too thank Jackie Robinson for the impact he had on my life and on the lives of all of us who grew up when he played in Brooklyn. In *Jackie Robinson: An Intimate Portrait,* his widow has recently written, simply but profoundly, "I believe that the singly most important aspect of Jack's presence was that it enabled white baseball fans to root for a black man, thus encouraging more whites to realize that all our destinies were inextricably linked."[11] *In Black Profiles in Courage,* in the tradition of Martin Luther King, Jr., and Jackie Robinson, Kareem Abdul-Jabbar similarly underscores the common destiny of blacks and whites in America: "we are *all* connected to each other in this country," he writes, "and should be busy reaffirming our connections, not our differences" (p. xx).

With racism on the rise in 1997, fifty years after Jackie Robinson broke the color barrier in baseball, with black churches once again burning throughout our country, which has witnessed over four hundred bias-motivated murders in the 1990s, Jackie's passion for justice and dedication to harmony among all races in America has a particular relevance. Jackie's ideas and the way he held them, his spirit and courage under fire shine forth through the fog of hatred and bigotry, like an ebony monstrance, a beacon, a symbol, a glowing example for all members of his race—the human race.

Notes

1. Kareem Abdul-Jabbar and Alan Steinberg, *Black Profiles in Courage: A Legacy of African-American Achievement* (New York: William Morrow, 1996), p. v. Additional page references are cited parenthetically in the text.
2. Kareem Abdul-Jabbar and Peter Knobler, *Giant Steps: The Autobiography of Kareem Abdul-Jabbar* (New York: Bantam, 1983).
3. Kareem Abdul-Jabbar with Mignon McCarthy, *Kareem* (New York: Random House, 1990), p. 190.
4. Peter Golenbock, *Bums: An Oral History of the Brooklyn Dodgers* (New York: Simon and Schuster, 1984), p. 281.
5. David Falkner, *Great Time Coming: The Life of Jackie Robinson, From Baseball to Birmingham* (New York: Simon and Schuster, 1995), p. 169.
6. Golenbock, *Bums,* p. 196. Falkner, relates the same incident in *Great Time Coming,* p. 173, as does Roger Kahn, in *The Era, 1947–1957: When the Yankees, the Giants and the Dodgers Ruled the World* (New York: Ticknor and Fields, 1993), p. 96. In *I Never Had It Made* (New Jersey: Ecco Press, 1997), Robinson does not mention Musial but does remark that "Slaughter deliberately went for my leg instead of the base and spiked me rather severely" (p. 68). Despite these firsthand accounts, Slaughter still denies that he spiked Robinson deliberately. In fact, he denied it publicly at the conference.

7. Red Barber, *1947: When All Hell Broke Loose in Baseball* (New York: Da Capo Press, 1982), p. 159.

8. Falkner, *Great Time Coming,* pp. 346, 237.

9. Roger Kahn, "Thousands Mourn Jackie Robinson," in *The Jackie Robinson Reader,* ed. Jules Tygiel (New York: Penguin Books USA, 1997), p. 277.

10. Red Barber with Robert Creamer, *Rhubarb in the Catbird Seat* (New York: Doubleday, 1968), pp. 272–273.

11. Rachel Robinson, *Jackie Robinson: An Intimate Portrait* (New York: Harry N. Abrams, 1996), p. 66.

22

Should We Rely on the Marketplace to End Discrimination? What the Integration of Baseball Tells Us

Robert Cherry

Introductory Remarks

At the popular level, the civil rights movement is thought to begin with the 1956 Birmingham bus boycott, initiated by Rosa Parks and led by Martin Luther King, Jr. Through militancy and heroism, the Student Nonviolent Coordinating Committee (SNCC) led the struggle that culminated in the 1964 Civil Rights Act. This ended any legal foundation for Jim Crow and other racial exclusionary policies in the United States. At a deeper level, however, the antiracist struggle has its roots in the decision in the 1930s of a section of the economic elite to integrate black Americans into American society. This decision had nothing to do with morality; it had everything to do with economic and political considerations.

At a political level, there was a growing anticapitalist movement, spearheaded by the U.S. Communist Party, which, through its efforts in the Scottsboro Case, had gained moral leadership in the struggle against bigotry. While this allowed the Party to make modest political gains among black Americans, its real significance was the prestige and sympathy gained among progressive white Americans. In contrast, the traditional reformist approach of the NAACP seemed totally ineffective, reducing its strength and standing.[1]

Second, the rise of Nazism caused at least some in the elite to realize that it was no longer possible to maintain the existing tensions between democratic ideals and the racist treatment of black Americans. The foundation of the Nazi race theory had been developed in the United States by elite academicians allied with the American Eugenics Movement. Genetic theories, which promoted the notion that there was a racial hierarchy of intelligence, dominated academic discourse. With a few exceptions, students in elite American universities in the 1920s were being taught essentially the same race theories as students in Nazi universities during the 1930s.[2]

Third, and probably most importantly, black Americans began leaving the South after World War I. The black population of New York, Chicago, Detroit, and Cleveland more than doubled between 1910 and 1920. With the closing of eastern and southern European immigration in 1924, the migration of black Americans to the Northeast and the Midwest accelerated. As a result, by 1930 over 20 percent of all black Americans lived in these regions, whereas fewer than 10 percent lived there in 1910. In addition, industrialists envisioned a growing black labor force as second-generation European immigrants, gaining enough upward mobility, would begin to shun industrial jobs. Thus, industrialists could no longer ignore the "race" question and consider it simply a southern problem.[3]

The decisive signal of this changing approach was the decision of the Carnegie Commission to fund a massive study on race in 1938. They chose Gunnar Myrdal to head this project, which had two major results. The Myrdal Report[4] undermined genetic notions of black inferiority which were pervasive. Instead, it proposed culture-of-poverty explanations which claimed that, through appropriate government policies and a reduction of discriminatory barriers, black Americans would in a generation or two become the equals of white Americans. Second, it reinvigorated the notion that reformist policies, led by the NAACP, would be sufficient to overcome discriminatory barriers faced by black Americans.

This new approach provided the backdrop for other legislative initiatives, which unfolded after World War II: the integration of the armed forces in 1948 and *Brown vs. Topeka Board of Education* in 1954. One of the most visible benchmarks of this changing landscape was the peaceful integration of baseball. As a result, it must be seen as one of the pillars constructed in the first decade after World War II, on which the later civil rights movement was constructed. Without minimizing its role in the sweep of the civil rights transformation, in many ways the integration of baseball had a more profound, lasting, and unexpected impact on the way economists have looked at the struggle for racial economic equality. Like other professional organizations during the early twentieth century, economics was marred by racist notions. The dominant positions in the profession held that both black

Americans and immigrants from southern and eastern Europe were inferior to native Americans of northern and western European descent. Virtually all the leading economists believed that black Americans were *genetically* inferior, though they were split about why the recent white immigrants were inferior. The "liberal" wing of the profession believed that cultural factors explained immigrants' inferiority, while the "conservative" wing believed that the newer immigrants were genetically inferior. The conservatives feared that continued unrestricted immigration would undermine the United States, and they characterized the pending doom as "race suicide." All the leading economics journals published articles presenting these viewpoints up through the early 1920s.[5]

During the 1930s, a growing antiracist movement took for granted that government intervention was necessary because capitalists benefited financially from racism. It claimed that by using racism to create divisiveness, capitalists weakened the ability of all workers to unite to form unions. Moreover, because of the persistent high unemployment among black workers, capitalists could use this reserve army as a constant threat against white workers. White workers would temper their demands because they implicitly knew that capitalists could replace them with black workers from the ranks of the unemployed.

The view that capitalism had a fundamental link to the persistence of racism was not accepted by corporate America, nor was the research they funded. Instead, Myrdal posited his "cumulative process" in which he adopted ideas that had been applied by the "liberal" wing of the economics profession to buttress their claims that the new immigrants were culturally not genetically inferior.

According to Myrdal, blacks were also culturally inferior and restrictive policies increased their dysfunctional behavior: laziness, reliance on criminal activities, and lax sexual mores. The growing dysfunctional behavior blacks exhibited, in turn, reinforced negative black stereotypes held by whites which only strengthened their support of racist policies. Thus, bigotry persisted because white racist attitudes were reinforced by the dysfunctional behavior blacks exhibited, not because of the capitalist profit motive.[6]

Despite Myrdal's protestations and further corporate funding to promote an alternative viewpoint, antiracist views that focused on benefits to corporations continued to enjoy broad support. It was not until Gary Becker's work that these antibusiness views began to wane. Becker[7] attempted to demonstrate that corporate profits are harmed when there are exclusionary employment clauses—when firms refuse to hire nonpreferred (black) workers. Since corporate profits are affected adversely, his pro-market model suggests that the natural workings of markets play a progressive role in the struggle against workplace discrimination. It suggests that antidiscrimination forces should ally themselves with forward-looking capitalists rather than the group of workers who are benefiting from the exclusionary barriers. Finally, this approach rejects the need for antidiscrimination legislation, such as affirmative action, since self-regulating mechanisms will be sufficient.

Becker's thesis is illustrated by a 1996 *National Review* article. Looking back at the integration of baseball in 1947, Steve Sailer emphasizes how the profit motive encouraged entrepreneurs to integrate baseball.

> Perhaps the least learned lesson of the saga of Jackie Robinson is that competition [among owners] can transform self-interest into an engine for racial fairness.... The integration of organized baseball *preceded* the civil rights revolution, and in reality baseball helped make later reforms politically feasible by giving white Americans black heroes with whom to identify.[8]

While Sailer recommends a laissez-faire policy with reliance on market mechanisms, he fears government agencies and unions. He contends,

> True, competition does restrain irrational [unprofitable] discrimination. But where competition is lacking—such as in government monopolies like police and fire departments, or in labor unions, which exist to negate competition—then quotas can sometimes be necessary to put a price on discrimination.

Are exclusionary employment practices against the interest of capitalists? Are profit-seeking capitalists the allies of antidiscrimination forces? Do unions and government cause discrimination to persist? This chapter will pursue these issues.

The Pro-Market Model

The pro-market model assumes that racist behavior arises from discriminatory attitudes—what Becker calls a preference for whites. Employers with these preferences weigh the psychic benefits from hiring additional white workers against any resulting productivity losses. Figure 22.1 helps illustrate this point. The marginal benefit (MB) schedule, indicates the psychic benefits from each additional white worker hired. This schedule is downward-sloping, indicating that each additional white worker hired provides somewhat less psychic benefits than the previous white workers. Eventually the employer has so many white workers that no further gains in psychic benefits from their further employment are possible. In Figure 22.1, this occurs when 95 percent of the firm's workforce are white workers. This

Figure 22.1 **The Pro-Market Theory of Discrimination**

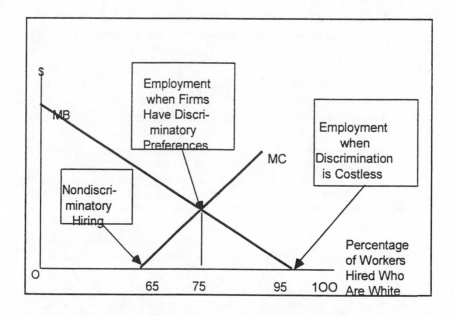

would be the employment decision if the firm could ignore the productivity of the workers hired and simply hire according to personal preferences.

When firms are profit-motivated, they must assess the productivity of their applicants. If they hire white workers when more qualified black workers are available, firms are sacrificing either some quality and/or some quantity of output. In Figure 22.1, this occurs after the firm's work force becomes more than 65 percent white. After that point, the firm incurs costs when hiring each additional white worker since it could have hired a more qualified black worker.

Let us assume that the firm is hiring 100 workers. The hypothetical data in Table 22.1 help us understand the marginal cost (MC) schedule. For example, the 63d-best white applicant has productivity equal to 84 units and the 37th-best black applicant has productivity equal to 74 units. As we go down the list of white applicants, productivity *declines*, since we are looking at successively *less* qualified applicants. As we go down the list of black applicants, productivity *rises*, since we are looking at successively *more* qualified applicants.

The most productive combination occurs when the firm hires 65 white and 35 black workers. At this point, the last black and the last white work-

Table 22.1

Comparing Productivity Among Applicants

White Applicants		Black Applicants	
Number	Productivity	Number	Productivity
63	84	37	74
64	82	36	77
65	80	35	80
66	78	34	83
67	76	33	86
68	74	32	89

ers hired each have the same productivity—80 units. Now suppose that the firm hires the 66th-best white worker instead of the 35th-best black worker. The 66th-best white worker's productivity equals 78 units while the 35th-best black worker's productivity equals 80 units. Thus, the hiring will cost the firm 2 units of output.

Table 22.1 illustrates why *each* additional white worker hired requires more productivity losses than the previous white worker hired. As the firm increases the share of its workforce which is white, it is hiring less and less qualified white workers by ignoring even more and more qualified black workers available. Now suppose that the firm hires the 67th-best white worker instead of the 34th-best black worker. The 67th-best white worker's productivity equals 76 units (2 less than the 66th-best white worker) while the 34th-black worker's productivity equals 83 units (3 more than the 35th-best black worker.) As a result, the hiring of this additional white worker will cost the firm 7 units of output. Thus, the marginal cost schedule, MC, in Figure 22.1 is upward sloping. While the firm suffers rising productivity losses for each additional discriminatory hiring, it will do so as long as the psychic benefits are greater. This occurs until the firm's workforce becomes 75 percent white. After that point, the psychic benefits from hiring additional white workers are no longer sufficient to compensate the firm for the additional productivity losses it would suffer. Thus, the firm finds it optimal to increase the white share of its workforce by 10 percentage points as a result of its discriminatory preferences.

Becker hypothesized that the profit losses from discriminatory hiring practices would depend upon industry structure. If the firm faced a less competitive environment, it could pass along to consumers a greater portion of the additional labor costs so that its profits would be less adversely

Figure 22.2 **Impact of Changing Market Structure**

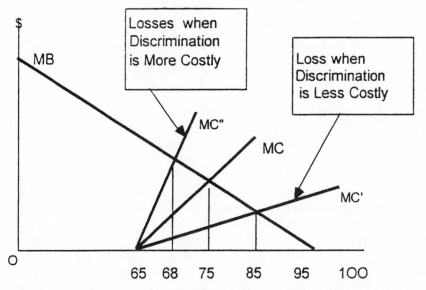

affected. With lower profit losses, the MC schedule shifts to MC ' in Figure 22.2, increasing white hirings to 85. Instead, if the firm faced a more competitive environment, it could only pass along to consumers a small portion of the additional labor costs so that its profits would be more adversely affected. With greater profit losses, the MC schedule shifts to MC " reducing white hirings to 68.

Becker and other conservatives have used this model to argue that the government is likely to be the most discriminating employer. The argument goes as follows. Since the government has no profit motive, it has no concern for productivity (i.e., MC = 0) and will hire solely on the basis of personal preferences. In Figures 22.1 and 22.2, this would result in the firm's employing a workforce that was 95 percent white. Conservatives point to the period prior to World War II when virtually no blacks were hired in a wide range of government occupations.

Since the civil rights acts of the 1960s, the government has disproportionately hired black workers. Between 1965 and 1982, 65 percent of all black professionals were hired by government and other nonprofit institutions. For many observers, this is evidence that the private sector had been slow to change its discriminatory policies. For many conservatives, however, there was an entirely different explanation: reverse discrimination. They argued that during this period, whites were politically passive, so that the demands of blacks and their liberal supporters were most pressing on politicians. As a result, the preference of the government shifted from favoring white to favoring black workers. Since its employment decisions are dominated by personal preferences rather than productivity concerns, the government began employing less qualified black workers.

The Baseball Industry

Conservatives like Sailer cite the experience in the baseball industry as evidence of the disciplining role of market forces. Though there was no civil rights legislation, by the early 1960s it seemed that competitive pressures had forced owners to integrate their baseball teams. Thus, at least within the mainstream of the economics profession, empirical evidence and the logic of the analysis were convincing; market forces would have eliminated exclusionary employment barriers.

Let us look more closely at the baseball example. Professional baseball was organized during the 1870s. A decade later, Cap Anson, a future Hall of Famer, refused to allow his team to play against black baseball players. In response, the major leagues became all-white. During the 1920s, with the popularity of Babe Ruth, baseball became the national pastime, and attendance and owners' incomes grew. As the pro-market model predicts, eventually the profit motive would encourage entrepreneurs to realize that they could increase their profit by integrating the baseball teams that they owned. In 1943, Bill Veeck wished to purchase weak teams and improve them by using black ballplayers. Sailer writes,

> Like all direct challenges, though, this was rebuffed by the autocratic Commissioner of Baseball, Judge Kenesaw Mountain Landis. After the Chicago Black Sox threw the 1919 World Series, the owners had restored faith in the game by appointing Landis, who was famed for his strict moral standards— one of which was Segregation Forever.[9]

After Landis' death in 1944, the new commissioner, "Happy" Chandler, refused to enforce any ban on black ballplayers, opening the way for profit-seeking owners. In 1947, the owner of the Brooklyn Dodgers, Branch Rickey, broke the color line in the National League by employing Jackie Robinson. When Veeck was able to purchase the Cleveland Indians in 1948, the color line was broken in the American League.

Table 22.2 summarizes the impact of integration on team performance. The average number of victories for each team during the years 1946–1949 is taken as a benchmark, since during this period integration had little impact on the competitiveness of teams. There are two measures of integration used: (1) the first year each team had a *starting* black player, and (2) the total number of starting positions each team filled with black players prior to 1960. Using

Table 22.2

Integration of Baseball

Team	Black Starters		Average Wins		
	First Year	1947–59	1946–49	1950–59	Difference
Milwaukee	1950	18	83.2	85.7	2.5
Brooklyn/Los Angeles	1947	27	92.0	91.6	− 0.4
New York/San Francisco	1950	22	75.8	81.8	6.0
Chicago—American League	1950	24	64.4	87.4	23.0
Cleveland	1948	25	85.2	90.2	5.0
Average					7.2
St. Louis	1958	2	88.0	77.7	−11.1
Philadelphia	1957	1	73.8	75.1	1.3
Washington	—	0	62.6	63.7	1.1
Detroit	—	0	87.4	71.4	−16.0
Boston	—	0	94.6	80.0	−14.6
New York	1959	2	94.6	94.1	− 0.5
Average					− 6.6
Pittsburgh	1955	6	67.2	63.2	− 4.0
Cincinnati	1956	7	66.4	75.0	8.6
Chicago—National League	1954	12	68.0	67.6	− 0.4
Baltimore	1955	5	59.2	63.8	4.6
Kansas City	1954	8	68.8	63.6	− 5.2
Average					0.9

either of these criteria, teams fell into three groups: those that were rapidly and strongly integrated, those that were delayed and modestly integrated, and those that had not really begun integration by 1959. For example, Cincinnati belonged to the middle group because it did not have its first starting black player until 1956 and used black players to fill only six starting positions before 1960.

According to the pro-market model, integration should have improved team performance since some black players available were better than some white players. Teams that remained segregated would be less productive and not perform as well. This expectation is confirmed by the data in Table 22.2. Teams which integrated rapidly averaged 7.2 *more* wins per year during the 1950s than during the benchmark years. In contrast, teams that were not meaningfully integrated by 1959 averaged 6.6 *fewer* wins yearly during the 1950s than during the benchmark years.

One might ask why the pace of integration was relatively slow. Why were there still a number of teams that had not integrated more than a decade after Jackie Robinson broke the color line? Pro-market theory suggests that it was because the profit motive was weak. Since team revenues and costs were quite low, winning or losing resulted in only small profit differences. Unlike Rickey and Veeck, most owners had made their fortunes elsewhere and considered baseball a hobby. They could easily afford to accept small financial losses so that they could hire according to their personal preferences.

In the 1960s, television increased salaries and potential revenues to owners. This increased dramatically the gains from having a winning team and the losses from having a losing one. No longer could owners afford to treat their teams as personal hobbies. Owners could maintain discriminatory preferences in their purely social activities, but they could no longer afford to act on them when employing ballplayers. By the mid-1960s all baseball teams were strongly integrated.

Alternative Assessments

Critics contend that, in conflict with the pro-market model, antiblack exclusionary policies persist in some government agencies, most prominently the Federal Bureau of Investigation (FBI).[10] Second, critics claim that the pro-market model minimizes the extent to which noncompetitive environments exist in the private sector. Critics look at the oil industry as an example of the persistence of exclusionary policies in the private sector and suggest that this phenomenon is quite prevalent. For this reason, this section begins by looking at the employment policies of Texaco and the FBI, where discrimination against nonwhite workers seems to persist more than twenty years after civil rights legislation was enacted.

Though these examples are not trivial, criticisms of the pro-market model generally focus on demonstrating that, even in competitive industries, many profit-motivated corporations still maintain exclusionary barriers. First, the cost of discrimination for these firms might be quite small so that market forces have a meager disciplining effect on their behavior. This is especially likely if there is a substantial cost to gathering productivity information on applicants. Second, there may be indirect benefits received by discriminating firms which more than offset the direct costs they bear. Finally, while acting individually they might suffer financial losses, at a broader level, all capitalists might benefit from exclusionary barriers if they sufficiently divide and weaken the political strength of the working class.

Texaco and the FBI

Civil rights advocates generally reject any notion that black government employment in recent years reflects discriminatory practices. Indeed, they note that a number of government agencies have continued to have limited nonwhite employment. In 1989, while 9 percent of FBI employees were black, only one of its field offices (Puerto Rico) was headed by a black and fewer than 2 percent of senior officers were black. In 1990, the FBI had to settle a class-action law suit with three hundred veteran black agents who were judged by a federal court to have been systematically denied promotions.

The most glaring example of abuse was the experience of Donald Rochon. A veteran of the Los Angeles police force, Rochon took a pay cut to join the FBI in 1983. At the Omaha office, he was subjected to numerous racist actions. For example, fellow agents destroyed a family photograph on his desk by taping a picture of an ape's head over his son's face. His supervisor told investigators that these pranks were "healthy" and a sign of an "esprit de corps." After Rochon transferred to the Chicago office, the harassment intensified. An agent forged Mr. Rochon's signature and handwriting on forms for two insurance polices in 1985, one for death and dismemberment coverage, the other for burial costs. When the FBI was forced to act after finding out the identity of the harassing officer, it decided that a fourteen-day suspension without pay was sufficient punishment. In response, white agents in the Chicago office chipped in to pay the penalized officer's salary for the two weeks. Recalling a three-year campaign of harassment by fellow agents, Mr. Rochon stated, "I couldn't believe this was happening. It was like I was in a time machine, and someone had turned the clock back from the 1980s to the 1950s."[11]

In 1990, Latino employees won a similar lawsuit against the FBI. Texas Federal District Judge Lucius Bunton found that "Hispanic agents tended to receive assignments that demanded Spanish language skills and offered no opportunity for career advancement." Rather than contest the ruling, FBI director William Sessions said, "Each of the 11 agents will be promoted to a position which best serves their needs and the needs of the FBI." Only 15 of the nearly 100 veteran Latino agents eligible to file did so, because of feared retaliation by non-Latino supervisors. "Listen, I might have gotten a promotion out of it, but they might have promoted me to Timbuktu as a form of punishment," said a Latino agent. "I wasn't going to risk that."[12]

Civil rights advocates also reject the claim that industries are generally competitive enough for the profit motive to be relied upon to eliminate discriminatory hiring practices. They note the persistence of employment discrimination in the oil industry. In 1996, Texaco was forced to settle a class-action lawsuit, agreeing to pay $176 million to its 1,400 black employees. The lawsuit noted that, due to the hostile environment, the percentage of black employees at Texaco fell from 9.8 to 8.3 percent between 1984 and 1995, and that blacks never represented more than 3.75 percent of its management staff. It was also noted that not one of the five hundred most senior oil industry executives is either black or Latino.[13]

Recent Texaco policies mirror its previous policies toward Jews. While there has been some improvement since the mid-1980s, the oil companies had the same exclusionary policies with respect to Jews. In a survey of the six major oil companies done in 1978, only 5 of the 300 top executives were Jewish. The study by Gissen[14] concluded that this resulted from "recruitment avoidance, promotion levels beyond which Jews cannot go, nonassignment to certain job areas, and stereotyped employment (i.e. in such departments as legal, accounting, and research)."

These findings were consistent with employment in many other industries dominated by a few large firms. For example, one 1970s study[15] did not find a single Jew among the 176 senior executives of the fifteen largest U.S. commercial banks, eight of which were headquartered in New York City. Even at middle-level management, there were only fourteen Jews out of 1,757 executives. A decade later, Simon Rifkin, a longtime Jewish leader and corporate director, still contended: "Jews have traditionally been successful bankers and yet if you look at most of the commercial banks you will not find a Jewish name at all. . . . The same is true of insurance companies. I would say the same is true of the bigger corporations."[16]

Slavin and Pradt[17] surveyed 1972–1973 recruitment patterns of major corporations. They document the recruitment avoidance mentioned in the Gissen study. They found a wide disparity between corporate interviewing at colleges with low Jewish enrollment and similar colleges with high Jewish enrollment. While corporations in the Fortune 500 made a total of more than 40 visits a year to colleges with a Jewish enrollment of less than 20 percent, they averaged less than 20 visits to comparable colleges with Jewish enrollment of more than 30 percent.

Limited Costs from Discrimination

In the pro-market model, firms suffer productivity losses because they could have hired more skilled black workers. These productivity losses are substantial in some occupations, like professional athletes. In baseball, there are starting center fielders who have a .250 batting average and hit only 3 home runs while others have a .300 batting average and hit 30 home runs. With *substantial* productivity differentials, it would be quite costly to hire on the basis of personal preferences. In these occupations, firms find it cost-effective to invest extensively in screening applicants. In baseball, this is reflected by the substantial scouting expenses incurred, as well as the funds allocated for fielding minor league teams. Thus, it is not surprising that once television revenues transformed baseball from a hobby to a business, owners were disciplined to separate their personal preferences from their business decisions in hiring players.

When there are small productivity differentials, however, they might not be sufficient to force owners to hire employers in a nondiscriminatory manner. Within baseball, we can distinguish between the employment of athletes and nonathletes—managers, coaches, and office personnel. Gerald Scully states,

> As blacks came to dominate professional team sports and earned handsome salaries, complaints of racism seemed ungracious. Nevertheless, it remains a fact that blacks largely have been confined to the playing field. Baseball has taken on the appearance of a white man's game which employs well-paid black gladiators.[18]

In 1987, looking at both the major and the minor leagues, there were only 75 blacks or Latinos employed in nonathletic position. After highly publicized racist remarks by a baseball executive, Commissioner of Baseball Peter Ueberroth prodded an additional 180 black and Latino hirings within the next year. However, virtually all these hirings were low level; few were to decision-making positions. Even after these affirmative action hirings, Scully notes,

> Of the 130 coaching positions, minorities hold a total of 16. There are no black trainers. There is no black umpire in the American League, and only six in the minors. . . . [Despite the urging by] Peter Ueberroth . . . to hire blacks as field managers and general managers [when] clubs appointed 13 new managers, general managers, and presidents, none were black.[19]

Though there has been modest improvement in the last decade, blacks and Latinos are still underrepresented in nonathletic positions within the baseball industry.

Even the relatively modest gains in baseball cannot be necessarily transposed to other professional athletes. In particular, arrangements in professional football reduce the financial benefits gained by having an improved team. Unlike baseball, there is only one television contract, which is negotiated collectively by the National Football League. As a result, each individual team receives the same television revenues regardless of its performance. For many years, this had the effect of muting concern for performance and there were many incidents when teams let go of superior athletes because of alleged "attitude" problems. Moreover, scouting was not as intense so that black players from smaller colleges were not as likely to gain employment as white players from football powerhouses. As a result, discrimination against black football players persisted long after it had ended in baseball. Only during the last decade, with the emergence of luxury box seats and sale of merchandise by individual teams, have the financial incentives to have a winning team become decisive.[20]

The football situation reinforces another aspect of the role of the profit motive. The owner of the Oakland Raiders, Al Davis, was able to field championship NFL teams during the period 1970–1985. Much of his success reflected a willingness to employ players with "attitude" problems who were cast off from other franchises. One possible explanation for this was that Davis, unlike most of the other football owners, had no outside sources of income. He was not a millionaire who had bought a football team as a "hobby." For him, the modest financial incentives of having a winning team were essential, whereas for many other owners, they were not. In this regard, Davis parallels Branch Rickey in Brooklyn and Bill Veeck in Cleveland, demonstrating that the profit motive is stronger for those who have a greater financial stake in the income generated from the sports enterprises they own. Once, however, financial incentives from winning increased for other football owners, Davis lost his edge. As a result, since the mid-1980s, Davis's team has not been able to maintain its excellence and has lost most of its "mystique."

In most employment situations, firms perceive their applicant pool as containing individuals whose skills are not dramatically different. Yes, there will be some truly exceptional talents, but at the margin, the difference between the last applicant hired and the last applicant not hired may be quite small. This may very well be the situation in professional sports for most nonathletic positions: coaches, trainers, umpires, and so on. This may explain why, even after forty years of integration, there was still substantial discrimination in baseball hirings for these positions. Thus, only in a small number of occupations in which productivity differentials are large will the profit motive discipline employers to separate their personal preferences from their hiring decisions.

Indirect Benefits

Women and black men continue to be disproportionately employed in lower-waged occupations. Studies also show that, within occupations, women and blacks have the least desirable jobs. Barbara Bergmann[21] has claimed that this disparity reflects exclusionary policies. She has argued that when firms exclude women and black men from desirable high-waged positions, these workers adapt. They shift their employment to less desirable occupations and firms. Thus, discriminated workers are "crowded" into undesirable jobs, increasing labor supply and, as a result, causing wages and working conditions to deteriorate.

The crowding model suggests that there are two different firms. Those "primary" firms, hiring workers for desirable jobs, which have exclusionary barriers and "secondary" firms which hire workers for less desirable jobs. It certainly follows that "secondary" capitalists benefit financially from the adaptation of nonpreferred workers. Let us now identify the way in which "primary" capitalists may also benefit indirectly from this crowding process.

First, it is inaccurate to make a dichotomy between primary and secondary capitalists. All firms have some desirable and some undesirable jobs. Firms that hire professionals also hire workers to be secretaries and janitors. As a result, the crowding model suggests that firms that exclude some workers from professional and managerial employment are compensated somewhat by the lower wages and the better-quality employees they can obtain from other employment categories. A simple example will illustrate this relationship.

Law firms do not hire only lawyers. They also hire paralegals and legal secretaries. For many years, major law firms had exclusionary barriers, refusing to hire female lawyers. This barrier caused many women who wished to enter law to adapt their career aspirations. Many of them reluctantly shifted to becoming paralegals and legal secretaries. Thus, law firms benefited indirectly by having somewhat better-qualified (and somewhat lower-paid) support service workers.

Exclusionary barriers can also create situations in which firms can hire nonpreferred workers into a lower track where the work is essentially equivalent but the pay and conditions are inferior to those of employees in the preferred track. The ability of capitalists to place black workers in secondary tracks within their companies was illustrated by the hiring practices of Henry Ford. During the 1930s, Henry Ford was the only automobile manufacturer who hired black workers. In his River Rouge plant, the largest automobile assembly plant in the world, black workers comprised 12 percent of the workforce. Within the automobile plants, however, some jobs were much less desirable, such as foundry work. It was to these positions that black workers were assigned. Thus, exclusionary policies indirectly benefited Ford since he was able to hire qualified workers for the most undesirable jobs.

Among law firms, once women were employed, a dual track developed. Sometimes called the "mommy track," it reflected inferior positions. In the main track, employees would have higher bonuses and the possibility of promotion to partner. In the mommy track, the number of hours worked was somewhat less demanding, enabling women to more easily balance career and family. While this reduced the number of female partners, potentially robbing the firm of some of its best managerial talent, it also reduced employment costs.

Even when firms do not employ those who adapt to exclusionary policies, they still might benefit indirectly. For example, suppose a firm has volatile demand. If it relied on its own internal production, the firm would have periods in which workers would have substantial overtime and other times when it would have high labor costs, resulting from maintaining employment when production is low. As an alternative, the firm can maintain stable employment and production in its own plants, staffed by primarily white male workers, and can outsource the volatile portion of its demand to contracting firms, staffed by white women and nonwhite workers. In addition, the firm might choose to purchase some of its inputs from firms in the secondary market that employ white women and nonwhite workers. Since these contracting and input-supplying firms are generally in competition environments, their lower labor costs cause them to lower their prices rather than raise their profits. As a result, it is the primary firms that benefit from the lowered labor costs in these secondary firms.

Divide-and-Conquer Strategies

Racial divisions foment and solidify divisions within the working class. These divisions can be beneficial to corporations in a number of ways. First, they may weaken the ability of workers to unite to form unions, enabling firms to keep wages down and profits up. For example, just after World War I, northern capitalists used blacks as strikebreakers to undermine union struggles. This culminated in race riots in the Chicago and St. Louis areas, where white workers invaded black areas. As a result, white workers' energies were sapped fighting black workers and capitalists were able to decimate a union movement.

Michael Reich[22] tested the hypothesis that racial unity impacts adversely on the income of capitalists. For income going to capitalists, he used the share of income in each area going to the richest 5 percent of households. For a measure of racial unity, he used the ratio of black to white family income in each area. Reich reasoned that the smaller the income gap, the more likely black and white families would be to find common grounds on which to unite.

Reich used regression analysis to demonstrate that this relationship was statistically significant. His results held even when he included other factors which might explain variations in the share of income going to capitalists

Figure 22.3 **Pattern of Taxation, 1969–1991**

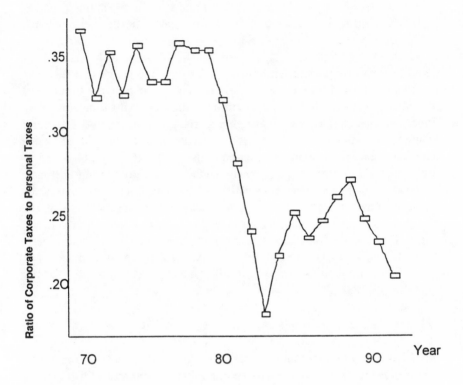

among areas. Moreover, just as the divide-and-conquer model would pre-
dict, Reich also found a statistically significant relationship between the
percentage of workers unionized and the degree of racial unity. In metropol-
itan areas where there was a greater degree of racial unity, there was also a
higher percentage of unionized workers.

Second, a racially divided working class is less able to defend social
spending programs. When spending on social services declines, so do the
taxes paid by upper-income households. This has clearly been the pattern
since 1980. The tax rate for households with income over $250,000 fell
from 90 percent in 1980 to 36 percent by 1986. It fell even further in 1997,
when legislation reduced the tax on capital gains from 32 to 18 percent.

In addition, corporations have been able to avoid federal taxation. Figure
22.3 indicates that, for most of the 1970s, corporate taxes were about one-
third the level of personal taxes. At the end of the 1970s, however, tax
changes began which lowered corporate taxes dramatically, so that by 1990,
federal corporate taxes were only one-fifth as much as personal taxes.

Finally, and maybe most importantly, racial divisions enable capitalists to scapegoat black Americans as the cause of social ills, deflecting the anger felt by white workers and their families away from the wealth-owning class. During the 1980s, there was a dramatic decline in the earnings and employment of adult men. For example, between 1979 and 1989, after adjusting for inflation, the usual weekly wage of the median male worker fell by 4 percent. For the male worker who was at the 25th percentile, the real wage fell by 11 percent. In addition, employment became more uncertain. The share of adult men who worked full-time in at least eight years fell from 79 percent for the period 1970–1979 to 70 percent for the period 1980–1989. The decline was even more dramatic for those with less education. Among high school graduates the decline was from 84 to 72 percent; among high school dropouts, from 52 to 30 percent.[23]

The resulting anger among male workers might have led to a united working-class movement to confront corporate greed. Instead, much of the white male anger was deflected to various scapegoats: foreigners, women, and blacks. In the 1988 presidential campaign, ideology was harnessed to shift concerns to black criminality, typified by a Willie Horton ad that focused on the perceived lenient treatment of convicted felons. During the 1992 presidential campaign, there was an attempt to shift concern to the perceived undermining of family values by feminists, typified by Dan Quayle's attack on Murphy Brown, a character in a TV situation comedy, for glorifying unwed mothers. During the 1996 campaign, the scapegoats became affirmative action beneficiaries and immigrants, typified by support for California initiatives to end affirmative action programs and to withhold government benefits from immigrants. Meanwhile corporate taxes continued to decline, working-class wages continued to stagnate, and capital gains tax reforms to benefit the richest households were promoted.

Concluding Remarks

The integration of baseball in 1947 must be seen in the context of the struggle against bigotry begun in the previous decade. This struggle required the heroic actions of individuals and antiracist organizations; without their efforts the gains would not have occurred. This chapter has indicated that while these efforts were necessary, their success was aided by the fact that elite industrialists did not have an economic stake in the perpetuation of racial exclusionary barriers.

Conservatives, however, have inflated the importance of these financial considerations. Though there were economic as well as political reasons for industrialists to favor integration, it is an exaggeration to claim that the profit motive alone would have been sufficient to eliminate racial exclusionary policies. After all, Jim Crow existed for seventy years in the South, though it was presumably against the interest of capitalists. Even when capitalists did begin to move away from accommodating exclusionary policies in the South in the late 1950s, their efforts were timid and limited. It was the actions of a militant antiracist movement, not simply the profit motive, which led to the 1964 Civil Rights Act overturning southern exclusionary policies.[24]

The reason the profit motive is not sufficient is simple. In only rare cases are the costs of discriminatory hiring practices sufficient to discipline owners. Often firms are in noncompetitive markets so that they can pass along the costs of their discriminatory behavior to consumers. In addition, firms are generally hiring in situations where there are only small productivity differences among their applicants, so that there is little cost if they hire according to personal preferences. Finally, firms may actually benefit from a discriminatory hiring environment since it may lower the cost of inputs they purchase or lower corporate taxes and labor costs by creating divisions within the working class. Thus, it would be foolish to rely on market forces if we truly desire fairness to triumph over bigotry in the workplace.

Notes

1. For a discussion of the role of the U.S. Communist Party in the Scottsboro case, see Hugh Murray, "The NAACP Versus the Communist Party: The Scottsboro Rape Cases, 1931-1932," in *Negro in Depression and War, 1930-1945,* ed. Bernard Sternsher (Chicago: Quadrangle Books, 1969), pp. 267-281. For general acceptance of communists, see St. Clair Drake and Horace Cayton, *The Black Metropolis* (New York: Harcourt and Brace, 1945).

2. For a history of the importance of genetic theories of racial inferiority and its relationship to Nazi theories, see John Higham, *Strangers in the Land* (New York: Atheneum, 1963); and Allan Chase, *The Legacy of Malthus* (New York: Alfred A. Knopf, 1977).

3. For a discussion of the growth in the size of the northern black population after World War I, see Gavin Wright, *Old South, New South* (New York: Basic Books, 1986).

4. Gunnar Myrdal, *An American Dilemma* (New York: Harper and Row, 1944).

5. For a detailed discussion of racial thought in the early economics profession, see Robert Cherry, "Racial Thought and the Early Economics Profession," *Review of Social Economy* 33 (October 1976), pp. 147-162.

6. For a detailed discussion of the origins of the culture-of-poverty thesis in the Myrdal Report, see Robert Cherry, "The Culture of Poverty Thesis and African Americans: The Views of Gunnar Myrdal and Other Institutionalists," *Journal of Economic Issues* 29 (December 1995): 1-14.

7. Gary Becker, *The Economics of Discrimination* (Chicago: University of Chicago Press, 1957).

8. Steve Sailer, "How Jackie Robinson Desegregated America." *National Review*

97 (8 April 1996), p. 38.

9. Ibid., p. 39.

10. Similar claims have been made concerning the Corps of Engineers; see Bob Herbert, "Bias Intensified by Inertia," *New York Times,* 14 January 1997, p. A24.

11. Phillip Shenon, "Black FBI Agent's Ordeal," *New York Times,* 25 January 1988, p. A1.

12. Phillip Shenon, "FBI to Promote 11 Hispanic Agents in Bias Case," *New York Times,* 20 September 1990, p. B4.

13. Series on Texaco by Peter Frisch and Allamma Sullivan, *Wall Street Journal,* 5 November 1996, p. B10; 11 November 1996, p. A3; 12 November 1996, p. A3.

14. Ira Gissen, "A Study of Jewish Employment Problems in the Big Six Oil Company Headquarters," *Rights* 9 (1978): 3.

15. American Jewish Committee, *Summary of Report on First Fifteen Banks* (New York: American Jewish Committee, 1973), p. 73.

16. Richard Zweigenhalf, "Recent Patterns of Jewish Representation in the Corporate and Social Elites," *Contemporary Jewry* 6 (1982), p. 42.

17. Stephen Slavin and Mary Pradt, *The Einstein Syndrome: Corporate Anti-Semitism in America Today* (Washington, DC: University Press of America, 1982).

18. Gerald Scully, *The Business of Major League Baseball* (Chicago: University of Chicago Press, 1989), p. 171.

19. Ibid., p. 172.

20. As with baseball, discrimination against nonwhites continues with respect to the hiring of nonplayer personnel. In 1997, ten new head football coaches were hired in the NFL; not one was nonwhite. This despite the fact that 65 percent of NFL football players and 35 percent of NFL assistant coaches are nonwhite.

21. Barbara Bergmann, *The Economic Emergence of Women* (New York: Basic Books, 1986).

22. Michael Reich, *Racial Inequality* (Princeton: Princeton University Press, 1981).

23. Lawrence Mishel, *The State of Working America* (Armonk, NY: M.E. Sharpe, 1997).

24. For further discussion on the attitude of capitalists on ending Jim Crow, see Wright, *Old South, New South,* and Robert Cherry, "Race and Gender in Radical Macroeconomic Models: The Case of the Social Structure of Accumulation Model," *Science and Society* 55 (Summer 1992), p. 60-78.

Part VII

Thank You, Jackie Robinson

Before discussing this final part of the book, it should be noted that the two chapters in it are transcripts of oral presentations given at the conference. Carl Erskine's speech was delivered via videotape and Roger Rosenblatt's was an extemporaneous keynote address subsequently converted to print from an audiotape. Thus, oddities of syntax or punctuation reflect the editors' decisions to capture the nuances of voice and expression and should not be construed as inattentiveness on the part of these two esteemed speakers.

Jackie Robinson, in Roger Rosenblatt's words, "turned an upside-down nation right side up." America's solution to its race problem differed from other nations because, as Rosenblatt cites Jackie Robinson, "It could not be a losing fight when it took place in a free society." Carl Erskine, a teammate of Robinson, delivered a talk which the reader may connect to the theme of the ripple effect raised in Part V. Erskine openly suggests that what Jackie Robinson started in this country was not only the concept of integration, but also that of inclusion. By way of example, Erskine introduces us to his own son, a champion of the Special Olympics. The most eloquent expression of Jackie Robinson's legacy may be the one offered by Erskine: "He really impacted America on social issues. . . . He caused America to reconnect itself to honor."

Thank you, Jackie Robinson.

23

Greetings

Carl Erskine

Well, hello, friends. Nice to see you today. Do you notice that I'm wearing my famous Brooklyn Dodgers cap with the famous "B?" The "B" reminds me that there will always be a Brooklyn where we had loyal supporters and wonderful friends. Brooklyn has a great history and I remember ten great seasons with the Brooklyn Dodgers. I want to tell you about my good friend and teammate of nine seasons: Jackie Robinson. Maybe I see Jackie differently. You say he broke the color line. But I say he didn't break anything. Jackie was a healer. He came to rectify a wrong, to heal a sore in America. He did a lot in that direction.

Jackie and I shared one strong thing. We both were raised by parents who instilled in us the dignity of individuals regardless of where they came from. We had a common bond. I would say to some people's surprise that Jackie was not a man of color. By that I mean he could have been a yellow man, a red man, a Scotsman, Irishman. He was for social justice for everybody.

The stage of baseball was perfect. The bright light of major leagues in the 1940s was a vehicle for affirmative action that Jackie showed in its purest form, the way it works the best. When Jack took the field, he got the opportunity that all in America should have. He did not have any help on the field. His mother, his beautiful wife Rachel, who helped him off the field, could not help him. When the ball was hit, he had to field it. Mr. Rickey could not help him. Jackie hit it; he threw it; he outran it; and he proved it. That's why he was accepted so quickly in baseball. The social side took a lot longer. And I have a feeling it's not there yet.

He was a special friend. He initiated our friendship. In 1948, I was a kid pitcher with Fort Worth, a Double A Dodger farm team. The big team, the Dodgers, were in town for an exhibition game. I started and pitched well even though we lost. After the game, Jackie Robinson came over to our bench. He said, "Young man, I hit against you today. I just want to tell you. With that stuff, you're not going to be in this league for very long." What a thrill! Later in the 1948 season, I was called up to the Brooklyn Dodgers. At Forbes Field in Pittsburgh, the first player to greet me was Jackie Robinson, who put out his hand and said, "I told you so. You couldn't miss." He reached out to me in friendship. And he still wasn't staying in the same hotels.

Later in my career, I had a lot of arm trouble. I was older. Jackie was older. He played third base. One Saturday afternoon, an article in a newspaper carried a report by a New York Giant scout stating that we were too old. Jackie's too old; Campy's too old. It also said that Erskine can't win with the garbage that he's throwing. In the game that day, Jackie made a great stop on a ball hit by Willie Mays. It saved a game which turned out to be a no-hitter. After the game, Jackie rushed to the Giants' dugout. With his usual intensity, he took the article out of his back pocket. Pointing to the scout on the Giants' bench, he waved the article and shouted, "How about that garbage?"

He was intense, too intense sometimes. Man, he was after you. Jackie was intense about social injustice too. He felt that change was too slow. Jackie Robinson wrote a book, *Wait till Next Year.* "I have only one life," he wrote, "to right wrongs." He really impacted America on social issues. He opened minds. He opened hearts. He could not wait. He caused America to reconnect itself to honor.

I want you to meet my son and my buddy, Jimmy. After . . . three healthy children, my fourth child, Jimmy, was born in 1960. The world was quite different then. Diagnosed as a mongoloid (remember those harsh terms?), he faced taboos and misunderstandings. Shut away. Misunderstood, mistreated, separated from society, many children like Jimmy suffered. In our lifetime, we have experienced tremendous change. He used to get "double takes" in public. For centuries, folks like Jimmy were shut away. Now, people come over in airports. Jimmy is so well received—even in Dodgertown during spring training. They see Jimmy as a Down's person. He is lovable and responsive. Along came special education. Jimmy attended school. He participated in Special Olympics. He excelled in swimming, bowling, track and field. At Indiana State University, Jimmy was pulled out of the water and hauled onto the stand and granted this Special Olympic gold medal.

Jackie's momentum is in that. Because of him, minds were opened, hearts were opened. He let people see what was right, what was just. He could not wait. He was intense, too intense. But thanks to him, people began to look around. I am wearing a World Series ring, the only one in Brooklyn in seventy-five years. I am proud of this ring. What a symbol! Jackie helped me get this ring. Jackie helped Jimmy get this medal. I think that's the contribution.

[Tearfully] Jackie's momentum lives. So I thank you for honoring Jackie Robinson. It's a wonderful tribute to baseball that [it] gave Jackie a stage. He pulled America out of deep and troubled waters. It's bigger than baseball, bigger than his own race. I feel it. America feels it. So I thank you for honoring Jackie. Thanks to you and God bless you.

24

Keynote Address

Roger Rosenblatt

This is my idea of an academic conference. I don't know where I get the authority to talk about Jackie Robinson. I did meet him once. I was renting a tuxedo when I was getting married. He was renting a tuxedo for some event. I was twenty-two. You see him and you lose all language, composure and everything else. And you feel like a jerk getting married anyway. But I mustered the courage and I went up and just talked to him. And I thought: It will never happen. I'll never be a man. That's a man!

And I have very little authority to talk about baseball. I was a pitcher in high school. My fastball was so slow that in my first varsity game, in the first inning, I hit a guy in the head. And I saw him trembling. He was holding his head. I went off the mound to see if he was OK until I saw he was laughing.

I have trouble with authority generally. A number of years ago, I moved my family up to Vermont for a year, for a year's rustication—mostly talk to woodchucks. Soon I wanted to get back to the city very much. I got a call from *Time* magazine to come work for them. I was really eager, but I didn't want to show it because I know that's always a mistake when one seeks a job. I drove down to New York for the interview. The editor of *Time* magazine was Ray Cave, a dour fellow, who looked like Captain Ahab. He also had the same sense of humor as Captain Ahab. So I talked to him. The salary was fine. Everything was fine. But in order to show him that I had some authority, that I wasn't just a rube, I said to him, "Wellll," my voice cracking because I was about to tell a lie, "Well, I'm used to four weeks vacation!" Now this was both true and not true. When I worked for the *Washington Post,* I got three weeks vacation, but I taught in a university before that and I got three months. So, I figured the whole thing averaged out. I look at him. He looks at me. I could tell that he could tell that he was dealing with a man of real authority. Finally, after the right pause, he says, "Fine, Roger. We ordinarily start with five weeks."

Authority or no, I am grateful, very grateful, for the invitation to be here, especially since I'm a lifelong Yankee fan. I've already gotten into five arguments this morning of the sort that I haven't enjoyed in twenty-five years. We all know how good that feels. I don't want to dwell on that. I don't really hate the sight of Johnny Podres. I'm just glad he's old! So to say a few things to Dodger fans, just to let you know nothing dies, I will give you the answers to settle a number of disputes.

The first answer is: five out of six! [Boos from the audience] Thank you!

The second: 1955 was a fluke!

The third answer which you will really love is: Mantle.

And finally, fret not Ralph Branca. After that terrible shot, we creamed the Giants.

But enough good will. The Dodger-Giant rivalry was much more severe. I remember Duke Snider saying that he so hated the Giants, whose colors were orange and black, that the whole Dodger team came to hate Halloween.

Roger Kahn tells this story. March 1946, exhibition game, Montreal Royals versus Indianapolis in Deland, Florida. As Jackie Robinson slid across home plate in the first inning, a local cop runs out on the field. Here is Roger Kahn:

> "Get off the field right now. I'm putting you in jail." Robinson claims that his first reaction was to laugh, so ludicrous did the situation seem. But he did not laugh. THEN, as always in the South, Robinson had attracted a huge crowd. And the crowd rose to its feet. The Indianapolis players stood stark still, watching. Then, Jackie turned and walked toward the dugout. And Clay Hopper [manager of the Montreal Royals] emerged from it.
> "What's wrong?" Hopper asked.
> "Ask the cop."
> The policeman: "We ain't having Negras and white boys mix in this town," the cop said. "You can't change our way of livin'! Negras and whites: they can't sit together. They can't play together. And you know damn well, they can't get married together!"[Not on the field, anyway.]

Fifty years later, we tend to laugh at this story. But fifty years ago only

Robinson felt the urge to laugh. And this is noteworthy. We celebrate fifty years of Jackie Robinson as the victory over . . . what? I suggest that it was the victory over absurdity, a victory over the ridiculous, over the ludicrous—that was in fact real.

The African-American experience in America has been terrible, shameful, a sin; but basically it has been absurd. It is the cop running out on the field, claiming nonsense, doing nonsense, and prevailing. If it weren't lethal—things like the Ku Klux Klan—it would be funny: murderous idiots dressed up in sheets calling each other wizards, doing deadly things.

So what we're celebrating in part is this. When Jackie Robinson played major league baseball, he turned an upside-down nation right side up. This is what black heroes have always done simply by being themselves. But it is hard because America often insists on remaining upside down and on making those who are right side up feel upside down. I give you an example from Richard Wright, the great black novelist, the author of *Native Son*. In his autobiography, *Black Boy*, he tells this story. As a young man in Memphis, he was working in an eyeglass factory, grinding glasses. And the white superior wanted to provoke a fight between Wright and Harrison, a black co-worker, who he said held a grudge against Wright. There was no grudge. No fight materialized. The white superior was disappointed. He persisted. "Settle your grudge in a boxing match. We'll pay you five bucks apiece." A lot of money in those days. Wright and Harrison decided to take the money and pull their punches.

The following afternoon, in front of an all-white crowd of men, they put on gloves. They start boxing. One jabs. The other jabs harder. One draws blood. The other retaliates. By the end of the fight, they beat each other senseless. They would not speak to each other afterward. Shamed, they had made the illogical, logical. They lived the lie. They were thrown into absurdity, encouraged by a world upside down.

African-American heroes in fiction sin in order to get salvation, die in order to live, murder in order to create. Take Ralph Ellison's *Invisible Man*. A senior in high school sits on stage, number 1 in his class. All the students are black, and are sitting next to a naked blonde white woman. They are wearing boxing gloves, as this is a battle royale. They hit each other. They knock each other silly. The white audience laughs. The invisible man emerges with a briefcase and an envelope. The letter reads, "To whom it may concern: Keep this nigger boy running."

Madness. Madness.

Leroi Jones, before he changed his name to Baraka, wrote that the black man in America is like a person kept in a one-room prison of a very large house. When he emerges from that one room, he knows the whole house.

The whites do not. Enter Jackie Robinson to show us the whole house. He ended the virulent nonsense of baseball's color line, and he was aided by fellow players like Pee Wee Reese, reporters like Marty Glickman, Stan Isaacs, Dick Schaap. The picture of the man that emerges is both unique and typical. He is an African-American everyman. He endures. He is asked to endure because without endurance nothing happens. Imagine a pitcher with a fastball. Picture it coming at your head, one hundred miles per hour. You hit the dirt, but you have to get up. They throw a black cat on the field. "Is that your relative, Jackie?" I suppose that's their idea of wit. He takes it.

Then [in 1949] he becomes the rebel. He begins to scowl, though he was never the scowler Bob Gibson was. There's the story about Gibson when he loaded the bases and Cardinal first baseman Bill White approached the mound to encourage the pitcher. Gibson told White to get back to first, barking, "The only thing you know about pitching is that you can't hit it!"

Always the fighter, Jackie Robinson fought the press. He instructed a journalist [Dick Young], "If you can't tell the truth, don't write." Imagine that. We'd be out of business in twenty minutes!

A base stealer, he stole home nineteen times. Not only that. He rattled the pitcher. His running style, crab-like, shoulders go up with tremendous speed not unlike Mantle, also an ex-football player. The stealer breaks the rules within the rules. That is the beauty of baseball. Rookie of the Year. MVP. He played every position except pitcher and catcher. During his ten-year career, the Dodgers averaged ninety-five wins a year. Amazing! A superstar. A truly great athlete. Baseball wasn't even his best sport. Others in the Negro Leagues were better. So we are talking about a genuine Hall of Famer. Nonsmoker, nondrinker, a Methodist. Supported Richard Nixon. A good husband, devoted to Rachel, good father. Died of a heart attack at age fifty-three. Picture him making a sophisticated speech and yet also telling Sal Maglie "to go fuck himself." In short, he was a man, an everyman, everybody. He played all the roles. He came out himself, in one piece. I suggest to you at the millennium that only two athletes will tower above the rest: Muhammad Ali and Jackie Robinson. To be sure, there are other outstanding athletes. Michael Jordan is the best ever at his game. Babe Ruth was also a great athlete. But compared to Ali and Robinson, they are only athletes. Ali and Robinson are more. Their colossal size drawn from character will carry them into the twenty-first century, leaving all the other great athletes behind—I believe.

We return to the cop on the field. Stupid. Even the meeting with Branch Rickey, where Robinson had to sign a contract not to fight back was ludicrous but grand. He was smart, upright. In a world upside down, he had to listen, to learn how to behave. He had to stand on his head in the beginning.

And so he did. The beauty of sport is simplicity. You win or lose. Near perfection, baseball is Eden waiting for errors. The poet May Swenson said, "It's about the ball, the bat, and the mitt," Simplicity helps. That's why writers—John Updike, Marianne Moore, a Dodger fan—are attracted. Undeniable. You can see it. The main attraction was that you could see Robinson steal, hit, field. You can't deny what you can see. Sports is clean, basically clean. Baseball equals freedom, freedom within limits, not chaos. Rickey Henderson is chaos. We don't like him because he represents chaos. We can take any rebellion within limits.

Who here would not like to go out this afternoon (not this evening) to watch one, two games and to eat orange ice and let the heat play over us? Baseball exists simultaneously in the present and the past. We remember last year's game, last year's series, a game ten years ago, and games that we never saw. I see that Bob Feller is going to be here today. I remember waiting for Bob Feller at Yankee Stadium. We were waiting for his autograph. He shoved us away. He was in a bad mood. He lost. Tough. I'm going to go up and ask him for his autograph. ["It'll cost you five dollars, Roger," came Elliot Abramson's gibe from the audience.] Yes. I'm afraid that might be so. I'll punch him in the face. The guy's got to be ninety.

A game lives in the past. That's why it's a game of records. The only tense we can know is the past. In Thornton Wilder's play, *The Skin of Our Teeth,* the gypsy comments, "Anybody can tell the future. The past. You want to know the past."

So now we go back, all of us here. We gather to look at the nonsense of the former world from the perspective of the nonsense of ours. It was simple and impossible to let Jackie play, impossible and inevitable. Here is what he said.

> I can say to my children that there is a chance for you, no guarantee but a chance. And this chance has come to be because there is nothing static with a free people. There is no Middle Ages logic so strong that it can stop the human tide from falling forward. I do not believe that every person in every walk of life can succeed in spite of any handicap. That would be perfection. But I do believe and with every fiber in me that what I was able to attain came because we put behind us—no matter how slowly—the dogmas of the past to discover the truth of today and perhaps the greatness of tomorrow.
>
> I believe in the human race. I believe in the warm heart. I believe in man's integrity. I believe in the goodness of a free society. I believe that society can remain good only as long as we are able to fight for it and fight against whatever imperfections may exist. My fight was against the barriers that kept Negroes out of baseball. It was the area where I found imperfection and where I was best able to fight. And I fought because I knew it was not going to be a losing fight. It could not be a losing fight when it took place in a free society.

Near the end of his life, very near the end of his life, he was blind. He was standing out on the field in the first game of the World Series between the Cincinnati Reds and the Oakland A's. My friend, Tom Callahan, a great sportswriter, watched him and told me this story. He was just standing out there before the game began. And all the players on both teams kind of wanted to touch him. But Joe Morgan, who was just tossing a ball back and forth behind him, seemed to pay no attention to Jackie. Then the announcement came that all people not in uniform had to leave the field. Everybody, including Jackie, started to go. And then Morgan went up to Jackie, not to face him but sort of standing behind him, and whispered, "Thank you." And Robinson said, "You're welcome." He left the field.

There was a sportswriter named Jim Murray from the *Los Angeles Times,* a great sportswriter. And Murray went up to Robinson and said,"Jackie! It's Jim Murray." Robinson said, "Oh Jim, oh Jim! I wish I could see you again." And Murray said, "Jackie, I wish I could see you again." Who does not?

Thank you.

About the Contributors

Ron Briley is an award-winning secondary school teacher at Sandia Preparatory School in Albuquerque, New Mexico. His published work on sports history and film has charted new territory in interdisciplinary studies. A consummate educator, Briley has earned praise from students and colleagues for extending the boundaries of history.

Robert Cherry is a professor of economics at Brooklyn College, where he has taught since 1977. Educated at Cornell, Purdue, and Kansas universities, he publishes widely on the issues of race, gender, and ethnicity. His book *Discrimination: Its Economic Impact on Blacks, Women, and Jews* (1989) is an important contribution to this growing field of inquiry.

Joseph Dorinson, educated at Columbia University, is a professor in the History Department (which he chaired, 1985–1997) at the Brooklyn Campus of Long Island University (LIU). Recipient of the first David E. Newton Award for Excellence in Teaching (1988), Dorinson has published numerous articles featuring his beloved borough, including "Brooklyn: The Elusive Image" in the *Long Island Historical Journal* (1989), "The Suburbanization of Brooklyn" in *Long Island: the Suburban Experience* (1990), and "Marianne Moore and the Brooklyn Dodgers" in *Long Island Women: Activists and Innovators* (1998), as well as studies of humor and ethnicity. He has organized conferences at LIU on Jackie Robinson (1997), Paul Robeson (1998), and Brooklyn: USA (1998). This is his first book.

Carl Erskine, affectionately known as "Oisk" in Brooklyn pitched for the Dodgers from 1948 to 1959. Because he hurt his arm as a rookie, Erskine pitched in pain for most of his career. Nevertheless, he compiled a solid record of 122 wins against 78 losses, an impressive .610 record. In 1953, a banner year, he won 20 games while only losing 6. Facing the New York Yankees in the third game of the World Series that same year, he struck out

14 opposing batsmen, a record that lasted for years. Only 5 feet 10 inches tall and weighing a shade over 160 pounds, Erskine used a sneaky fastball, a wicked curve, and a brilliant change-up to baffle the hitters. His ability to change speeds on his curve and an indomitable spirit led Erskine to hurl two no-hitters: one against the Chicago Cubs on June 19, 1952; the other against the rivals across the river, the New York Giants, on May 12, 1956. After baseball, Erskine became a highly successful banker. Currently a top executive at the Star Financial Bank in Anderson, Indiana, Erskine devotes much time and energy to raising money for the Special Olympics, in which his fourth son, Jimmy Erskine, excels.

Henry D. Fetter was born in New York City in 1949. After graduating from Harvard College and Harvard Law School, he moved to Los Angeles, where he currently practices business and entertainment litigation. He is writing a business history of the National League from 1921 to 1957.

Henry Foner retired in 1988 after twenty-seven years as president of the Fur, Leather & Machine Workers Union and as editor of the union's prize-winning newspaper. Since then, he has taught labor history at the Harry Van Arsdale, Jr., School of General Studies, the City College Center for Worker Education, and the Brooklyn College Institute for Retired Professionals and Executives. He has served as president of the National Association for Visually Handicapped, and as vice-president of the Brooklyn Philharmonic Symphony Orchestra. He is presently a trustee of the Paul Robeson Foundation, a member of the executive board of the New York Labor History Association, and a columnist for *Jewish Currents* magazine. He recently completed the Newspaper in Education Curriculum Guide on Paul Robeson for the *New York Times*.

Sidney Gendin was thirteen years old when he first watched Jackie Robinson in his 1947 rookie season. A philosophy professor at Eastern Michigan University, he earned his Ph.D. from New York University. He has edited several philosophy anthologies and has written dozens of articles, principally in ethics and philosophy of law, which have appeared in leading journals.

Peter Golenbock is one of America's preeminent sports biographers. Born in New York City, he earned a B.A. degree with honors at Dartmouth College and a law degree at New York University. Averse to legal practice, he turned to his first love, writing. Golenbock honed his craft on the staffs of various newspapers in Connecticut and in New Jersey. His first major book, *Dynasty: The New York Yankees, 1949–1964* (1975), made the *New York Times* best seller list and was followed in rapid succession on the charts by *The Bronx Zoo,* with Sparky Lyle (1979); *Guidry,* with Ron Guidry (1980); *Number 1,* with Billy Martin (1980); *Teammates* (1990); and, a perennial favorite, *Bums: The Brooklyn Dodgers, 1947–1957: An Oral History* (1983). Since then, Golenbock has continued to write on sports issues, to the endless joy and satisfaction of baseball fans.

Bob Gruber is an investment relations executive. A Manhattan resident, he was educated at the University of Rhode Island and the University of Minnesota where he gained a master's degree in journalism. The research for this paper proved to be a profoundly emotional experience. It enabled Gruber to revisit his adolescence in postwar Brooklyn and to recall Jackie Robinson's heroic achievement with even more appreciation today.

Ivan Hametz grew up in Greenpoint/Williamsburg, not too far from the location where Bette Smith's tree emerged from the asphalt. Educated at Queens College, he became a computer expert at the dawn of the technological era. Preferring a vocation with a more humanistic bent, he turned to another pursuit, the law, which he mastered at the Brooklyn Law School while raising a family. Hametz is now a successful attorney on Long Island.

Tom (Tommy) Hawkins was the first African-American to star in basketball at Notre Dame University. Known for his tremendous leaping ability, he vaulted into a successful ten-year professional career primarily with the Los Angeles Lakers. Following the sterling example of Jackie Robinson and prodded by his beloved mother, Hawkins went on to a successful post-athletic career as a broadcaster and business executive. He currently holds the position of vice-president for communications with the Los Angeles Dodgers. Hawkins dedicates the poem which opens this book to the memory of his mother, Juanita.

Patrick Henry grew up in Queens, New York. He now teaches French at Whitman College in Walla Walla, Washington. His latest two books are edited volumes: *An Inimitable Example: The Case for La Princesse de Cleves* (1992) and *Approaches in Montaigne's Essays* (1994). His "Jackie Robinson: Athlete and American Par Excellence" was the lead article in the spring 1997 issue of the *Virginia Quarterly Review*.

Peter Levine is a professor of history at Michigan State University. He is the author of *A. G. Spaulding and the Rise of Baseball, American Sport: A*

Documentary History (1986) and the editor of *Baseball History, 1986–91* (1990). His definitive study, *Ellis Island to Ebbets Field: Sport and the American Jewish Experience* (1992), was named Best Book of the Year for 1992 by the North American Society for Sport History. In association with celebrated sports journalist Robert Lipsyte, Levine wrote: *Idols of the Game: A Sporting History of the American Century* (1995).

Lee Lowenfish holds a master's degree and a Ph.D. in American history from the University of Wisconsin–Madison. He is currently an adjunct professor in both history and music at the Brooklyn Campus of Long Island University. He is the author of three baseball books: *The Imperfect Diamond: A History of Baseball's Labor Wars* (1991), Tom Seaver's *The Art of Pitching* (1994), and *The Professional Baseball Athletic Trainers Fitness Book* (1988). From 1982 to 1991, he hosted *Seventh Inning Stretch*, a sports program on WBAI–Pacifica Radio in New York City.

Bill Mardo was born in Manhattan but escaped to Brooklyn at age six, later graduating from Lafayette High School. Combining a passion for sports and politics, Mardo began writing for the *New York Daily Worker*. In this communist newspaper, he launched a campaign to end Jim Crow in American sports. He was joined in this good fight by Lester Rodney. Together, this dynamic duo helped bring down the barriers. Later, hounded by "Red Scare" advocates, he pursued a literary career elsewhere. Now a robust seventy-four years of age, Mardo is completing his memoirs and considers the fight to bring Jackie Robinson into baseball "the best years of my life."

Jack B. Moore is a professor in both the English and the American studies departments at the University of South Florida, and a member of the Institute on Black Life. Among his scholarly publications are books on Joe DiMaggio, W.E.B. DuBois, Maxwell Bodenheim, and American skinheads.

Robert A. Moss was born in Brooklyn in 1940. Educated at Brooklyn College, the University of Chicago, and Columbia University, Dr. Moss is an outstanding chemist. Since 1964, he has taught at Rutgers University, where he holds the Louis P. Hammett Chair of Chemistry, and has published extensively. His passion for baseball, particularly the Brooklyn Dodgers, derives from the indelible impressions made upon him by Jackie Robinson and the "boys of summer," during his childhood.

Samuel O. Regalado received his Ph.D. in 1987 from Washington State University. He has published several articles concerning Latins in American professional baseball as well as on the Japanese-American Nisei generation and sports. Regalado was a 1994 Smithsonian Faculty Fellow. He is the author of *Viva Baseball!: Latin Major Leaguers and Their Special Hunger* (1998). Rooted in Los Angeles's San Fernando Valley, Regalado is currently professor of history at California State University, Stanislaus. He is the nephew of former Cleveland Indian baseball player, Rudy Regalado.

Lester Rodney was born in New York City in 1911. A founding sports editor of the *New York Daily Worker*, where he worked from 1936 to 1957, he also served in the U.S. Army from 1942 to 1946. After moving west, Rodney continued to write and to edit in California, including features for the *Santa Monica Outlook,* copy for Stiller/Hunt Advertising, and features and editorial work for the *Long Beach Press-Telegram* of the Knight-Ridder chain. He is also an outstanding tennis player who garners many laurels in senior play, and may be considered the youngest octogenarian in America.

Roger Rosenblatt is a "Renaissance man." Educated at Harvard University, he has taught at his alma mater (1968–1973) and has written articles, essays, books, and plays. His voice and word pictures are familiar to millions who have listened to and watched *The MacNeil/Lehrer News Hour* on PBS since 1983. After serving in public administration as director of education for the National Endowment of the Humanities (1973–1975), he moved on to the *New Republic* as literary editor (1975–1978), to the *Washington Post* as columnist and editorial board member (1976–1979), and finally to *Time* as magazine senior writer (1980–1988). In addition, he has worked as contributing editor at the *New York Times Magazine,* the *New Republic,* and *Vanity Fair.* His books include *Black Fiction* (1974); *Children of War* (1983, winner of the Robert F. Kennedy Book Prize); *Witness: The World Since Hiroshima* (1985); *Life Itself: Abortion in the American Mind* (1992); and *The Man in the Water* (1994). Also a playwright, Rosenblatt is the author of *Free Speech in America* (1991); *And* (1992); and *Bibliomania* (1993). His numerous awards include a Fullbright to Dublin, Ireland; a George Foster Peabody award; an Emmy; and two George Polk awards, bestowed by Long Island University, his workplace since 1995. In that year, LIU broke precedent and appointed Rosenblatt to its first-ever endowed chair, the Parsons Family University Professorship of Writing. United Press International called Dr. Rosenblatt, "a national treasure." He teaches at the Southampton Campus of Long Island University.

Kelly E. Rusinack was born and raised near Uniontown, Pennsylvania. She earned a B.A. degree in history in 1987 from Chatham College in Pittsburgh, and an M.A. in history from Clemson University in South Carolina. A promising young scholar, she is continuing her research on the *Daily Worker* sports page and other sports-related history.

David Shiner serves as dean of Shimer College in Waukegan, Illinois (the birthplace of comedian Jack Benny), where he has been a member of the faculty for over twenty years. He has studied with several influential contemporary American philosophers, including Joseph Margolis and Amelie Oksenberg Rorty. His articles on a wide range of topics have been published in *Continuing the Conversation, Business Ethics Quarterly,* and other journals.

Lyle Spatz began his long love affair with baseball in 1945, and his fascination with opening days in 1949. He later attended Brooklyn College, where he majored in economics. After working at the U.S. Department of Commerce as an economist for thirty-three years, he retired to devote more time to his passion for baseball. Lyle chairs the records committee of SABR (The Society for American Baseball Research). He has published numerous articles in *Baseball Weekly* and *Baseball Digest.* He recently published a book, *New York Yankee Openers* (1997).

Joram Warmund is a professor in the history department of the Brooklyn Campus of Long Island University. He earned a B.A. from Queens College, an M.A. from Columbia University, and a Ph.D. from New York University. He has worked at Long Island University since 1963, first teaching history and later serving in several key administrative posts. In 1994, he returned to the history department after ten years as provost of the Rockland Campus of LIU. Warmund is a two-time recipient of the Fulbright-Hays Fellowship and was also awarded the D.A.A.D. (*Deutscher Akademischer Austauschdienst).* His fields of specialty include modern German and diplomatic histories. His service as co-director of the Jackie Robinson Conference and co-editor of this book has paralleled a growing interest in comparative United States–German histories and in post–World War II cultures.

Peter Williams, educated at Yale, Columbia, and Michigan universities, is the son of the classic sportswriter Joe Williams, whose baseball columns he collected in *The Joe Williams Baseball Reader* (1989). He has also published a study of sports myth, *The Sports Immortals* (1994), and a biography of Bill Terry called *When the Giants Were Giants* (1994), as well as numerous articles about baseball. Professor Williams lives and teaches college in New Jersey.

Index